ISTEP+ Coach Mathematics Grade 5

Triumph Learning®

Jerome D. Kaplan, Ed.D.

ISTEP+ Coach, Mathematics, Grade 5
164IN
ISBN-10: 1-60471-429-8
ISBN-13: 978-1-60471-429-6

Author: Jerome D. Kaplan, Ed. D.
Cover Image: Indiana has a long and rich auto racing history. © Designpics/Punchstock

Triumph Learning® 136 Madison Avenue, 7th Floor, New York, NY 10016
Kevin McAliley, President and Chief Executive Officer

Printed in the United States of America.

10 9 8 7 6 5 4 3 2 1

Table of Contents

To the Student

This book is called ***The ISTEP+ Coach, Mathematics, Grade 5***. It will help you prepare for the ISTEP+ in Mathematics.

Here is how *The ISTEP+ Coach, Mathematics, Grade 5* can help you:

- It shows you what the math questions on the ISTEP+ Test are like.
- It tells you what you need to know to do well on the test.
- Finally, it gives you practice on the kind of math that will be on the test.

The ISTEP+ Test in Math has many **multiple-choice questions**. They are like most of the questions you will work with in this book. After each question there are four possible answers. Only one is correct. The others are wrong. You must mark the one correct answer for each question.

The ISTEP+ also has **open-ended questions**—short answer questions and questions that require explanations. On these questions, you will have to write your answers in your test booklet as clearly as you can.

Here are some tips that will help when you work in this book and when you take the test:

- Read each question completely.
- Work as carefully as you can.
- Make sure you answer the question that is asked.
- Ask yourself if the answer makes sense.
- On multiple-choice questions, if you cannot decide on the answer, make the best guess you can. There is no penalty for guessing.
- On open-ended questions, write the answer clearly. Write a full explanation when you are asked to explain your answer.
- Answer as many questions as you can.

Use these tips throughout the book and when you take the test.

Standard

1 Number Sense

1 Ordering Whole Numbers

5.1.3: Compare whole numbers

You can use place value to compare and order numbers.

Example

Write these numbers in order from least to greatest.

6,258; 6,398; and 6,342

STRATEGY: **Use place value.**

STEP 1: Compare the thousands places.

6,258 **6**,398 **6**,342

All three numbers have 6 thousands.

STEP 2: Compare the hundreds places.

6,**2**58 6,**3**98 6,**3**42

Two hundreds are less than 3 hundreds. So 6,258 is the least number.

STEP 3: Compare the tens places of the remaining numbers.

6,3**9**8 6,3**4**2

Four tens are less than 9 tens. So 6,342 is less than 6,398.

SOLUTION: **The order of the numbers from least to greatest is 6,258; 6,342; and 6,398.**

Sample Test Questions

1 Which set of numbers is in order from least to greatest?

Ⓐ 3,343; 3,243; 2,343

Ⓑ 4,646; 4,666; 4,466

Ⓒ 3,085; 3,805; 3,508

Ⓓ 5,014; 5,104; 5,410

2 What is the greatest number that can be made using all of these digits?

2, 4, 1, 8

Ⓐ 8,412

Ⓑ 8,421

Ⓒ 8,124

Ⓓ 8,214

3 If the following numbers were listed in order from greatest to least, which would be second in the list?

256,108; 256,112; 256,192; 256,602

Ⓐ 256,108

Ⓑ 256,112

Ⓒ 256,192

Ⓓ 259,602

4 Order the days from least to greatest in school attendance.

Day	Attendance
Monday	605
Tuesday	625
Wednesday	602
Thursday	598
Friday	615

Ⓐ Thursday, Wednesday, Monday, Friday, Tuesday

Ⓑ Thursday, Monday, Wednesday, Tuesday, Friday

Ⓒ Thursday, Monday, Tuesday, Wednesday, Friday

Ⓓ Monday, Wednesday, Friday, Tuesday, Thursday

5 Gerald researched the population of four cities as part of a social studies project.

Aurora, Colorado	276,393
Corpus Christi, Texas	277,454
Newark, New Jersey	273,546
Raleigh, North Carolina	276,093

If he lists the populations from greatest to least, which city's population will be third on the list? Explain.

____

____

____

____

2 Prime and Composite Numbers

5.1.6: Describe and identify prime and composite numbers

Prime Numbers

A number is a prime number if its only factors are 1 and itself.

For example, 7 is a prime number because its only factors are 1 and 7.

$1 \times 7 = 7$

Composite Numbers

A number that is not a prime number is called a composite number.

8 is a composite number because it has more than two factors.

The factors of 8 are 1, 2, 4, and 8.

$1 \times 8 = 8$
$2 \times 4 = 8$

Note: 2 is the only even prime number.

1 is special. It is neither a prime number nor a composite number.

Division

An operation on two numbers that tells how many groups or how many in each group.

How to Write a Division Problem

There are two ways to write a **division** problem.

$63 \div 9 = 7$

```
                  7   ← quotient
divisor  →  9)63      ← dividend
             − 63
                0
```

Division with Remainders

Divide $502 \div 6$.

Divide $50 \div 6$.
Since $6 \times 8 = 48$, there are 8 tens.

Subtract $50 - 48$.
Bring down the 2 ones.

Divide $22 \div 6$.
Since $6 \times 3 = 18$, there are 3 ones.
Subtract $22 - 18$.

```
    83 R4
  6)502
  − 48↓
     22
   − 18
      4
```

The **remainder** is 4. A remainder is a number less than the divisor that remains after division is completed.

Division by Multidigit Divisors

Divide $926 \div 34$.

Divide the tens.
Multiply 34×2.
Subtract $92 - 68$.
Bring down the 6 ones.

Multiply 34×7.
Subtract $246 - 238$.
The remainder is 8.

```
     27 R8
  34)926
   − 68
     246
   − 238
       8
```

Divide.

1. $8\overline{)425}$

2. $26\overline{)636}$

ANSWERS: 1. 53 R1 **2.** 24 R12

Sample Test Questions

1 Which of the following is a prime number?

Ⓐ 22

Ⓑ 21

Ⓒ 20

Ⓓ 19

2 Which number is prime?

Ⓐ 72

Ⓑ 71

Ⓒ 70

Ⓓ 69

3 Which of the following is a composite number?

Ⓐ 17

Ⓑ 19

Ⓒ 23

Ⓓ 33

4 Look at the pairs of numbers. Which pair includes a prime number and a composite number?

Ⓐ 21, 27

Ⓑ 41, 43

Ⓒ 5, 46

Ⓓ 23, 29

5 What are all the prime numbers between 30 and 40?

Ⓐ 31, 33, 37

Ⓑ 31, 35, 37

Ⓒ 31, 39

Ⓓ 31, 37

6 How many prime numbers are there between 60 and 70?

Ⓐ 0

Ⓑ 1

Ⓒ 2

Ⓓ 3

7 List the prime numbers between 70 and 100. Explain how you identified the prime numbers.

____

____

____

____

____

3 Interpreting Fractions

5.1.5: Explain different interpretations of fractions

One way to interpret a fraction is to think of the fraction as part of a whole.

Example 1

What fraction of this circle is shaded?

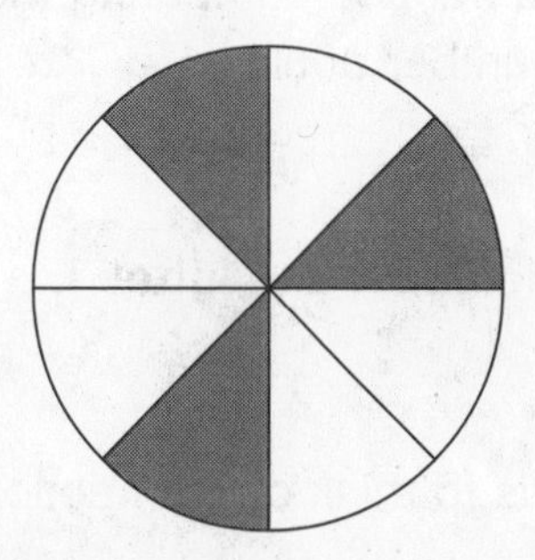

STRATEGY: **Compare the part that is shaded to the whole figure.**

STEP 1: Identify the whole.

The whole is the circle, which is divided into 8 equal regions.

STEP 2: Identify the part.

The part is the 3 regions that are shaded.

STEP 3: Write a fraction comparing the part to the whole.

$\frac{3}{8}$ ← shaded regions / ← regions in the whole

SOLUTION: **$\frac{3}{8}$ of the circle is shaded.**

Another way to interpret a fraction is to think of the fraction as part of a set.

Example 2

What fraction of the tiles in this set have the letter T?

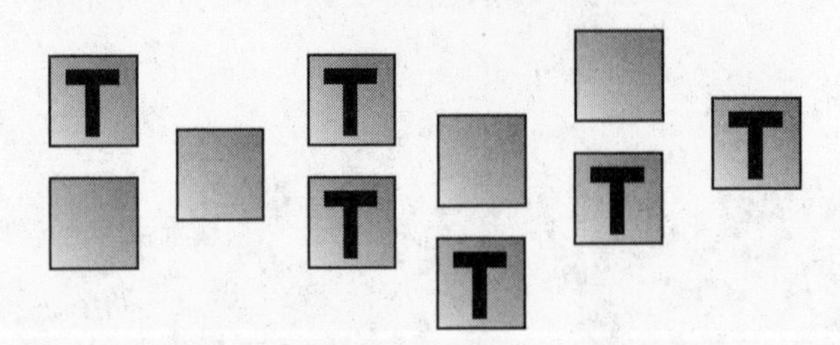

STRATEGY: **Compare the tiles with the letter T to the total number of tiles.**

STEP 1: Find the number of tiles in the set with the letter T.

There are 6 tiles with the letter T.

STEP 2: Find the total number of tiles in the set.

There are 10 tiles in the set.

STEP 3: Write a fraction comparing the number of tiles with T with the total number of tiles.

$\frac{6}{10}$

SOLUTION: **$\frac{6}{10}$, or $\frac{3}{5}$ of the tiles have the letter T.**

A third way to interpret a fraction is to think of the fraction as division.

Example 3

Write the fraction that represents $5 \div 12$.

STRATEGY: **Use the dividend as the numerator and the divisor as a denominator.**

STEP 1: Identify the dividend and the divisor.

The dividend is 5, and the divisor is 12

STEP 2: Write the fraction.

$\frac{5}{12}$

SOLUTION: **The fraction $\frac{5}{12}$ represents $5 \div 12$.**

Sample Test Questions

1 Which fraction of this rectangle is shaded?

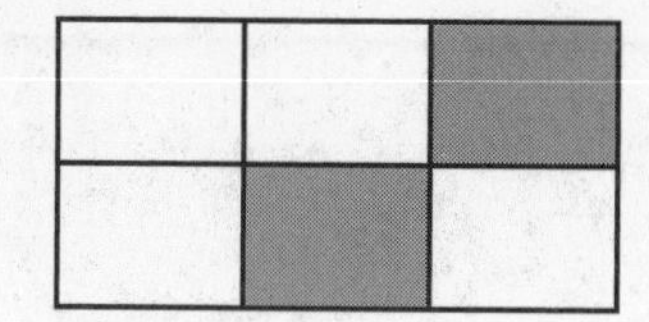

Ⓐ $\frac{1}{6}$

Ⓑ $\frac{1}{3}$

Ⓒ $\frac{1}{2}$

Ⓓ $\frac{2}{3}$

2 Dennis cut his birthday cake into 10 equal pieces. George ate 2 pieces. What fraction of the cake did George eat?

Ⓐ $\frac{1}{5}$

Ⓑ $\frac{1}{4}$

Ⓒ $\frac{4}{5}$

Ⓓ $\frac{10}{2}$

3 Connie spent 4 hours on her math project and 5 hours on her history project. What fraction of the total hours did she spend on the history project?

Ⓐ $\frac{4}{9}$

Ⓑ $\frac{5}{9}$

Ⓒ $\frac{4}{5}$

Ⓓ $\frac{5}{4}$

4 There are 4 pounds of trail mix to be divided equally among 18 students on a field trip. How much trail mix will each student get?

Ⓐ $\frac{2}{9}$ pound

Ⓑ $\frac{2}{7}$ pound

Ⓒ $\frac{7}{9}$ pound

Ⓓ $\frac{9}{2}$ pound

5 What fraction of a pizza will each person get when 5 pizzas are divided equally among 20 people? Explain how you determined your answer.

____

____

____

____

____

4 Place Value of Whole Numbers and Decimals

5.1.1: Convert between numbers in words and numbers in figures

This place-value chart shows the value of each digit in the number 7,359,284. The value of a digit depends on its place. The groupings are millions, thousands, and ones.

Millions	Hundred Thousands	Ten Thousands	Thousands	Hundreds	Tens	Ones
7	3	5	9	2	8	4

Read the number as:

Seven million, three hundred fifty-nine thousand, two hundred eighty-four.

The commas indicate where new groupings start in the numbers.

Example 1

In the year 2000, the population of Indiana was 6,080,485. Write the population in word form.

STRATEGY: **Think of the place value of each digit.**

STEP 1: There is a 6 in the millions place. → *six million*

STEP 2: There is an 8 in the ten thousands place. → *eighty thousand*

STEP 3: There is a 4 in the hundreds place. → *four hundred*

STEP 4: There is an 8 in the tens place. → *eighty*

STEP 5: There is a 5 in the ones place. → *five*

SOLUTION: **In words, the population is six million, eighty thousand, four hundred eighty five.**

Example 2

In the year 1990, the population of Indiana was five million, five hundred forty-four thousand, one hundred fifty-nine. Write the population in standard form.

STRATEGY: **The location of the commas can help you find the groupings.**

SOLUTION: **The population is 5,544,159.**

This is a place-value chart showing decimals. It shows the value of each digit for the number 65.934.

Tens	Ones	Decimal Point	Tenths	Hundredths	Thousandths
6	5	.	9	3	4

Read this number as:

Sixty-five and nine hundred thirty-four thousandths.

The word *and* goes where the decimal point is. It separates the whole number part from the decimal part.

Example 3

What is the value of 3 in 48.823?

STRATEGY: **Use a place-value chart.**

STEP 1: Write 48.823 in the chart.

Tens	Ones	Decimal Point	Tenths	Hundredths	Thousandths
4	8	.	8	2	3

STEP 2: Look above the 3 to find its value.

SOLUTION: **The value of the 3 is 3 thousandths.**

Example 4

The diameter of a plastic pipe is two and three hundred seventy-five thousandths inches. Write this number in standard form.

STRATEGY: **Put a decimal point in place of the word *and*, which separates the whole number part from the decimal part.**

STEP 1: What is the whole number part before *and*?

The whole number is 2. Write 2 before the decimal point.

2.?

STEP 2: Determine the number of places after the decimal point.

The decimal part reads thousandths, so there are three places after the decimal point.

STEP 3: Write 375 after the decimal point 2.375.

SOLUTION: **The number in standard form is 2.375.**

Sample Test Questions

1 What is 5,075,189 in words?

Ⓐ five hundred seventy-five thousand, one hundred eighty-nine

Ⓑ five million, seventy-five thousand, one hundred ninety-eight

Ⓒ five million, seventy-five thousand, one hundred eighty-nine

Ⓓ five million, seventy-five hundred, one hundred eighty-nine

2 Express the number in standard form.

nine million, five hundred sixteen thousand, forty-three

Ⓐ 9,560,430

Ⓑ 9,516,043

Ⓒ 9,501,643

Ⓓ 9,051,643

3 What is the value of the 9 in 60.394?

Ⓐ 9 tenths

Ⓑ 9 hundredths

Ⓒ 9 thousands

Ⓓ 9 hundreds

4 Which is the word form of the number?

65.067

Ⓐ Sixty-five and sixty-seven hundredths

Ⓑ Sixty-five and sixty-seven thousandths

Ⓒ Sixty-five and sixty-seven ten-thousandths

Ⓓ Sixty-five thousand sixty-seven tenths

5 What number does this place-value chart show?

Hundreds	Tens	Ones	Tenths	Hundredths	Thousandths
5	0	6	4	3	9

Ⓐ 5.06439

Ⓑ 50.6439

Ⓒ 506.439

Ⓓ 5,604.39

6 Which shows this number in standard form?

seven and three hundred five thousandths

Ⓐ 73,500

Ⓑ 7,305

Ⓒ 73,005

Ⓓ 7.305

7 In the number 517.936, the 3 is in which place?

Ⓐ tenths place

Ⓑ hundredths place

Ⓒ thousandths place

Ⓓ ten-thousandths place

8 What is the value of the 5 in 0.352?

Ⓐ 5 tens

Ⓑ 5 tenths

Ⓒ 5 hundredths

Ⓓ 5 thousandths

9 What is the value of each digit in 2.915? Explain your answer.

____

____

____

____

____

5 Comparing Decimals

5.1.3: Compare decimals

Example 1

Place these decimal numbers in order from least to greatest.

9.42, 3.2, 4.08, and 11.2

STRATEGY: **Compare the whole number parts.**

STEP 1: Place the whole numbers in order.

3, 4, 9, and 11

STEP 2: Place the decimal numbers in the same order.

3.2, **4**.08, **9**.42, **11**.2

SOLUTION: **The decimals in order from least to greatest are 3.2, 4.08, 9.42, and 11.2.**

Example 2

Which of these numbers is the least? Which is the greatest?

7.35, 6.98, 7.03

STRATEGY: **When two or more numbers have the same whole-number parts, compare tenths.**

STEP 1: Compare the whole-number parts first.

The least whole number is 6.

Two numbers have 7 as the whole number part.

STEP 2: Compare tenths.

The digit in the tenths place of 7.35 is 3.

The digit in the tenths place of 7.03 is 0.

$0 < 3$

So, $7.03 < 7.35$. (7.03 is less than 7.35.)

SOLUTION: **The least number is 6.98, and the greatest is 7.35.**

Sample Test Questions

1 Kim's highest jumps were 2.3 meters, 2.6 meters, and 2.1 meters. Which shows the correct ordering?

Ⓐ $2.1 < 2.6 < 2.3$

Ⓑ $2.3 < 2.6 < 2.1$

Ⓒ $2.1 < 2.3 < 2.6$

Ⓓ $2.6 < 2.3 < 2.1$

2 Which number represents the greatest distance?

Ⓐ 0.75 kilometer

Ⓑ 0.6 kilometer

Ⓒ 0.51 kilometer

Ⓓ 0.62 kilometer

3 Tim weighed a thumbtack 4 times and got these readings:

1.24 g, 1.26 g, 1.22 g, and 1.2 g.

Which measurement is smallest?

Ⓐ 1.24 grams

Ⓑ 1.26 grams

Ⓒ 1.22 grams

Ⓓ 1.2 grams

Use the following information to answer Questions 4 and 5.

Last week, Stuart kept a record of how far he walked each day.

Monday	4.3 miles
Tuesday	5.7 miles
Wednesday	3.7 miles
Thursday	3.5 miles
Friday	4.1 miles

4 On which day did Stuart walk the shortest distance?

Ⓐ Monday

Ⓑ Tuesday

Ⓒ Wednesday

Ⓓ Thursday

5 On which day did he walk the longest distance?

Ⓐ Monday

Ⓑ Tuesday

Ⓒ Wednesday

Ⓓ Thursday

6 Which shows the correct order?

Ⓐ $5.27 > 5.21 > 5.38$

Ⓑ $5.27 > 5.21 > 5.2$

Ⓒ $5.27 > 5.2 > 5.3$

Ⓓ $5.27 > 5.22 > 5.24$

7 What number is 0.1 greater than 3.25?

Ⓐ 4.25

Ⓑ 3.26

Ⓒ 3.35

Ⓓ 3.15

8 What number is 0.01 less than 5.38?

Ⓐ 5.27

Ⓑ 5.37

Ⓒ 5.28

Ⓓ 5.39

9 Which set shows the decimals in order from greatest to least?

Ⓐ 0.7, 0.62, 0.76

Ⓑ 0.62, 0.7, 0.76

Ⓒ 0.76, 0.7, 0.62

Ⓓ 0.62, 0.76, 0.7

10 List these numbers in order from least to greatest.

19.345 19.35 19.3 19.4

Explain your answer.

____

____

____

____

____

6 Percents

5.1.4: Interpret percents as part of a hundred. Find decimal and percent equivalents for common fractions

Percent means "of 100." So percents are fractions with denominators of 100.

Fractions with Denominators of 100

Example 1

Write $\frac{23}{100}$ as a percent.

STRATEGY: **Look at the denominator of the fraction. It is 100.**

Since the denominator of $\frac{23}{100}$ is 100, the percent is the same as the numerator.

SOLUTION: $\frac{23}{100}$ **= 23%** **% is the symbol for percent.**

Example 2

Write 0.07 as a percent.

STRATEGY: **Think of place value.**

0.07 is 7 hundredths.

7 hundredths is $\frac{7}{100}$.

SOLUTION: **0.07 = 7%**

Fractions with Denominators That Are Not 100

Example 3

Write $\frac{4}{5}$ as a percent.

STRATEGY: **Change $\frac{4}{5}$ to a fraction with a denominator of 100.**

STEP 1: Multiply the denominator by a number to get 100.

$5 \times 20 = 100$

STEP 2: Multiply the numerator by the same number.

$4 \times 20 = 80$

STEP 3: Write the new fraction.

$\frac{80}{100}$

$\frac{4}{5}$ is equivalent to $\frac{80}{100}$.

STEP 4: Use the numerator of the new fraction to write the percent.

$\frac{80}{100} = 80\%$

SOLUTION: $\frac{4}{5} = 80\%$

Example 4

Write $\frac{3}{4}$ as a decimal and as a percent.

STRATEGY: **Change $\frac{3}{4}$ to a percent with a denominator of 100.**

STEP 1: Multiply 4 by a number to get 100.

$4 \times 25 = 100$

STEP 2: Multiply 3 by 25.

$3 \times 25 = 75$

STEP 3: Write the new fraction.

$\frac{75}{100}$

SOLUTION: $\frac{75}{100} = 0.75 = 75\%$

Using a Table

The table shows common fractions and their equivalent decimals and percents. You can save time by memorizing the table.

Fraction, Decimal, and Percent Equivalents

Fraction	Decimal	Percent	Fraction	Decimal	Percent
$\frac{1}{10}$	0.10	10%	$\frac{3}{5}$	0.60	60%
$\frac{1}{5}$	0.20	20%	$\frac{2}{3}$	0.66... or $0.\overline{6}$	$66\frac{2}{3}\%$
$\frac{1}{4}$	0.25	25%	$\frac{7}{10}$	0.70	70%
$\frac{3}{10}$	0.30	30%	$\frac{3}{4}$	0.75	75%
$\frac{1}{3}$	0.33... or $0.\overline{3}$	$33\frac{1}{3}\%$	$\frac{4}{5}$	0.80	80%
$\frac{2}{5}$	0.40	40%	$\frac{9}{10}$	0.90	90%
$\frac{1}{2}$	0.50	50%			

Example 5

George ate 1 of the 4 equal parts of his birthday cake. What decimal and what percent of the cake did he eat?

STRATEGY: **Write the fraction for the part that George ate. Then use the table.**

STEP 1: Find the fraction of the cake that George ate. George ate 1 of 4 equal parts of the cake, so he ate $\frac{1}{4}$ of the cake.

STEP 2: Convert the fraction to a decimal and a percent by using the table.

$\frac{1}{4} = 0.25 = 25\%$

SOLUTION: **George ate 0.25 or 25% of the cake.**

Sample Test Questions

Write the equivalent number.

1 $\frac{37}{100} =$

Ⓐ 3700%

Ⓑ 370%

Ⓒ 37%

Ⓓ 3.7%

2 $\frac{6}{100} =$

Ⓐ 6%

Ⓑ 60%

Ⓒ 600%

Ⓓ 6000%

3 $\frac{2}{5} =$

Ⓐ 0.35

Ⓑ 0.4

Ⓒ 0.6

Ⓓ 0.75

4 0.02 =

Ⓐ $\frac{1}{50}$

Ⓑ $\frac{1}{5}$

Ⓒ $\frac{1}{20}$

Ⓓ $\frac{1}{2}$

5 80% =

Ⓐ $\frac{2}{10}$

Ⓑ $\frac{2}{5}$

Ⓒ $\frac{5}{10}$

Ⓓ $\frac{4}{5}$

6 $33\frac{1}{3}\% =$

Ⓐ $\frac{2}{3}$

Ⓑ $\frac{3}{5}$

Ⓒ $\frac{33}{100}$

Ⓓ $\frac{1}{3}$

7 Fred ate $\frac{2}{8}$ of a pizza last night. What percent of the pizza did he eat?

Ⓐ $37\frac{1}{2}\%$

Ⓑ 28%

Ⓒ 25%

Ⓓ $12\frac{1}{2}\%$

8 Marion spelled 20 of her 40 words correctly. What percent of her words did she spell correctly?

Ⓐ 5%

Ⓑ 50%

Ⓒ 30%

Ⓓ 20%

9 In Jeff's town, it rains 0.8 of the time. What percent is 0.8?

Ⓐ 8%

Ⓑ 18%

Ⓒ 80%

Ⓓ 88%

10 Shade the grid below to show 70%. Then on the lines below the grid, tell what decimal and what fraction you shaded.

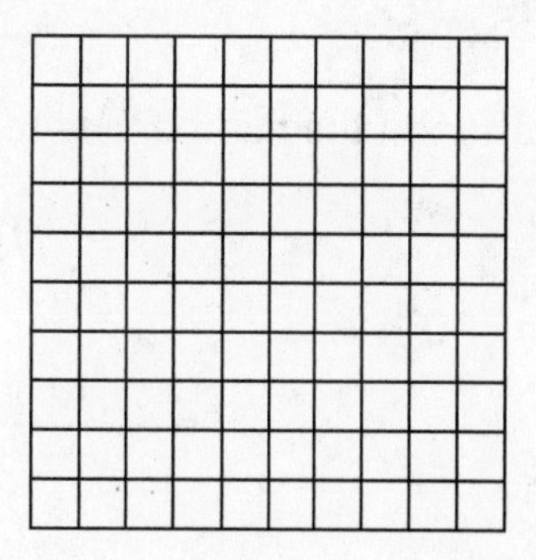

____

____

____

____

____

7 Locating Numbers on a Number Line

5.1.7: Identify on a number line the relative position of simple positive fractions, positive mixed numbers, and positive decimals.

Example

Each letter on the number line represents one of these numbers.

$\frac{29}{50}$ 0.182 $1\frac{2}{3}$ 0.812

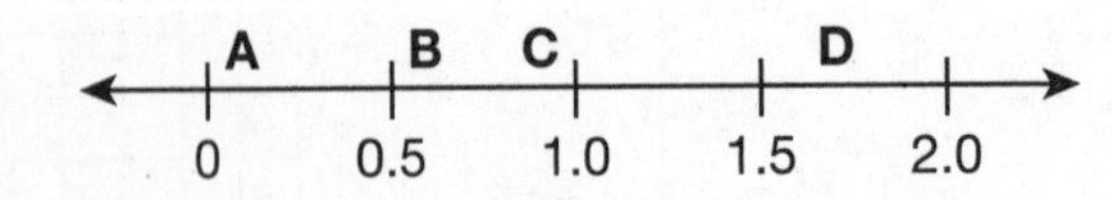

Identify the number represented by each letter.

STRATEGY: **Change each fraction to a decimal.**

STEP 1: $\frac{29}{50} = \frac{50}{100} = 0.58$

STEP 2: $1\frac{2}{3} = 1.6666...$

STEP 3: Locate the numbers.

A is between 0 and 0.5. The number 0.182 is also between 0 and 0.5, so A = 0.182.

B is greater than 0.5 and less than halfway between the 0.5 and 1, so B is 0.58.

C is greater than 0.75 and less than 1.0, so C = 0.812.

D is greater than 1.5, so D = 1.6666...

SOLUTION: **The four numbers are A = 0.182, B = $\frac{29}{50}$, C = 0.812, and D = $1\frac{2}{3}$.**

Sample Test Questions

1 Which number does X represent on the number line?

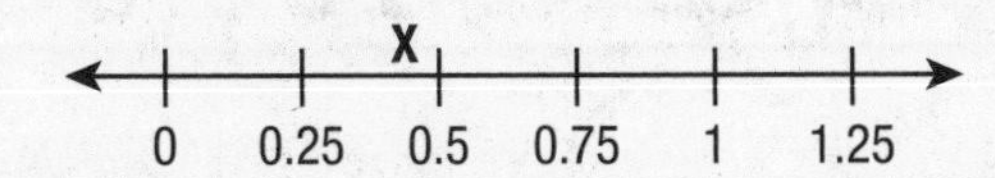

Ⓐ $\frac{7}{25}$

Ⓑ $\frac{1}{5}$

Ⓒ $\frac{3}{8}$

Ⓓ 0.29

2 Which number does Y represent on the number line?

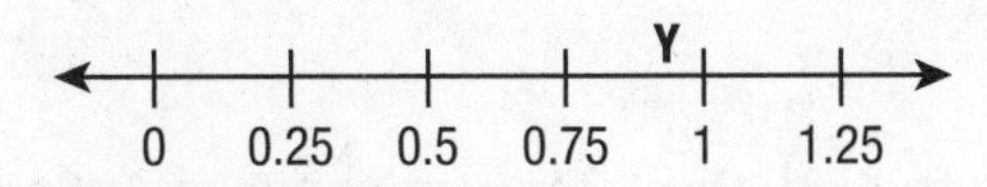

Ⓐ 0.85

Ⓑ $\frac{19}{25}$

Ⓒ $\frac{3}{4}$

Ⓓ 0.94

3 Which number does Z represent on the number line?

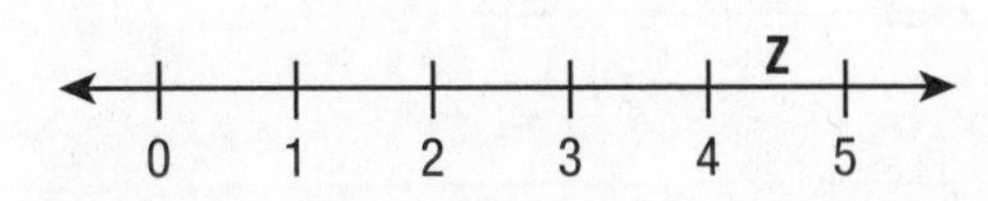

Ⓐ 4.05

Ⓑ 4.5

Ⓒ $4\frac{1}{5}$

Ⓓ $4\frac{17}{20}$

4 Which number is not represented by the letter T on the number line?

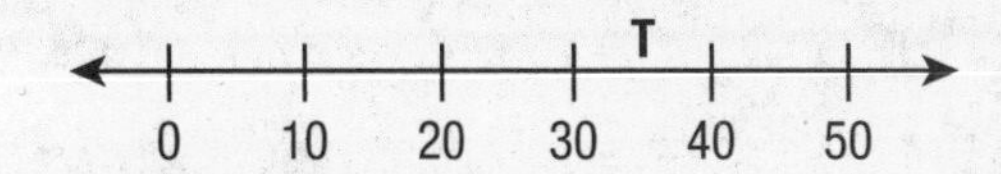

Ⓐ $\frac{175}{5}$

Ⓑ 30.5

Ⓒ 35

Ⓓ $\frac{70}{2}$

5 Graph and label each point on this number line.

$A = 1\frac{3}{4}$

$B = 3.2$

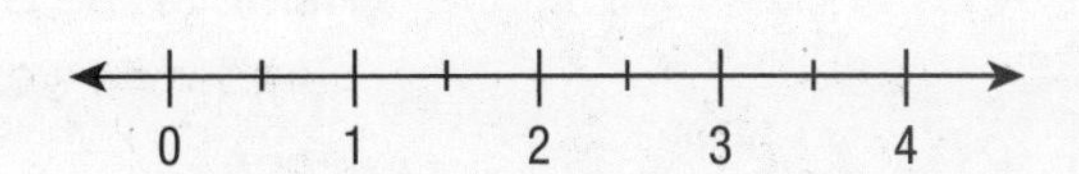

Explain how you graphed each point.

____

____

____

____

____

8 Rounding Numbers to the Nearest 10, 100, 1,000, 10,000, and 100,000

5.1.2: Round whole numbers to any place

Example 1

A house sold for $165,230. Round this number to the nearest thousand.

STRATEGY: **Find the number of thousands that is closest to this number.**

STEP 1: Underline the thousands place of the number.

16<u>5</u>,230

STEP 2: Remove the digits to the left of the thousands place. What number do you get?

5,230

STEP 3: 5,230 is between which two thousands?

5,230 is between 5,000 and 6,000.

STEP 4: Which is 5,230 closer to—5,000 or 6,000?

5,230 is closer to 5,000 than to 6,000.

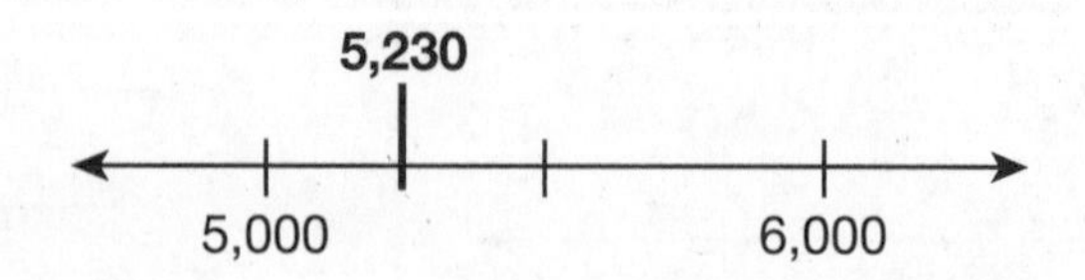

SOLUTION: **So, 165,230 rounded to nearest thousand is 165,000.**

Example 2

Round 1,267,945 to the nearest hundred thousand.

STRATEGY: **Find the number of hundred thousands that is closest to this number.**

STEP 1: Underline the hundred thousands place of the number.

1,<u>2</u>67,945

STEP 2: Remove the digit to the left of the hundred thousands place. What number do you get?

267,945

STEP 3: 267,945 is between which two hundred thousands?

267,945 is between 200,000 and 300,000.

STEP 4: Which is 267,945 closer to—200,000 or 300,000?

267,945 is closer to 300,000 than to 200,000.

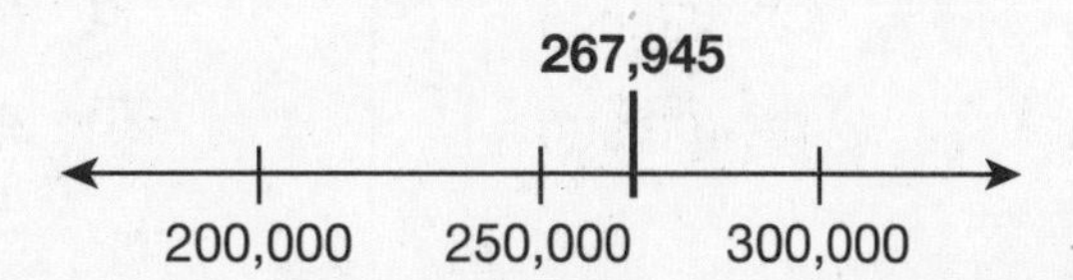

SOLUTION: **So, 1,267,945 rounded to the nearest hundred thousand is 1,300,000.**

> **NOTE:** If a number is halfway between two numbers on a number line, round up to the greater number.

Sample Test Questions

Round the numbers in Questions 1–3 to the nearest thousand.

1 6,702

Ⓐ 6,000 Ⓒ 6,700

Ⓑ 6,500 Ⓓ 7,000

2 14,703

Ⓐ 15,000 Ⓒ 14,500

Ⓑ 14,700 Ⓓ 14,000

3 349,065

Ⓐ 300,000 Ⓒ 350,000

Ⓑ 349,000 Ⓓ 400,000

Round the numbers in Questions 4–6 to the nearest ten thousand.

4 775,205

Ⓐ 700,000 Ⓒ 780,000

Ⓑ 770,000 Ⓓ 800,000

5 60,500

Ⓐ 60,000 Ⓒ 61,500

Ⓑ 61,000 Ⓓ 70,000

6 1,253,066

Ⓐ 1,200,000 Ⓒ 1,253,000

Ⓑ 1,250,000 Ⓓ 1,254,000

Round the numbers in Questions 7–9 to the nearest hundred thousand.

7 2,394,650

Ⓐ 2,400,000

Ⓑ 2,390,000

Ⓒ 2,350,000

Ⓓ 2,300,000

8 24,447,392

Ⓐ 24,400,000

Ⓑ 24,440,000

Ⓒ 24,450,000

Ⓓ 25,500,000

9 7,859,000

Ⓐ 7,800,000

Ⓑ 7,850,000

Ⓒ 7,860,000

Ⓓ 7,900,000

10 Is 2,704,310 closer to 2,000,000 or 3,000,000? Explain your answer.

____

____

____

____

____

9 Rounding Decimals

5.1.2: Round decimals to any place value

Rounding on a Number Line

Example 1

A living room is 4.75 meters long. Round 4.75 meters to the nearest whole number.

STRATEGY: **Find the whole number 4.75 is closest to.**

STEP 1: Place 4.75 on the number line, which shows intervals of $\frac{1}{2}$.

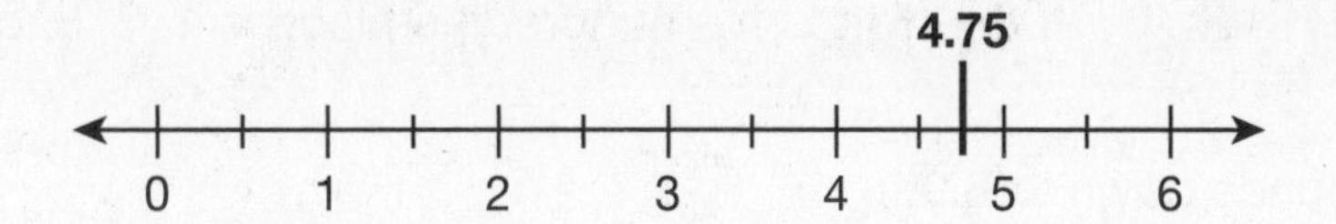

STEP 2: Is 4.75 closer to 4 or 5?

4.75 is closer to 5.

SOLUTION: **4.75 rounded to the nearest whole number is 5. The living room is about 5 meters long.**

Example 2

Paul took 17.5 hours to finish a project. Round 17.5 to the nearest whole number.

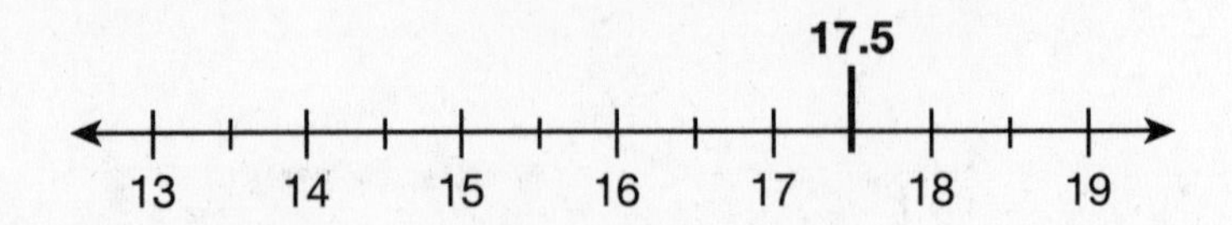

STRATEGY: **Use the following rule:**

If a number is exactly halfway between two whole numbers, round UP.

17.5 is exactly halfway between 17 and 18. So, round up to 18.

SOLUTION: **17.5 rounded to the nearest whole number is 18. So Paul took about 18 hours to finish the project.**

Rounding to the Nearest Tenth

Here are two rules for rounding to the nearest tenth:

RULE 1: If the digit in the hundredths place is 1, 2, 3, or 4, round DOWN.

8.93 rounds down to 8.9.

761.84 rounds down to 761.8.

RULE 2: If the digit in the hundredths place is 5, 6, 7, 8, or 9, round UP.

3.28 rounds up to 3.3.

43.85 rounds up to 43.9.

Example 3

Round 23.68 to the nearest tenth.

STRATEGY: **Follow the rules above.**

STEP 1: The decimal 23.68 has 2 decimal places:
6 is in the tenths place, and 8 is in the hundredths place.

STEP 2: By Rule 2, round 23.68 UP to 23.7.

SOLUTION: **23.68 rounded to the nearest tenth is 23.7.**

Rounding to the Nearest Hundredth

These are two rules that you can use to round decimals to the nearest hundredth:

RULE 1: If the digit in the thousandth position is 4 or less, round DOWN.

56.724 rounds down to 56.72.

105.081 rounds down to 105.08.

RULE 2: If the digit in the thousandths place is 5 or more, round UP.

12.749 rounds up to 12.75.

0.055 rounds up to 0.06.

Example 4

Round 537.724 to the nearest hundredth.

STRATEGY: **Use the rules from the previous page.**

STEP 1: The decimal 537.724 has three decimal places:

7 is in the tenths place; 2 is in the hundredths place; and 4 is in the thousandths place.

STEP 2: By Rule 1, round 537.724 DOWN to 537.72

SOLUTION: **537.724 rounded to the nearest hundredth is 537.72.**

Rounding to the Nearest Dollar

Here are two rules for rounding to the nearest dollar.

RULE 1: If the cents part of a money amount is less than 50 cents, round DOWN.

RULE 2: If the cents part of a money amount is 50 cents or more, round UP.

Example 5

Round $215.34 to the nearest dollar.

STRATEGY: **Use the rules above.**

STEP 1: For $215.34, the amount 34 cents is less than 50 cents.

STEP 2: By Rule 1, round DOWN.

SOLUTION: **$215.34 rounded to the nearest dollar is $215.**

Sample Test Questions

1 Which of these decimals is closest to 4?

Ⓐ 3.5

Ⓑ 3.75

Ⓒ 4.5

Ⓓ 4.8

2 Round 34.81 to the nearest tenth.

Ⓐ 34.9

Ⓑ 34.8

Ⓒ 34.7

Ⓓ 34.6

3 Round 9.45 to the nearest whole number.

Ⓐ 9

Ⓑ 9.4

Ⓒ 9.5

Ⓓ 10

4 Denny said that 10,000 meters is about 6.2 miles. Which of the following numbers is rounded to 6.2?

Ⓐ 6.27

Ⓑ 6.25

Ⓒ 6.21

Ⓓ 6.14

5 The bill at the paper supply company was $87.43. Round $87.43 to the nearest dollar.

Ⓐ $87

Ⓑ $87.50

Ⓒ $88

Ⓓ $90

6 Anna rounded off the amount of money she had in her purse to the nearest dollar and got $80. Which of these amounts could she have?

Ⓐ $79.25

Ⓑ $79.48

Ⓒ $79.75

Ⓓ $80.50

7 Tanya spent $8.49 for lunch. Round this amount to the nearest dollar.

Ⓐ $9

Ⓑ $8.50

Ⓒ $8.40

Ⓓ $8

8 Which of these amounts rounds to $40 when rounded to the nearest dollar?

Ⓐ $39.45

Ⓑ $39.49

Ⓒ $40.49

Ⓓ $40.50

9 Round 67.205 to the nearest hundredth.

Ⓐ 67.21

Ⓑ 67.20

Ⓒ 66.50

Ⓓ 65.50

10 Round 0.955 to the nearest hundredth.

Ⓐ 0.95

Ⓑ 0.96

Ⓒ 0.97

Ⓓ 0.98

11 Name the least amount of money that rounds to $20 when rounded if you round to the nearest dollar. Name the greatest amount of money that rounds to $20 if you round to the nearest dollar. Explain how you found your answers.

____

____

____

____

____

Progress Check for Lessons 1–9

1 If you are rounding to the nearest 100,000, which number does not round to 200,000?

Ⓐ 156,487

Ⓑ 187,940

Ⓒ 240,307

Ⓓ 250,000

2 Which statement is true?

Ⓐ $0.07 > 0.7$

Ⓑ $0.85 < 0.59$

Ⓒ $0.6 < 0.64$

Ⓓ $0.88 < 0.8$

3 Which number is closest to 2?

Ⓐ 1.75

Ⓑ 2.10

Ⓒ 2.05

Ⓓ 1

4 Which set of numbers is in order from least to greatest?

Ⓐ 6.4, 6.02, 6.2, 6.04

Ⓑ 6.04, 6.02, 6.4, 6.2

Ⓒ 6.04, 6.02, 6.2, 6.4

Ⓓ 6.02, 6.04, 6.2, 6.4

5 What decimal is equivalent to $4\frac{9}{100}$?

Ⓐ 4.9

Ⓑ 4.90

Ⓒ 4.09

Ⓓ 4.009

6 Which is a prime number?

Ⓐ 27

Ⓑ 51

Ⓒ 52

Ⓓ 53

7 Which set of numbers is in order from greatest to least?

Ⓐ 451,705; 451,750; 455,705

Ⓑ 455,705; 455,704; 454,704

Ⓒ 455,710; 455,703; 455,709

Ⓓ 405,701; 406, 701; 408,701

8 What percent is equivalent to $\frac{3}{5}$?

Ⓐ 25%

Ⓑ 40%

Ⓒ 60%

Ⓓ 80%

9 Round 6.275 to the nearest hundredth.

Ⓐ 6.28

Ⓑ 6.3

Ⓒ 6.27

Ⓓ 6.0

10 Write 253.147 in word form.

Ⓐ two hundred fifty-three and one hundred forty-seven hundredths

Ⓑ two hundred fifty-three thousand, one hundred forty-seven

Ⓒ two hundred fifty-three and one hundred forty-seven tenths

Ⓓ two hundred fifty-three and one hundred forty-seven thousandths

11 Which numbers are graphed on this number line?

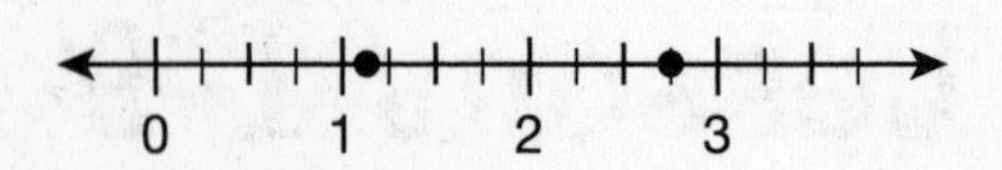

Ⓐ 7.8 and 3.25

Ⓑ $1\frac{1}{8}$ and 2.5

Ⓒ $1\frac{1}{2}$ and 2.75

Ⓓ $1\frac{1}{8}$ and 2.75

12 Igor packed 3 apples, 4 pears, and 5 oranges for a family picnic. What fraction of the fruit were pears?

Ⓐ $\frac{1}{3}$

Ⓑ $\frac{1}{2}$

Ⓒ $\frac{2}{3}$

Ⓓ $\frac{2}{1}$

Standard 1
Open-Ended Questions

1 a) List all the prime numbers greater than 30 but less than 50.

b) Choose any two of the numbers you listed in part a. and add them. Is the sum a prime number? Will the sum of any two prime numbers from your list ever be prime? Explain.

c) Multiply any two of the numbers you listed in part a. Is the product a prime number? Will the product of any two prime numbers from your list ever be prime? Explain.

2 a) Delores rounded 29, 745 to the nearest thousand and got 29,000. What is the correct answer?

b) Write a list of directions Dolores could follow to get the correct answer.

3 Look at these numbers.

$5.5, 7.75, 6\frac{1}{4}, 8.5, 9\frac{3}{4}$

Plot each number on the number line below.
Be sure to label each point with its value.

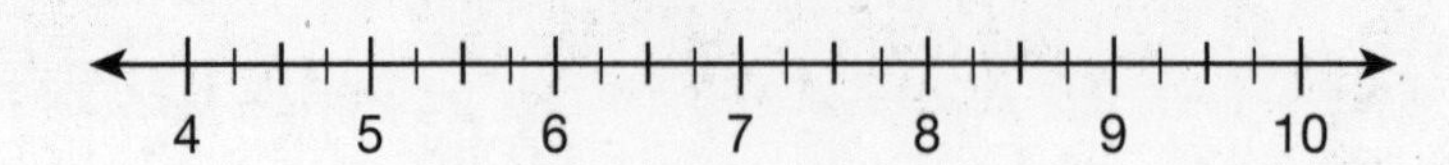

4 Shade the grid to show 20%. Then write what fraction and what decimal you shaded.

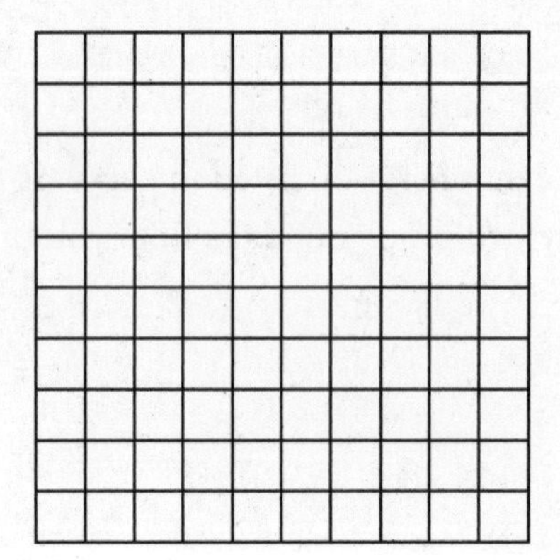

Fraction: ____________

Decimal: ____________

Standard

2 Computation

10 Multiplying By Two-Digit Whole Numbers

5.2.1: Solve problems involving multiplication and division of any whole numbers
5.2.6 Use estimation to decide whether answers are reasonable in addition, subtraction, and multiplication problems

Note: Do not use a calculator with this lesson. Do all your work with paper and pencil.

This lesson shows you one way to multiply any whole number by a two-digit whole number.

Example

Find the product: $59 \times 27 = ?$

STRATEGY: **Multiply and regroup.**

STEP 1: Multiply the ones.

$$\begin{array}{r} 59 \\ \times\ 27 \\ \hline \end{array}$$

$7 \times 9 = 63$

Think of 63 as 6 tens and 3 ones.

Write the 3 in the ones place of the answer and write the 6 in the tens column above the 5.

$$\begin{array}{r} {\scriptstyle 6} \\ 59 \\ \times\ 27 \\ \hline 3 \end{array}$$

STEP 2: Multiply the ones of the bottom number by the tens of the top number.

7×5 (tens) = 35 (tens)

Add the 6 tens shown above the 5 in the tens column. Cross out the 6.

$35 + 6 = 41$ (tens)

Write 41 (tens) in the answer.

$$\begin{array}{r} \not{6} \\ 59 \\ \times\ 27 \\ \hline 413 \end{array}$$

STEP 3: Multiply the tens of the bottom number by the ones of the top number.

2 (tens) $\times 9 = 18$ (tens)

Think of this number as 18 tens, or 180.

Write the 8 in the answer in the tens column and write the 1 above and to the left of the 5.

$$\begin{array}{r} 1\not{6} \\ 59 \\ \times\ 27 \\ \hline 413 \\ 8 \end{array}$$

STEP 4: Multiply the tens.

2 (tens) $\times$ 5 (tens) = 10 (hundreds)

Add the 1 that you wrote above the 5.

10 (hundreds) + 1 (hundreds) = 11 (hundreds)

Write 11 (hundreds) in the answer.

$$\begin{array}{r} 1\not{6} \\ 59 \\ \times\ 27 \\ \hline 413 \\ 118 \end{array}$$

STEP 5: Add to find the product.

$$\begin{array}{r} {}^{1\not{6}} \\ 59 \\ \times\ 27 \\ \hline 413 \\ +118 \\ \hline 1593 \end{array}$$

SOLUTION: **The product is 1,593.**

NOTE: You can use this technique to multiply any two whole numbers.

You can use estimation to check your answer. Round each of the factors in Example 1 to the greatest place and then multiply the rounded numbers:

59 rounds to 60.

27 rounds to 30.

$60 \times 30 = 1{,}800$

Since 59 and 27 were both rounded up, it makes sense that the estimate—1,800—is greater than the actual product—1,593.

Sample Test Questions

1 $46 \times 32 = ?$

Ⓐ 1,362

Ⓑ 1,372

Ⓒ 1,462

Ⓓ 1,472

2 $32 \times 94 = ?$

Ⓐ 3,108

Ⓑ 3,008

Ⓒ 2,908

Ⓓ 2,808

3 $162 \times 63 = ?$

Ⓐ 9,906

Ⓑ 10,106

Ⓒ 10,206

Ⓓ 11,206

4 $307 \times 95 = ?$

Ⓐ 28,165

Ⓑ 29,165

Ⓒ 4,865

Ⓓ 3,515

5 $23{,}117 \times 6 = ?$

Ⓐ 138,702

Ⓑ 138,712

Ⓒ 138,732

Ⓓ 138,762

6 $54 \times 79 = ?$

Ⓐ 4,366

Ⓑ 4,236

Ⓒ 4,166

Ⓓ 4,266

7 Which of the following is the best estimate of 68×41?

Ⓐ 2,800

Ⓑ 2,600

Ⓒ 2,400

Ⓓ 1,800

8 Which of the following is the best estimate of 198×71?

Ⓐ 16,000

Ⓑ 14,000

Ⓒ 12,000

Ⓓ 7,000

9 a) Multiply: 2,087 × 45

b) Explain your method.

____

____

____

____

c) How could you explain to someone that your answer is reasonable?

____

____

____

____

11 Dividing By Two-Digit Divisors

5.2.1: Solve problems involving multiplication and division of any whole numbers
5.2.6: Use estimation to decide whether answers are reasonable in addition, subtraction, multiplication and division problems

Note: Do not use a calculator with this lesson. Do all your work with paper and pencil.

Each number in a division problem has a name.

$$\text{divisor}\overline{)\text{dividend}}^{\text{quotient}}$$

In other words, the dividend, divided by the divisor, equals the quotient. Sometimes the answer includes a remainder.

Example 1

Find the quotient and remainder.

$23\overline{)1495}$

This means 1,495 divided by 23.

STRATEGY: **Estimate to find the quotient.**

STEP 1: How many times does the 2 of 23 divide the 14 of 1,495?

7 This is the first estimate.

Multiply 23 by 7.

$23 \times 7 = 161$, which is more than 149. So, 7 is too great.

STEP 2: Try 6.

Multiply 23×6.

$23 \times 6 = 138$, which is less than 149. So, 6 is the first digit of the quotient.

$$23\overline{)1495}\quad \text{quotient: } 6$$

STEP 3: Subtract 138 from 149. Bring down the 5.

$$\begin{array}{r} 6 \\ 23\overline{)1495} \\ -\,138 \\ \hline 115 \end{array}$$

STEP 4 : How many times does the 2 of 23 divide the 11 of 115?

5 This is the second estimate.

Multiply 23×5.

$23 \times 5 = 115$

STEP 5: Subtract 115 from 115.

$$\begin{array}{r} 65 \\ 23\overline{)1495} \\ -\,138 \\ \hline 115 \\ -\,115 \\ \hline 0 \end{array}$$

The remainder is 0.

SOLUTION: **The quotient is 65, and the remainder is 0.**

Example 2

Divide.

$76\overline{)6387}$

This means 6,387 divided by 76.

STRATEGY: **Estimate to find the quotient.**

STEP 1: How many times does 76 divide 6387?

Estimate by answering: What is 63 divided by 7?

Answer: 9

Multiply 9×76

$9 \times 76 = 684$, which is greater than 638. So 9 is too big.

STEP 2: Try 8.

$8 \times 76 = 608$, which is less than 638. So 8 works.

Write 8 as the first digit of the quotient.

$$\begin{array}{r} 8 \\ 76\overline{)6387} \end{array}$$

STEP 3: Subtract 608 from 638. Include the next digit.

$$\begin{array}{r} 8 \\ 76\overline{)6387} \\ -\,608 \\ \hline 307 \end{array}$$

STEP 4: How many times does 76 divide 307?

Estimate by answering: What is 30 divided by 7?

Answer: 4

Multiply $4 \times 76 = 304$

304 is less than 307, so 4 works.

Write 4 in the quotient.

$$\begin{array}{r} 84 \\ 76\overline{)6387} \\ -\,608 \\ \hline 307 \end{array}$$

STEP 5: Subtract 304 from 307.

$$\begin{array}{r} 84 \\ 76\overline{)6387} \\ -\,608 \\ \hline 307 \\ -\,304 \\ \hline 3 \end{array}$$

The remainder is 3.

SOLUTION: **The quotient is 84, and the remainder is 3.**

NOTE: The answer to Example 2 is often written as 84 R3. The R stands for remainder.

Another way to write this answer is $84\frac{3}{76}$.

You can use estimation to help you decide whether the answer to a division problem makes sense. In Example 2 above, you can round 76 to 80 and round 6,387 to 6,400. The numbers 6,400 and 80 are called compatible numbers because they are easy to divide: $6{,}400 \div 80 = 80$. Since 80 is close to 84 R3, the answer is reasonable.

Sample Test Questions

1 Divide: 252 ÷ 12

Ⓐ 20

Ⓑ 21

Ⓒ 22

Ⓓ 31

2 Divide: 493 ÷ 17

Ⓐ 29

Ⓑ 29 R1

Ⓒ 29 R2

Ⓓ 39

3 $35\overline{)4676}$

Ⓐ 133

Ⓑ 133 R21

Ⓒ 133 R22

Ⓓ 133 R31

4 $18\overline{)7877}$

Ⓐ 437 R11

Ⓑ 437 R10

Ⓒ 437 R9

Ⓓ 437

5 $42\overline{)8723}$

Ⓐ 27 R9

Ⓑ 27 R29

Ⓒ 207

Ⓓ 207 R29

6 $23\overline{)4853}$

Ⓐ 210 R22

Ⓑ 211

Ⓒ 211 R21

Ⓓ 211 R2

7 Which is the best estimate of 5,499 ÷ 88?

Ⓐ 60

Ⓑ 80

Ⓒ 600

Ⓓ 700

8 Which is the best estimate of 3,702 ÷ 13?

Ⓐ 30

Ⓑ 37

Ⓒ 300

Ⓓ 500

9 a) Find the answer: 8463 ÷ 38.

b) Explain your method for finding the quotient.

____

____

____

____

c) How could you explain to someone that your answer is reasonable?

____

____

____

____

12 Adding and Subtracting Decimals

5.2.5: Add and subtract decimals
5.2.7: Use mental arithmetic to add or subtract simple decimals
5.5.7: Add and subtract with money in decimal notation

How to Add or Subtract Two Decimals

1. Write one number under the other.
2. Make sure the decimal points line up.
3. Add or subtract each place, starting at the right.
4. Place the decimal point in the sum or difference, lined up under the other decimal points.

Example 1

Lorraine walked 2.7 miles on Wednesday and 4.2 miles on Thursday. How far did she walk on the two days?

STRATEGY: **Follow the steps above.**

$$\begin{array}{r} 2.7 \\ +\ 4.2 \\ \hline 6.9 \end{array}$$

SOLUTION: **Lorraine walked 6.9 miles on the two days.**

Example 2

Manny weighed two paper clips. A red paper clip weighed 3.75 grams and a yellow paper clip weighed 2.53 grams. How much more did the red paper clip weigh?

STRATEGY: **Follow the steps for adding and subtracting decimals.**

$$\begin{array}{r} 3.75 \\ -\ 2.53 \\ \hline 1.22 \end{array}$$

SOLUTION: **The red paper clip weighs 1.22 grams more.**

You may be able to add or subtract decimals mentally when the numbers are easy to work with. For example, in Examples 1 and 2 above, there was no regrouping, so you could have used mental math.

You can use estimation to check the reasonableness of your answers when adding and subtracting decimals. In Example 2 above, round 3.75 to 4 and round 2.53 to 3: $4 - 3 = 1$. Since 1 is close to 1.22, the difference 1.22 is reasonable.

You can use the rules for adding and subtracting decimals when you solve problems involving adding and subtracting money.

Example 3

Ginny paid $7.35 for lunch. She gave the cashier a $10 bill. How much change will she get?

STRATEGY: **Subtract the money amounts the same way you would subtract decimals.**

STEP 1: Write $10 so that it has the same number of decimal places as $7.35.

$10.00

STEP 2: Subtract.

$$\begin{array}{r} \$10.00 \\ -\ 7.35 \\ \hline \$2.65 \end{array}$$

SOLUTION: **She will get $2.65 in change.**

Sample Test Questions

In Questions 1–4, use mental math to find the sum or difference.

1 $2.9 + 3.1 = ?$

Ⓐ 5.0

Ⓑ 5.8

Ⓒ 6.0

Ⓓ 6.8

2 $0.003 + 0.033 = ?$

Ⓐ 0.030

Ⓑ 0.036

Ⓒ 0.063

Ⓓ 0.333

3 $0.047 - 0.003 = ?$

Ⓐ 0.017

Ⓑ 0.044

Ⓒ 0.050

Ⓓ 0.473

4 $9.057 - 0.003 = ?$

Ⓐ 0.054

Ⓑ 0.060

Ⓒ 9.054

Ⓓ 9.060

5 Carolyn practiced her flute for 1.5 hours on Saturday. She practiced for 1.2 hours on Sunday. How many more hours did she practice on Saturday than on Sunday?

Ⓐ 0.3 hours

Ⓑ 1.3 hours

Ⓒ 1.5 hours

Ⓓ 5.7 hours

6 Richard drank 2.57 liters of water at the beach. He drank 3.25 liters of water in the mountains. How many liters did Richard drink altogether?

Ⓐ 4.82 liters

Ⓑ 4.92 liters

Ⓒ 5.82 liters

Ⓓ 5.92 liters

7 Kathleen spent 2.9 hours doing homework last week. She spent 4.1 hours doing homework this week. How many fewer hours did Kathleen spend doing homework last week than this week?

Ⓐ 0.8 hours

Ⓑ 1.2 hours

Ⓒ 2.2 hours

Ⓓ 2.8 hours

8 Tom has 6.89 inches of string. If he cuts off a piece of string that is 4.99 inches long and uses it for a project, how much string will he have left?

Ⓐ 1.09 inches

Ⓑ 1.90 inches

Ⓒ 2.09 inches

Ⓓ 2.90 inches

9 There are two bags of macaroni. One weighs 3.45 kg. The other weighs 4.67 kg. What is the total weight of the two bags of macaroni?

Ⓐ 8.12 kg

Ⓑ 8.02 kg

Ⓒ 7.12 kg

Ⓓ 7.02 kg

10 $13.58 − $1.43 = ?

Ⓐ $11.15

Ⓑ $12.15

Ⓒ $14.01

Ⓓ $15.01

11 Ashley's best time for running 100 yards is 13.47 seconds. Her friend Kayla's best time is 15.19 seconds. How much slower is Kayla's time than Ashley's?

Ⓐ 11.72 seconds

Ⓑ 2.72 seconds

Ⓒ 1.72 seconds

Ⓓ 1.62 seconds

12 $13.67 + $3.20 = ?

Ⓐ $16.87

Ⓑ $16.89

Ⓒ $16.99

Ⓓ $45.67

13 Eric bought a CD that cost $14.45 including tax. He gave the cashier a $20 bill. How much change did he get?

Ⓐ $5.45

Ⓑ $5.55

Ⓒ $6.45

Ⓓ $6.55

14 Tara had $49.27 in her wallet. She took her friend to lunch and paid $30.88 including tax and tip. How much money did she have left in her wallet after lunch?

Explain why your answer is reasonable.

____

____

____

____

____

13 Adding and Subtracting Fractions With Unlike Denominators

5.2.2: Add and subtract fractions with different denominators

Note: Do not use a calculator with this lesson. Do all your work with paper and pencil.

LESSON STRATEGY: **Find a common denominator. Then use these rules when adding and subtracting two fractions.**

Sum of Two Fractions With a Common Denominator	Difference of Two Fractions With a Common Denominator
$\frac{\text{Sum of numerators}}{\text{Common denominator}}$	$\frac{\text{Difference of numerators}}{\text{Common denominator}}$
Example: $\frac{2}{7} + \frac{3}{7} = \frac{5}{7}$	Example: $\frac{5}{8} - \frac{3}{8} = \frac{2}{8}$

Example 1

$\frac{3}{5} + \frac{1}{4} = ?$

STRATEGY: **Find a common denominator.**

STEP 1: Find the least common multiple of 5 and 4. What numbers do the denominators 5 and 4 divide evenly?

5 and 4 evenly divide 20, 40, 60, and so forth—they are common multiples of 5 and 4. They can be used as common denominators.

STEP 2: Choose the least of the common denominators. The least common denominator is 20.

STEP 3: Change the two fractions $\frac{3}{5}$ and $\frac{1}{4}$ to equivalent fractions with 20 as a denominator.

$\frac{3}{5} = \frac{12}{20}$ and $\frac{1}{4} = \frac{5}{20}$

STEP 4: Use the rule in the lesson strategy for adding two fractions with the same denominator.

$\frac{12}{20} + \frac{5}{20} = \frac{17}{20}$

SOLUTION: **The sum is $\frac{17}{20}$.**

> **NOTE:** The lowest common denominator for two consecutive integers, such as 5 and 4, is their product.

Example 2

$4\frac{5}{8} - 2\frac{3}{4} = ?$

STRATEGY: **Find a common denominator. You may have to rename the greater number.**

STEP 1: What numbers do the denominators 8 and 4 divide evenly?

8 and 4 evenly divide 8, 16, 24, and so forth—common multiples of 8 and 4. They are common denominators for 8 and 4.

STEP 2: Choose the least of the common denominators.

The least common denominator is 8.

STEP 3: Change $\frac{3}{4}$ to an equivalent fraction with 8 as a denominator.

$\frac{3}{4} = \frac{6}{8}$

STEP 4: Set up the subtraction with the denominators of 8. Then check to see if subtraction in the fractions column is possible.

$$\begin{array}{r} 4\frac{5}{8} \\ -\ 2\frac{6}{8} \\ \hline \end{array}$$

Notice that $\frac{5}{8} - \frac{6}{8}$ is not possible because $\frac{6}{8}$ is greater than $\frac{5}{8}$.

STEP 5: Rename 4 as $3 + \frac{8}{8}$; then add $\frac{8}{8}$ to $\frac{5}{8}$

$4\frac{5}{8} = 3 + \frac{8}{8} + \frac{5}{8} = 3\frac{13}{8}$.

STEP 6: Subtract using the renamed mixed number. Use the rule from earlier this lesson to subtract the fractions, then subtract the whole numbers.

$$\begin{array}{r} 3\frac{13}{8} \\ -\ 2\frac{6}{8} \\ \hline 1\frac{7}{8} \end{array}$$

SOLUTION: **The difference is $1\frac{7}{8}$.**

Remember to examine your answers to see if the fraction can be expressed in lower terms. For example, if a sum is $2\frac{8}{12}$, you should express the fraction part of the mixed number in lowest terms. Divide both the numerator and denominator by their greatest common factor.

$$2\frac{8}{12} = 2 \times \frac{8 \div 4}{12 \div 4} = 2\frac{2}{3}$$

Sample Test Questions

1 $\frac{9}{10} - \frac{3}{10} = ?$

Ⓐ $\frac{3}{10}$

Ⓑ $\frac{3}{5}$

Ⓒ $\frac{6}{5}$

Ⓓ $\frac{2}{5}$

2 $\frac{3}{5} + \frac{3}{10} = ?$

Ⓐ $\frac{9}{10}$

Ⓑ $\frac{4}{5}$

Ⓒ $\frac{3}{5}$

Ⓓ $1\frac{1}{10}$

3 $4\frac{1}{2} - 2\frac{3}{4} = ?$

Ⓐ $2\frac{3}{4}$

Ⓑ $2\frac{1}{2}$

Ⓒ $2\frac{1}{4}$

Ⓓ $1\frac{3}{4}$

4 $4\frac{1}{5} + 3\frac{7}{10} = ?$

Ⓐ $8\frac{1}{10}$

Ⓑ $7\frac{9}{10}$

Ⓒ $7\frac{7}{10}$

Ⓓ $\frac{9}{10}$

5 $10 - 3\frac{3}{8} = ?$

Ⓐ $6\frac{3}{8}$

Ⓑ $6\frac{5}{8}$

Ⓒ $6\frac{7}{8}$

Ⓓ $7\frac{5}{8}$

6 $2\frac{3}{5} + 7\frac{9}{10} = ?$

Ⓐ $10\frac{7}{10}$

Ⓑ $10\frac{3}{5}$

Ⓒ $10\frac{1}{2}$

Ⓓ $9\frac{1}{2}$

7 $8\frac{2}{3} - \frac{5}{6} = ?$

Ⓐ $7\frac{5}{6}$

Ⓑ $7\frac{2}{3}$

Ⓒ $7\frac{1}{2}$

Ⓓ $7\frac{1}{3}$

8 $7\frac{1}{10} - 6\frac{3}{5} = ?$

Ⓐ $\frac{3}{5}$

Ⓑ $\frac{1}{2}$

Ⓒ $\frac{2}{5}$

Ⓓ $\frac{3}{10}$

9 $10\frac{5}{8} - \frac{1}{2} = ?$

Ⓐ $9\frac{7}{8}$

Ⓑ $10\frac{1}{8}$

Ⓒ $10\frac{1}{4}$

Ⓓ $10\frac{3}{8}$

10 $100 - 22\frac{7}{8} = ?$

Ⓐ $76\frac{3}{4}$

Ⓑ $77\frac{1}{8}$

Ⓒ $76\frac{7}{8}$

Ⓓ $77\frac{1}{4}$

11 $17\frac{3}{8} - 16\frac{3}{4} = ?$

Ⓐ $1\frac{1}{2}$

Ⓑ $1\frac{1}{4}$

Ⓒ $\frac{7}{8}$

Ⓓ $\frac{5}{8}$

12 Elena is $5\frac{1}{4}$ ft tall She is $\frac{5}{12}$ ft taller than her brother Ricky. How tall is Ricky?

Explain how you found your answer.

____

____

____

____

____

14 Multiplying and Dividing Fractions and Mixed Numbers

5.2.3: Use models to show an understanding of multiplication and division of fractions
5.2.4: Multiply and divide fractions to solve problems

Multiplying Fractions

Between fractions, the word "of" means to multiply.

$\frac{1}{3}$ of $\frac{1}{2} = \frac{1}{3} \times \frac{1}{2}$

You can use models to help you understand how to multiply fractions.

Draw a rectangle and divide it into rows that represent thirds and columns that represent halves.

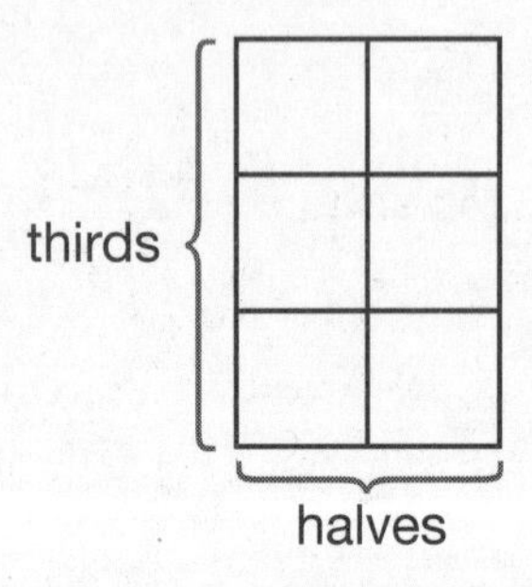

Shade one of the rows to represent $\frac{1}{3}$ and one of the columns to represent $\frac{1}{2}$.

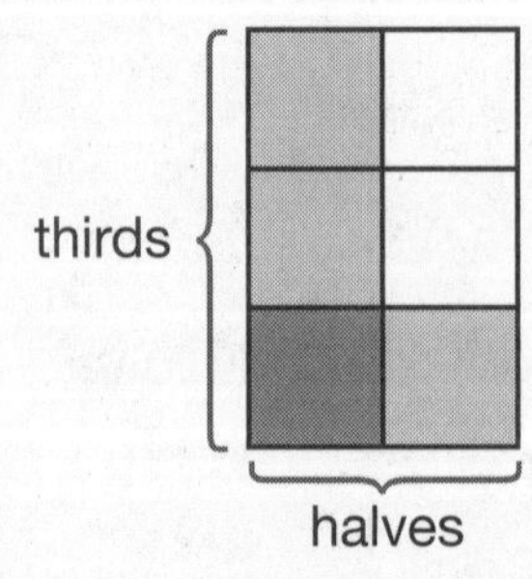

The part of the rectangle shaded twice represents $\frac{1}{3}$ of $\frac{1}{2}$, or the product $\frac{1}{3} \times \frac{1}{2}$. It is $\frac{1}{6}$ of the large rectangle, so $\frac{1}{3} \times \frac{1}{2}$ is $\frac{1}{6}$.

Rule: How to Multiply Two Fractions

$$\frac{1}{3} \times \frac{1}{2} = ?$$

STEP 1: Multiply the two numerators $(1 \times 1 = 1)$

STEP 2: Multiply the two denominators $(3 \times 2 = 6)$

STEP 3: Form this fraction from Steps 1 and 2:

$$\frac{\text{product of numerators}}{\text{product of denominators}} = \frac{1}{6}$$

STEP 4: Simplify the fractions if necessary: $\frac{1}{6}$ cannot be simplified.

Example 1

Multiply $1\frac{1}{2} \times 12$.

STRATEGY: **Use the rule for multiplying two fractions.**

STEP 1: Change the mixed number $1\frac{1}{2}$ to an improper fraction.

$1\frac{1}{2} = \frac{3}{2}$

STEP 2: Write the whole number 12 in fractional form.

$12 = \frac{12}{1}$ (All integers can be written in fractional form by using 1 as a denominator.)

STEP 3: Multiply the two fractions. Simplify if necessary.

$\frac{3}{2} \times \frac{12}{1} = \frac{3 \times 12}{2 \times 1} = \frac{36}{2} = 18$

SOLUTION: $\mathbf{1\frac{1}{2} \times 12 = 18}$

Dividing Fractions

Example 2

Juanita divided a pizza into sixths. How many sixths are there in $\frac{1}{3}$ of the pizza?

STRATEGY: **Draw a diagram of a pizza.**

STEP 1: Draw a diagram of a pizza divided into 6 equal parts.

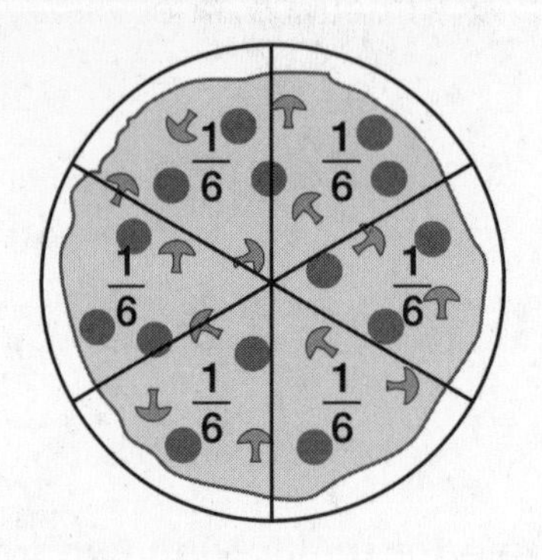

Each part is $\frac{1}{6}$ of the pizza.

STEP 2: Shade $\frac{1}{3}$ of the pizza.

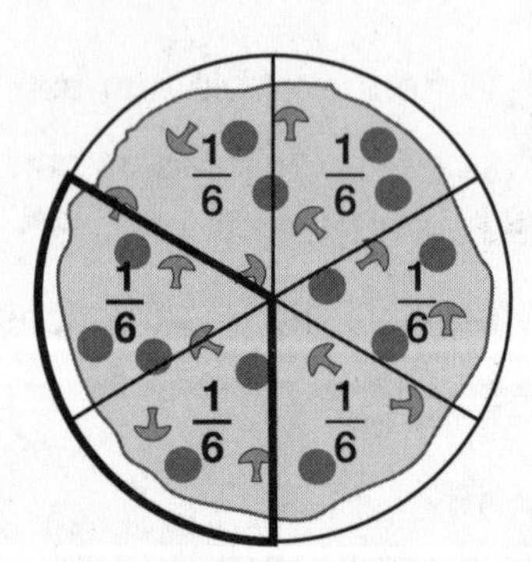

STEP 3: Count the number of sixths in $\frac{1}{3}$ of the pizza.

SOLUTION: **There are 2 sixths in $\frac{1}{3}$ of the pizza.**

Example 2 finds the quotient $\frac{1}{3} \div \frac{1}{6} = ?$

Rule: How to Divide Two Fractions

1. Find the reciprocal of the second fraction.

   (That means "flip" the fraction, with the numerator taking the denominator's place, and vice versa: $\frac{3}{5}$ becomes $\frac{5}{3}$).
2. Multiply the first fraction by the flipped fraction.
3. Simplify, if necessary.

Try Example 2 following this Rule.

$\frac{1}{3} \div \frac{1}{6} = \frac{1}{3} \times \frac{6}{1} = \frac{6}{3} = 2$

Example 3

Divide: $\frac{3}{4} \div \frac{1}{2} = ?$

STRATEGY: **Follow the rule for dividing two fractions.**

$\frac{3}{4} \div \frac{1}{2} = \frac{3}{4} \times \frac{2}{1} = \frac{6}{4} = \frac{3}{2} = 1\frac{1}{2}$

SOLUTION: $\frac{3}{4} \div \frac{1}{2} = 1\frac{1}{2}$

Sample Test Questions

1 Find $\frac{1}{5}$ of $\frac{1}{2}$.

Ⓐ $\frac{1}{20}$

Ⓑ $\frac{1}{2}$

Ⓒ $\frac{1}{10}$

Ⓓ $\frac{4}{5}$

2 Divide $\frac{1}{2} \div \frac{3}{4} = ?$

Ⓐ $\frac{2}{3}$

Ⓑ $\frac{3}{8}$

Ⓒ $\frac{5}{6}$

Ⓓ $\frac{3}{2}$

3 Multiply $\frac{3}{4} \times \frac{1}{3} = ?$

Ⓐ 5

Ⓑ $\frac{1}{4}$

Ⓒ $\frac{5}{3}$

Ⓓ $\frac{15}{4}$

4 Divide $\frac{3}{5} \div 3 = ?$

Ⓐ $\frac{5}{5}$

Ⓑ $\frac{5}{9}$

Ⓒ $\frac{9}{5}$

Ⓓ $\frac{1}{5}$

5 Multiply: $3 \times 3\frac{2}{3} = ?$

Ⓐ $\frac{3}{11}$

Ⓑ 11

Ⓒ $\frac{11}{3}$

Ⓓ $\frac{11}{9}$

6 Divide: $\frac{2}{3} \div 1\frac{1}{3} = ?$

Ⓐ $\frac{1}{2}$

Ⓑ $\frac{1}{3}$

Ⓒ $\frac{1}{4}$

Ⓓ $\frac{4}{5}$

7 a) Shade this rectangle to show $\frac{3}{5} \times \frac{2}{3}$.

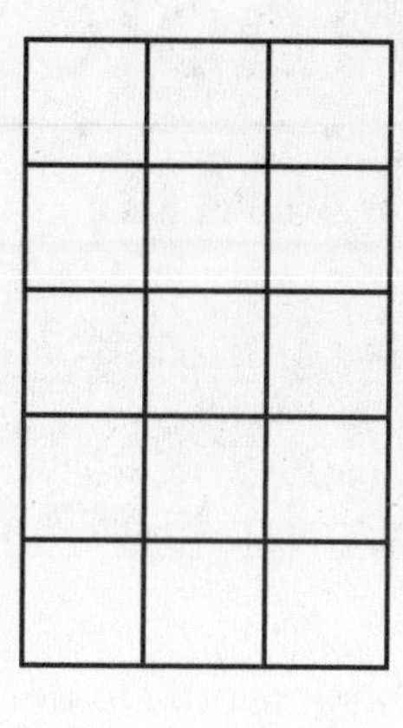

b) Explain how the shaded region shows the product.

____

____

____

____

____

c) What is the product in simplest form?

____

15 Solving Problems With Whole Number Operations

5.2.1: Solve problems involving multiplication and division of any whole numbers
5.2.6: Use estimation to decide whether answers are reasonable in addition, subtraction, multiplication and division problems
5.5.7: Add and subtract with money in decimal notation

Note: Do not use a calculator with this lesson. Do all your work with paper and pencil.

In this lesson you will apply whole-number operations.

Example 1

As principal of Farley School, Mrs. Aaron will give each of the 4 sixth-grade classrooms an equal amount of the $356 in the parents' fund. How much money will each classroom receive?

STRATEGY: **Read the problem carefully. Then determine the operation that will help solve this problem.**

STEP 1: Which operation will solve the problem?

The operation is division, since the money will be divided equally among the four classrooms.

STEP 2: Set up the division.

$4\overline{)356}$

This means "divide 356 by 4."

STEP 3: Do the computation.

$$\begin{array}{r} 89 \\ 4\overline{)356} \\ -32 \\ \hline 36 \\ -36 \\ \hline 0 \end{array}$$

SOLUTION: **Each classroom will receive $89.**

Example 2

Malcolm delivers soda for a cola company. On Monday, he delivered 127 cases of soda. Each case has 24 cans. How many cans of soda did he deliver?

STRATEGY: **Read the problem carefully and determine the operation that will help solve this problem.**

STEP 1: Which operation will solve the problem?

Since there are 127 cases of soda, with 24 cans in each case, you need to multiply.

STEP 2: Set up the multiplication.

$$\begin{array}{r} 127 \\ \times\ 24 \\ \hline \end{array}$$

STEP 3: Do the computation.

$$\begin{array}{r} 127 \\ \times\ 24 \\ \hline 508 \\ +\ 2540 \\ \hline 3048 \end{array}$$

SOLUTION: **Malcolm delivered 3,048 cans of soda.**

Sample Test Questions

1 Maria has spent 1,054 days in school since kindergarten. Her little brother has spent 716 days in school. How many more days has Maria spent in school than her brother?

Ⓐ 328

Ⓑ 338

Ⓒ 348

Ⓓ 368

2 Eric carried 37 boxes of pencils to school last Friday. Each box had 25 pencils. How many pencils did Eric bring to school?

Ⓐ 725

Ⓑ 825

Ⓒ 925

Ⓓ 1,205

3 Dana placed 154 movie cards into 9 equal piles. How many cards were in each pile? How many were left over?

Ⓐ 16 in each pile, 1 left over

Ⓑ 16 in each pile, 2 left over

Ⓒ 17 in each pile, 1 left over

Ⓓ 17 in each pile, 2 left over

4 The attendance at the last two basketball games at the Franklin High School were 2,704 and 6,348. How many people came to these games?

Ⓐ 9,052

Ⓑ 9,042

Ⓒ 8,952

Ⓓ 8,052

5 An inventory at a supermarket shows that it has 1,206 magic markers. They come in boxes of 6 each. How many boxes are there altogether?

Ⓐ 21

Ⓑ 101

Ⓒ 102

Ⓓ 201

6 How many seconds are in a week?

Ⓐ 25,200

Ⓑ 100,800

Ⓒ 604,800

Ⓓ 10,080

7 Kyra spent $47.26 at the mall. She started out with $50. How much did she have left?

Ⓐ $3.84

Ⓑ $2.84

Ⓒ $3.74

Ⓓ $2.74

8 Devin has to read 128 pages of his social studies textbook. He decided to read 25 pages each night for the next 5 nights. After he has done this, how many more pages will he have to read?

Ⓐ 1

Ⓑ 2

Ⓒ 3

Ⓓ 4

9 Tina bought the following equipment to go with her new computer:

Keyboard	$ 89
Monitor	$305
Printer	$296
Scanner	$212

All prices included tax. She paid with a $1,000 gift certificate. She expected to have $187 left over.

a) Without finding the exact answer, explain why her expectation is wrong.

____

____

____

____

____

b) Find the exact amount she paid for the computer equipment.

Progress Check for Lessons 10–15

1 Divide 8,423 by 21

Ⓐ 401

Ⓑ 401 R1

Ⓒ 401 R2

Ⓓ 401 R19

2 $\frac{5}{8} - \frac{1}{2} = ?$

Ⓐ $\frac{2}{5}$

Ⓑ $\frac{2}{3}$

Ⓒ $\frac{1}{4}$

Ⓓ $\frac{1}{8}$

3 Students counted all the pencils in Lantern School. There were 914 pencils. Then the students placed the pencils in boxes that held 24 pencils each. How many boxes did they fill completely?

Ⓐ 381

Ⓑ 39

Ⓒ 38

Ⓓ 37

4 $\frac{6}{8} - \frac{1}{3} = ?$

Ⓐ $\frac{2}{5}$

Ⓑ $\frac{5}{12}$

Ⓒ $\frac{3}{8}$

Ⓓ $\frac{1}{4}$

5 $1\frac{3}{4} \times \frac{5}{8}$

Ⓐ $1\frac{3}{32}$

Ⓑ $1\frac{3}{16}$

Ⓒ $1\frac{3}{8}$

Ⓓ $1\frac{3}{4}$

6 Tim takes money out of an automated teller machine every Tuesday morning. He never takes more than \$50 and never takes less than \$25. After five weeks, what is a reasonable range for the amount of money he withdrew from his account?

Ⓐ less than \$125

Ⓑ between \$125 and \$250

Ⓒ between \$250 and \$350

Ⓓ more than \$350

7 $36 \times 72 = ?$

Ⓐ 2,503

Ⓑ 2,562

Ⓒ 2,582

Ⓓ 2,592

8 Martha paid her \$45.92 electricity bill and her \$81.66 telephone bill. What was the total of both bills?

Ⓐ \$126.58

Ⓑ \$127.58

Ⓒ \$128.58

Ⓓ \$126.68

9 The ball Smith hit traveled 403 feet. The ball Jones hit traveled 295 feet. What is a reasonable estimate of how many more feet Smith's ball traveled?

Ⓐ 100 feet

Ⓑ 150 feet

Ⓒ 200 feet

Ⓓ 250 feet

10 What product does this model show?

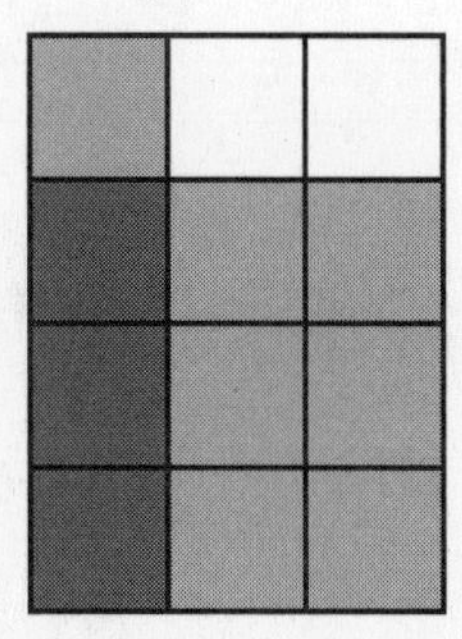

Ⓐ $\frac{1}{3} \times \frac{1}{4}$

Ⓑ $\frac{2}{3} \times \frac{1}{4}$

Ⓒ $\frac{1}{3} \times \frac{2}{4}$

Ⓓ $\frac{1}{3} \times \frac{3}{4}$

11 Use mental math to find the difference:

$\$4.95 - \$3.05 = ?$

Ⓐ \$0.35

Ⓑ \$0.45

Ⓒ \$1.35

Ⓓ \$1.90

Standard 2
Open-Ended Questions

1 Each minute, Bobby pours $1\frac{1}{4}$ cups of broth into the soup he is making. The soup needs 10 cups of broth. How many minutes will it take Bobby to pour the broth into the soup? Show your work.

2 You have $2\frac{3}{4}$ pizzas left over after a party. How many slices are left if each slice is $\frac{1}{8}$ of a pizza? Use words and/or pictures to explain your answer.

3 Idalia's teacher has a school supply budget of $300. She plans to spend $67.50 for pencils, $203 for writing pads, and $43.50 for pens. Will she be able to buy all these items and keep within her budget? Use words or symbols to explain your reasoning.

4 Beth has $2\frac{1}{2}$ yards of trim to make costumes for the class play. She needs another $3\frac{2}{3}$ yards of trim to complete the costumes. How many yards of trim will she use in all? Explain.

Standard

3

Algebra and Functions

16 Translating Word Problems Into Expressions and Sentences

5.3.1: Use a variable to represent an unknown number

You need to know how to write word sentences in problems as number sentences. Use a variable to represent an unknown quantity in an expression or sentence.

Here are some common words and phrases and their mathematical translations.

Phrases That Mean ADDITION

x plus 4	$x + 4$
Add y and 8	$y + 8$
2 more than z	$z + 2$

Phrases That Mean SUBTRACTION

a minus 4	$a - 4$
Subtract 3 from b.	$b - 3$
c less 5	$c - 5$

(Be careful. In subtraction, the order of the numbers is important.)

Phrases That Mean MULTIPLICATION

twice a number	$2x$
5 times a number	$5y$
the product of a number and 8	$8z$

Phrases That Mean DIVISION

the quotient of a number and 7	$n \div 7$ or $\frac{n}{7}$
a number divided by 6	$n \div 6$ or $\frac{n}{6}$

Example 1

Which expression has the same value as 6 more than x?

A $6 - x$
B $x - 6$
C $x + 6$
D $x \times 6$

STRATEGY: **Follow these steps:**

STEP 1: Look for the phrase "more than" in the table on the prior page.

The answer you want will be an addition problem.

STEP 2: Look at your answer choices.

Find the number expression that uses addition.

SOLUTION: **This is Answer C. $x + 6$ is the same as "6 more than x."**

Some expressions can involve more than one operation.

Example 2

Write an expression for the following sentence.

A number is divided by 4 and then 6 is subtracted.

STRATEGY: **Find the phrases in the table.**

STEP 1: Choose a variable to represent the number.

Let n represent the number.

STEP 2: Show the number divided by 4.

$\frac{n}{4}$

STEP 3: Show 6 subtracted from the quotient.

$\frac{n}{4} - 6$

SOLUTION: **An expression for the word sentence is $\frac{n}{4} - 6$.**

Some word sentences can be translated into equations.

Example 3

Write an equation for the following word sentence.

When a number is multiplied by 6 and then 8 is added, the result is 26.

STRATEGY: **Find the key words in the table.**

STEP 1: Choose a variable to represent the number.

Let x represent the number.

STEP 2: Show the number multiplied by 6.

$6x$

STEP 3: Show 8 added to the product.

$6x + 8$

STEP 4: Translate "the result is" as "equals."

$6x + 8 = 26$

SOLUTION: **An equation for the sentence is $6x + 8 = 26$.**

Sample Test Questions

In Questions 1–3, choose the mathematical expression for each word expression.

1 The product of a number and 3

Ⓐ $n + 3$

Ⓑ $3n$

Ⓒ $n - 3$

Ⓓ $\frac{n}{3}$

2 Nine more than a number

Ⓐ $x + 9$

Ⓑ $9x$

Ⓒ $x \div 9$

Ⓓ $9 - x$

3 Eight less than the product of a number and 7

Ⓐ $8 - 7n$

Ⓑ $(8 - 7)n$

Ⓒ $7n - 8$

Ⓓ $\frac{n}{7} - 8$

In Questions 4 and 5, choose the equation for each word sentence.

4 When a certain number is doubled and then 7 is added, the result is 19.

Ⓐ $n + 2 + 7 = 19$

Ⓑ $n + 2 = 19 + 7$

Ⓒ $2n + 7 = 19$

Ⓓ $2n - 7 = 19$

5 When a certain number is increased by 9 and then 4 is subtracted, the result is 12.

Ⓐ $9n - 4 = 12$

Ⓑ $n + 9 - 4 = 12$

Ⓒ $n - 9 - 4 = 12$

Ⓓ $\frac{n}{9} - 4 = 12$

6 Let x stand for the unknown number and write an equation for this word sentence:

> When a number is multiplied by 8 and then 5 is subtracted, the result is 21.

Explain how you found your equation.

____

____

____

____

____

17 Evaluating Algebraic Expressions

5.3.2: Write simple algebraic expressions in one or two variables and evaluate them by substitution

Variables

Letters that stand for numbers are called variables. The letters a, b, c, x, y, and z are often used for variables. Here are some of the ways you may see variables.

Multiply 3 and a.	$3a$
Multiply 4, a, and b, and then add a.	$4ab + a$
Multiply $\frac{1}{3}$, x, y, and z.	$\frac{1}{3}xyz$

Evaluating Expressions

To evaluate expressions, replace variables with specific numbers and do the math.

Example 1

a) If $c = 5$, what is $4c$?

b) If $t = 3$, what is $16t$?

c) If $x = 4$, what is $\frac{x}{2}$?

STRATEGY: **Replace each variable with its value.**

SOLUTIONS: **a) If $c = 5$, then $4c = 4(5) = 20$**

b) If $t = 3$, then $16t = 16(3) = 48$

c) If $x = 4$, then $\frac{x}{2} = \frac{4}{2} = 2$

Example 2

Evaluate $4x + y$ if $x = 5$ and $y = 3$.

STRATEGY: **Substitute and compute.**

STEP 1: Substitute 5 for x and 3 for y.

$4x + y = 4(5) + 3$

STEP 2: Compute.

$4(5) + 3 = 20 + 3 = 23$

SOLUTION: **The result is 23.**

Example 3

A phone company uses this formula to calculate the cost of a phone call:

$C = 1 + 0.20m$

where $1 is a fixed cost, m is the number of minutes of the call, and C is the total cost of the call. Use this formula to compute the cost of a call that lasts 40 minutes.

STRATEGY: **Substitute and compute.**

STEP 1: Substitute.

$C = 1 + 0.20(40)$

STEP 2: Multiply the whole number and the decimal.
Multiply the numbers as if there were no decimals. Then count the total number of decimal places and put that many decimal places in the answer.

$$\begin{array}{r} 0.20 \\ \times\ 40 \\ \hline 8.00 \end{array}$$

STEP 3: Compute.

$C = 1 + 8 = 9$

SOLUTION: **The cost is $9.**

Sample Test Questions

1 Evaluate this expression if $x = 2$ and $y = 1$.

$3x + 2y$

Ⓐ 2

Ⓑ 4

Ⓒ 6

Ⓓ 8

2 Evaluate this expression if $y = 1$ and $z = 3$.

$5z - 11y$

Ⓐ 3

Ⓑ 4

Ⓒ 5

Ⓓ 6

3 Find the value of z if $r = 4$, and $s = 3$.

$z = \frac{1}{4}r + s$

Ⓐ 4

Ⓑ 6

Ⓒ 8

Ⓓ 10

4 What does this expression mean?

$6xy + 6y$

Ⓐ Multiply 6, x, and y.

Ⓑ Multiply 6, x, and y and then add the result of multiplying 6 and y.

Ⓒ Add the product of 6 and y to 6.

Ⓓ Multiply 6, x, and y and then subtract the result of multiplying 6 and y.

5 Find the value of p if $W = 3$ and $L = 4$.

$p = 2L + 2W$

Ⓐ 7

Ⓑ 10

Ⓒ 11

Ⓓ 14

6 Evaluate this expression if $x = 4$, $y = 10$, and $z = 6$.

$xy - xz$

Ⓐ 12

Ⓑ 16

Ⓒ 18

Ⓓ 20

7 A taxi company uses this expression to calculate the cost of a trip:

$2 + 0.50t$

where $2 is a fixed charge and t is the time in minutes. Use this expression to compute the cost of a trip that lasts 30 minutes.

Ⓐ $15

Ⓑ $16

Ⓒ $17

Ⓓ $20

8 The cost of a meal at Smith's Deli depends on the weight of the main course. This is the expression the deli uses to determine the cost of a meal:

$3 + 0.40w$

where $3 is a fixed cost and w is the weight of the main course in ounces. What is the cost of a meal if the main course weighs 14 ounces?

Ⓐ $5.60

Ⓑ $6.00

Ⓒ $7.60

Ⓓ $8.60

9 Tammy repairs television sets. She charges $25 for a house call and $18 per hour.

a) Write an expression to find the total amount Tammy earns for a repair job. Let h represent the number of hours she works.

b) Use your expression in part a) to find the total amount Tammy earns for a repair job that takes 2 hours.

18 The Distributive Property

5.3.3: Use the distributive property in numerical equations and expressions

This is an example of the distributive property of multiplication and addition:

$6 \times (4 + 7) = 6 \times 4 + 6 \times 7$.

This same rule can also be used with a variable.

Example 1

Multiply $7 \times (y + 9)$ using the distributive property.

STRATEGY: **Think of y as a number and follow the rule shown above.**

$7 \times (y + 9) = 7 \times y + 7 \times 9 = 7 \times y + 63$

SOLUTION: $\mathbf{7 \times (y + 9) = 7 \times y + 63}$

NOTE: Another way to write $7 \times (y + 9)$ is $7(y + 9)$, and another way to write $7 \times y + 63$ is $7y + 63$. You can drop the $\times$ sign between a number and a variable.

Example 2

Use the distributive property to multiply 60×103.

STRATEGY: **Rewrite the number 103 as a sum.**

STEP 1: Rewrite the number 103.

$103 = 100 + 3$

STEP 2: Use the distributive property.

$60 \times 103 = 60 \times (100 + 3) = 60 \times 100 + 60 \times 3$

STEP 3: Do the math.

$60 \times 100 + 60 \times 3 = 6{,}000 + 180 = 6{,}180$

SOLUTION: **$60 \times 103 = 6{,}180$**

Sample Test Questions

1 Multiply $3(y + 4)$ using the distributive property.

Ⓐ $3y + 4$

Ⓑ $y + 12$

Ⓒ $3y + 12$

Ⓓ $3y + 7$

2 If you use the distributive property to multiply 70×404, which is the best first step?

Ⓐ Write 70 as $60 + 10$.

Ⓑ Write 404 as $400 + 40$.

Ⓒ Write 404 as $400 + 4$.

Ⓓ Write 404 as $354 + 50$.

3 Use the distributive property.

$9(q + 4) = ?$

Ⓐ $9q + 4$

Ⓑ $9q + 36$

Ⓒ $9q + 13$

Ⓓ $q + 36$

4 Multiply $7(3 + s)$ using the distributive property.

Ⓐ $10 + 7s$

Ⓑ $10 + s$

Ⓒ $21 + 7s$

Ⓓ $21 + s$

5 Which shows how the distributive property can be used to make the computation 30×203 easier?

Ⓐ $30 \times (200 + 30) = 30 \times 200 + 30 \times 30$

Ⓑ $30 \times (200 + 3) = 30 \times 200 + 30 \times 3$

Ⓒ $30 \times (200 + 3) = 200 + 30 \times 3$

Ⓓ $30 \times (200 + 3) = 30 \times 300 + 30 \times 4$

6 Multiply $w(3 + 21)$ using the distributive property.

Ⓐ $3w + 21$

Ⓑ $w + 21w$

Ⓒ $3w + 21w$

Ⓓ $3 + 21w$

7 Tom had to find the following product to complete a math problem.

15×203

Write directions for Tom showing how he can use the distributive property to rewrite the expression and find the answer using mental math.

____

____

____

____

____

19 Ordered Pairs and Linear Equations

5.3.4: Identify and graph ordered pairs of positive numbers
5.3.5: Find ordered pairs that fit a linear equation, graph the ordered pairs and draw the line they determine

What is an ordered pair of numbers?

An ordered pair of numbers is a set of two numbers such as (3,5).

3 is the first number of the ordered pair

5 is the second number of the ordered pair.

The first number is called the ***x*-coordinate.**

The second number is called the ***y*-coordinate.**

Each ordered pair can be represented on a grid like the one shown below.

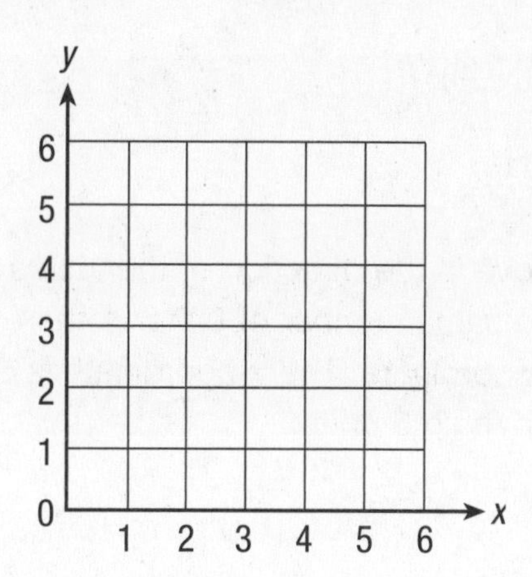

On the grid the lines with arrows are called **axes.**

The horizontal axis is called the ***x*-axis.**

The vertical axis is called the ***y*-axis.**

The point where the two axes cross (0) is called the **origin.**

Example 1

Locate the point on the grid for the ordered pair (3,5).

STRATEGY: **Move in the direction of the x-axis first and then in the direction of the y-axis.**

STEP 1: Start at the origin.

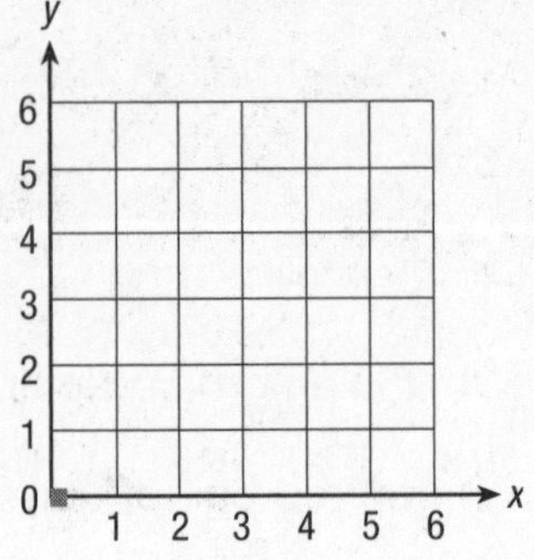

STEP 2: Move to the right along the x-axis the number of units named by the x-coordinate. The x-coordinate is 3. So move 3 units to the right of the origin along the x-axis.

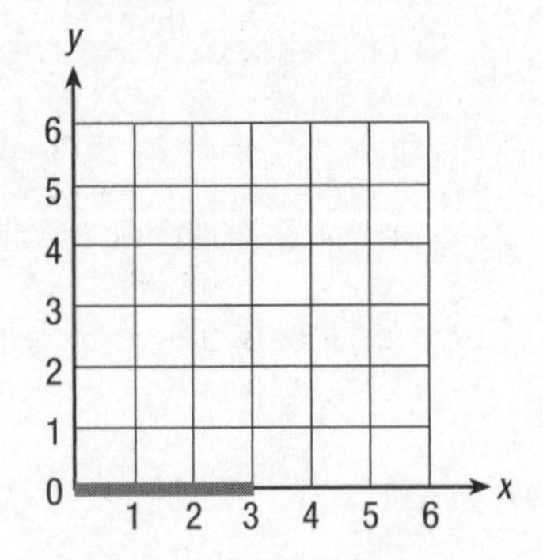

STEP 3: Move in the direction of the y-axis the same number of units as the y-coordinate. The y-coordinate is 5. Move up 5 units.

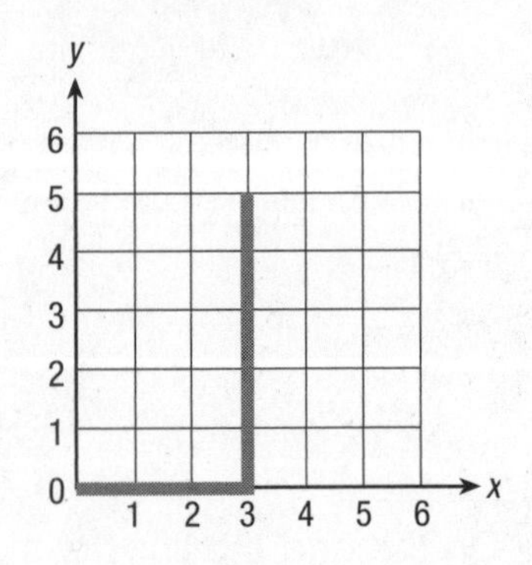

SOLUTION: **Place a dot at (3,5).**

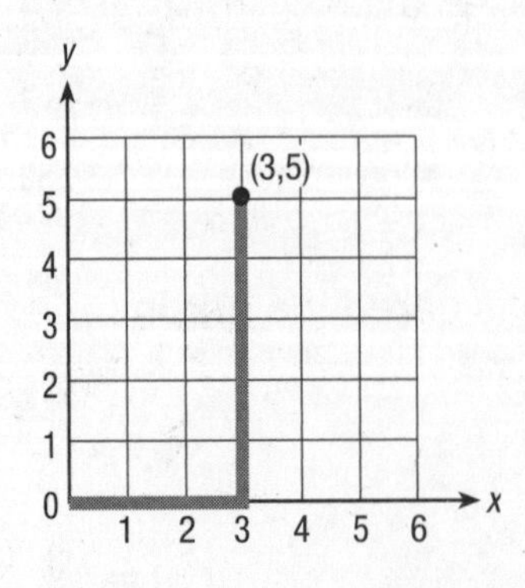

Rules for Locating Ordered Pairs on a Grid

For x-coordinate, move to the right.

For y-coordinates, move up.

You can graph a relationship between x and y by plotting several points on a grid. You need to find several ordered pairs to see what the graph looks like.

A linear equation has a graph that is a straight line. Here are some examples of linear equations.

$$y = x \qquad y = 3x \qquad y = x + 2 \qquad y = 2x + 5$$

You can graph a linear equation by making a table to find several ordered pairs, graphing the ordered pairs, and then drawing a line through the points.

Example 2

Draw the graph of this linear equation $y = 3x$.

STRATEGY: **Find 5 points (ordered pairs) for the graph.**

STEP 1: Start with x values and use a table.

Make a table for these x values. (Note that you could choose any x values.)

x	y
0	
1	
2	
3	
4	

STEP 2: Find the *y* values for the *x* values.

x	*y*
0	0
1	3
2	6
3	9
4	12

STEP 3: List the ordered pairs from the table.

The ordered pairs from the table are (0,0), (1,3), (2,6), (3,9), and (4,12).

STEP 4: Plot these ordered pairs on a grid.

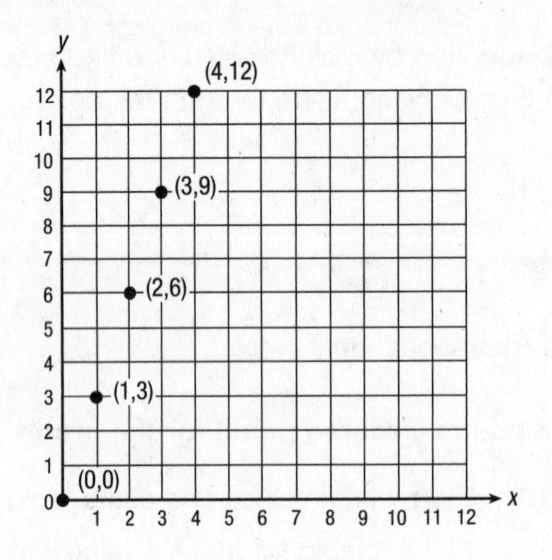

STEP 5: Connect the points.

SOLUTION:

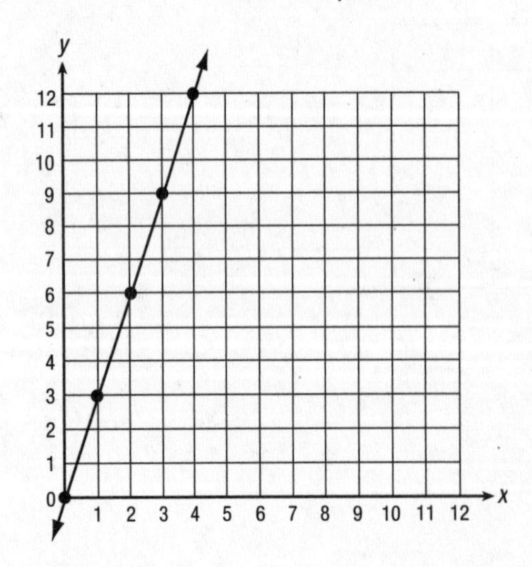

Sample Test Questions

1 What does the point at (5,3) on the grid map represent?

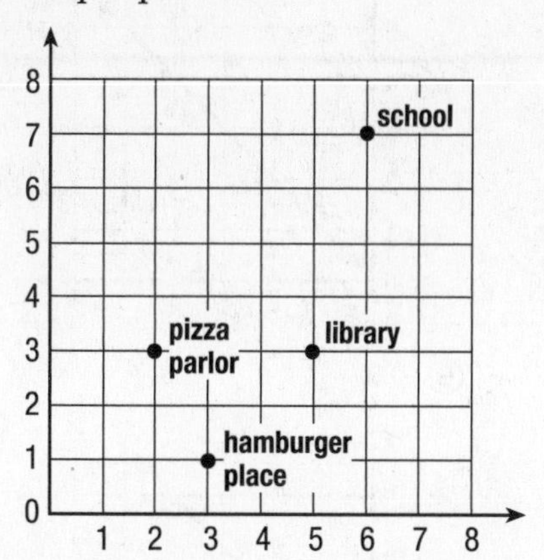

Ⓐ the library

Ⓑ the school

Ⓒ the hamburger place

Ⓓ the pizza parlor

2 You are playing a game called Find the City. Four cities are located at W, X, Y, and Z. If you named the position of City W, what location did you name?

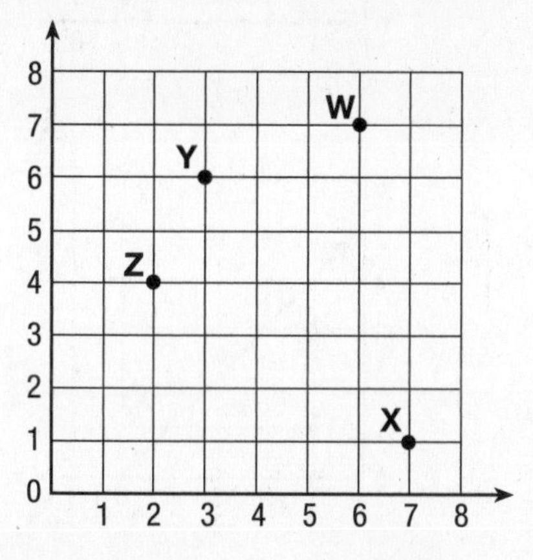

Ⓐ (2,4)

Ⓑ (7,1)

Ⓒ (3,6)

Ⓓ (6,7)

3 If you connect the following points, what figure do you get?

(4,1), (8,5), (5,8), (1,4)

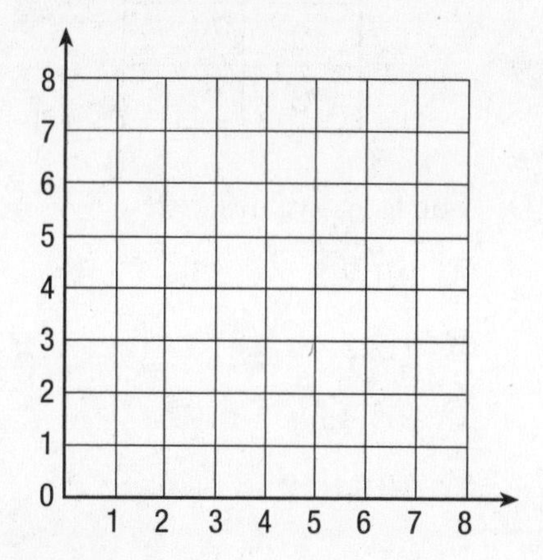

Ⓐ square

Ⓑ rectangle

Ⓒ triangle

Ⓓ trapezoid

4 What is the location of the baseball field on the grid map below?

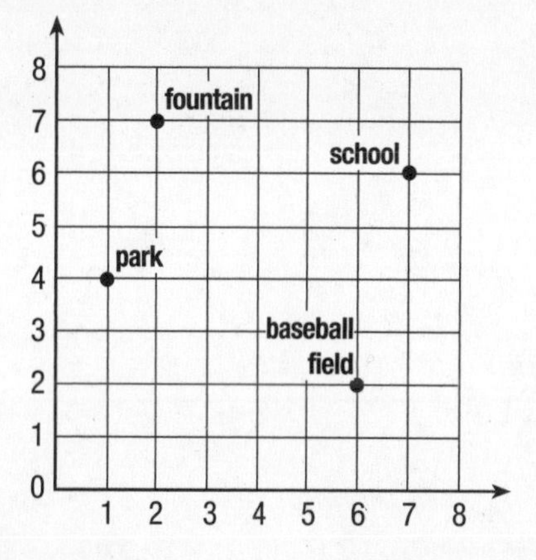

Ⓐ (1,4)

Ⓑ (2,8)

Ⓒ (6,2)

Ⓓ (7,6)

5 For the relationship, $y = x + 1$, fill in the table for the y values.

x	y
0	
1	
2	
3	

The four y values are:

Ⓐ 0,1,2,3

Ⓑ 1,2,3,4

Ⓒ 2,3,4,5

Ⓓ 10,11,12,13

6 Which of these lines is the graph of $y = x + 1$?

Ⓐ
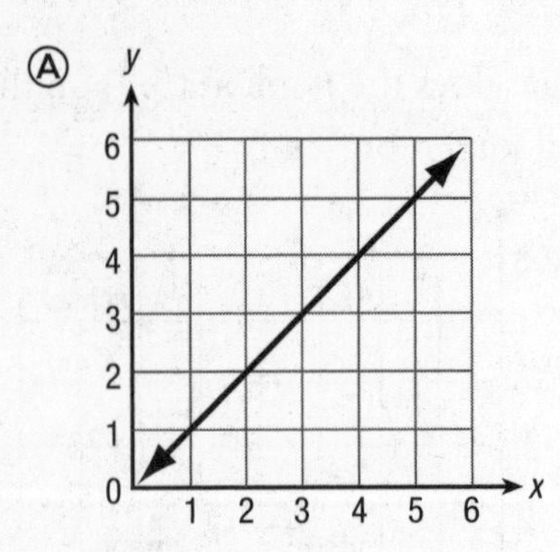

Ⓑ
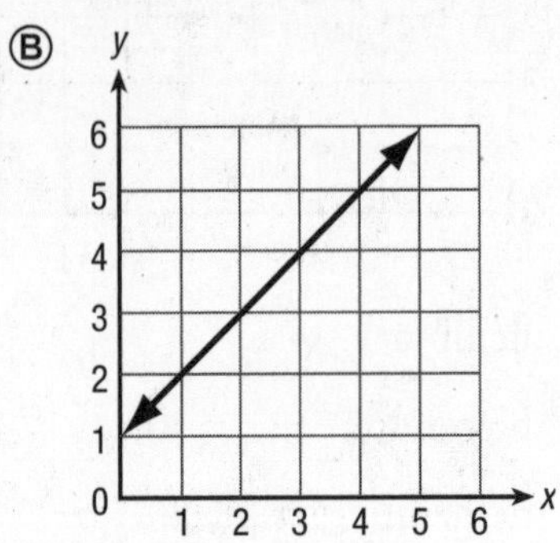

Ⓒ
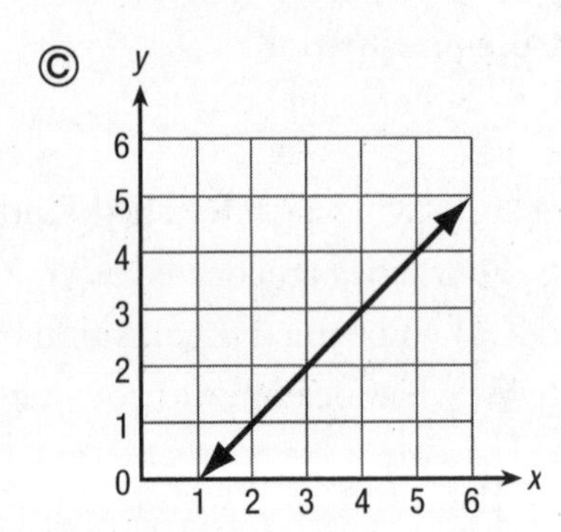

Ⓓ
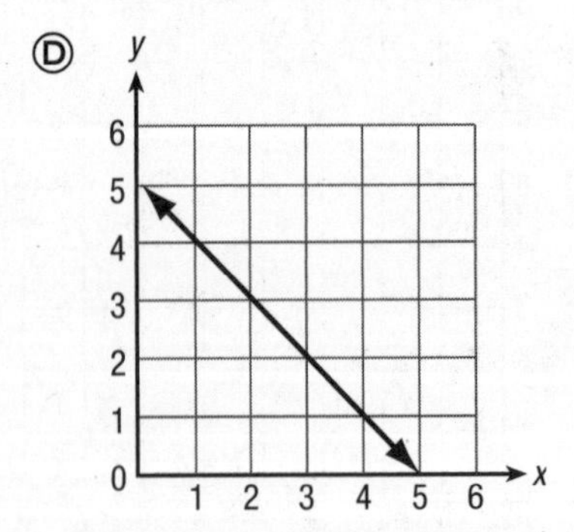

7 a) Use the linear equation $y = 2x + 1$ to complete this table of values.

x	y
0	
1	
2	
3	

b) Graph the linear equation on this grid.

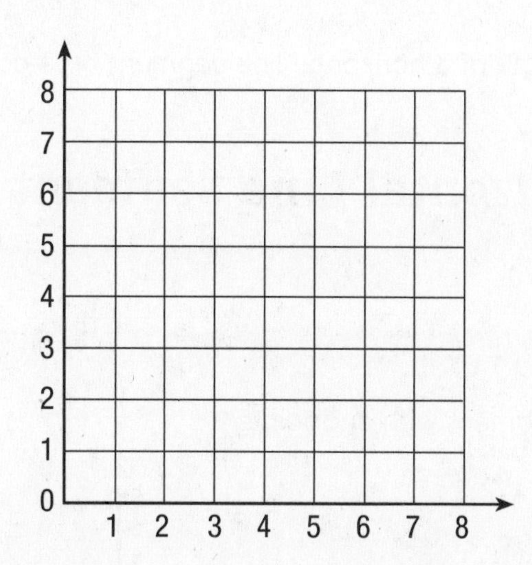

20 Length of Horizontal and Vertical Line Segments

5.3.6: Understand that the length of a horizontal line segment on a coordinate place equals the difference between the *x*-coordinates and that the length of a vertical line segment on a coordinate plane equals the difference between the *y*-coordinates

How do you find the length of a horizontal line segment on a coordinate plane?

Length of Horizontal Line Segment

Example 1

Find the length of the segment with endpoints A = (3,5) and B = (8,5).

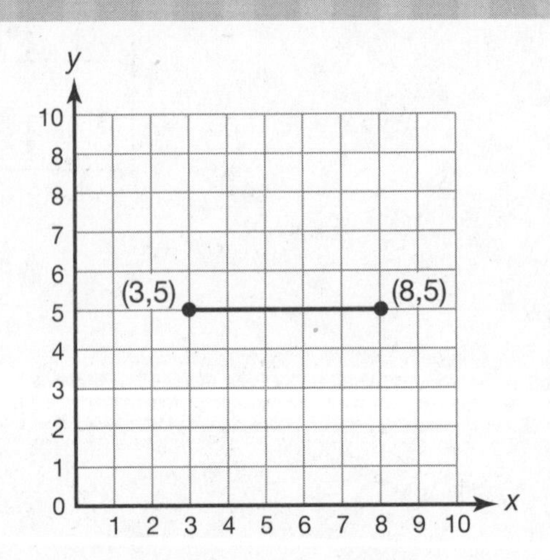

STRATEGY: **Use the *x*-coordinates of the endpoints to find the length.**

STEP 1: Identify the *x*-coordinates of the endpoints A and B.

The *x*-coordinates of the endpoints are 3 and 8.

Because the segment is horizontal, the *y*-coordinates are the same.

STEP 2: The segment starts at 3 and ends at 8. Subtract to find the horizontal length.

$8 - 3 = 5$

SOLUTION: **The segment is 5 units long.**

Example 1 illustrates this rule: To find the length of a horizontal segment, subtract the lesser *x*-coordinate from the greater *x*-coordinate.

Length of a Vertical Line Segment

Example 2

Find the length of the segment with endpoints C = (4,1) and D = (4,10).

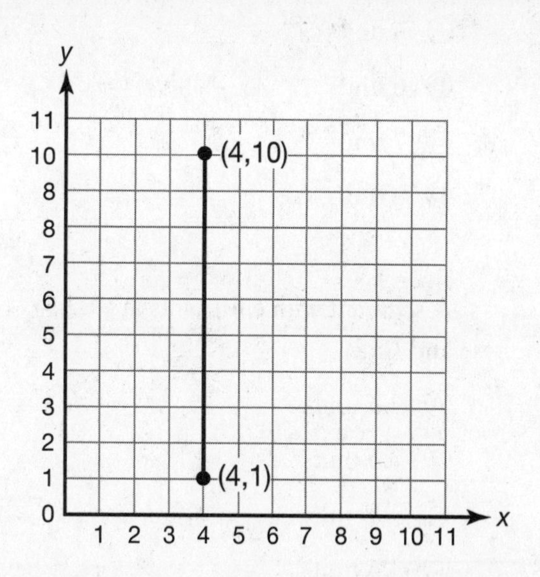

STRATEGY: **Use the *y*-coordinates of the endpoints.**

STEP 1: Identify the *y*-coordinates of the endpoints C and D.

The *y*-coordinates of the endpoints are 1 and 10.

Because the segment is vertical, the *x*-coordinates are the same.

STEP 2: The segment starts at 1 and ends at 10. Subtract to find the vertical length.

$10 - 1 = 9$

SOLUTION: **The segment is 9 units long.**

Example 2 illustrates this rule: To find the length of a vertical segment, subtract the lesser *y*-coordinate from the greater *y*-coordinate.

Sample Test Questions

In Questions 1–4, find the length of each segment.

1 A segment with endpoints at (6,2) and (6,9)

Ⓐ 5 units

Ⓑ 6 units

Ⓒ 7 units

Ⓓ 8 units

2 A segment with endpoints at (0,7.5) and (0,2)

Ⓐ 9.5 units

Ⓑ 7.5 units

Ⓒ 5.5 units

Ⓓ 3.5 units

3 A segment with endpoints at (10.5,2) and (6.5,2)

Ⓐ 4 units

Ⓑ 5 units

Ⓒ 16 units

Ⓓ 17 units

4 A segment with endpoints at (3,8) and (3,0)

Ⓐ 10 units

Ⓑ 9 units

Ⓒ 8 units

Ⓓ 0 units

5 What is the length of horizontal leg *PR* of the right triangle *PQR*?

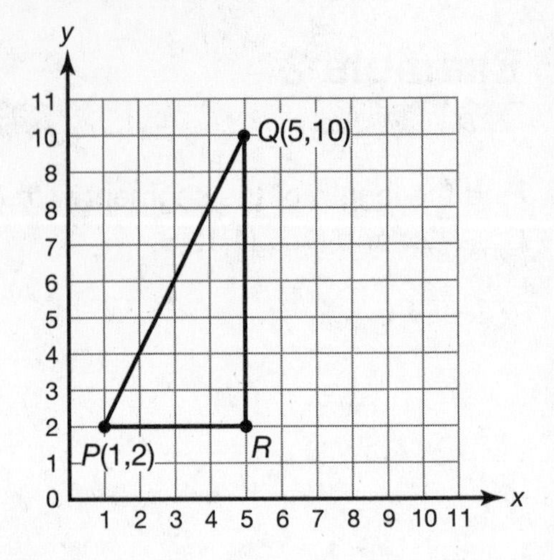

Ⓐ 8

Ⓑ 7

Ⓒ 6

Ⓓ 4

6 On the grid below, draw four segments that are each 3 units long, each with one endpoint at (5,4). Label the coordinates of the endpoints.

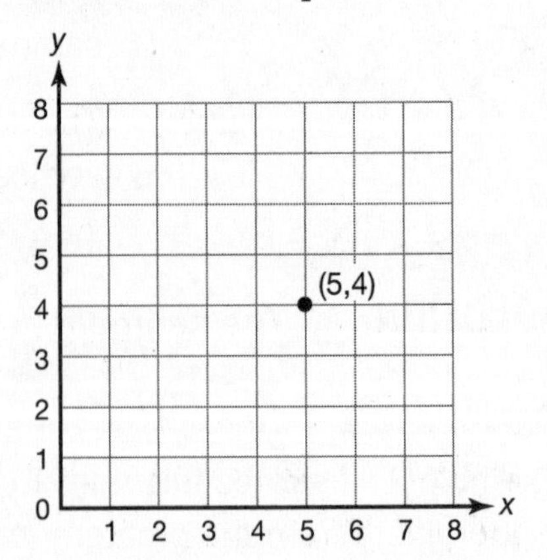

21 Using Information From a Graph or Equation

5.3.7: Use information from a graph or equation to answer questions about a problem situation

You can use graphs or equations to solve some problems.

Example 1

This graph shows how far a family traveled away from home in their car over five days.

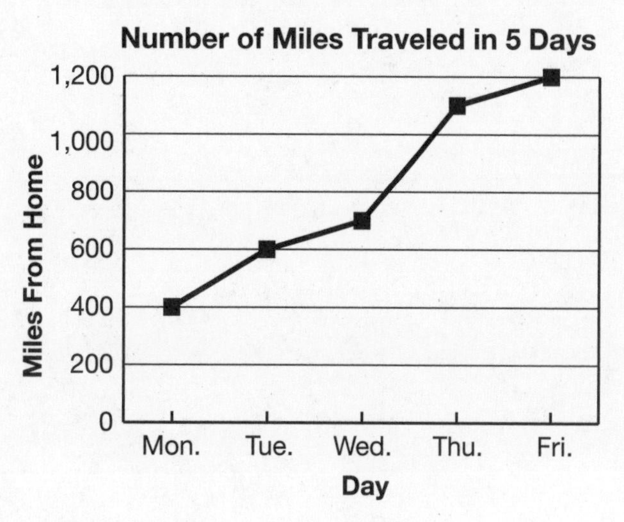

How many miles from home was the family on Tuesday?

STRATEGY: **Find Tuesday and check the distance.**

STEP 1: Find Tuesday on the bottom scale.

Tuesday is the second day listed on the bottom scale.

STEP 2: Put your finger on the line graph directly above Tuesday.

STEP 3: Look at the scale on the left to find the number of miles the family drove.

SOLUTION: **The family was 600 miles from home on Tuesday.**

Example 2

The equation tells how many books children in Jefferson School must read during the school year. G stands for the grade of the child and B stands for the number of books.

$$B = 3G$$

How many books must a child in Grade 5 read during the school year?

STRATEGY: **Substitute for the known variable in the equation.**

Use $G = 5$ in the equation.

$$B = 3G = 3(5) = 15$$

SOLUTION: **A child in Grade 5 must read 15 books this year.**

Sample Test Questions

Use the graph to answer Questions 1–4. It shows how much money was in Julia's savings account as her age increased.

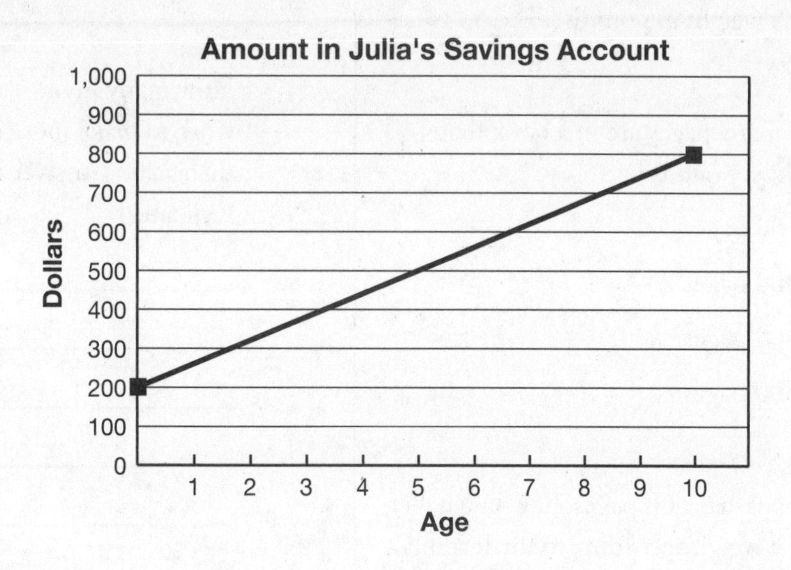

1 How much money was in the account when Julia was born?

Ⓐ $0

Ⓑ $200

Ⓒ $400

Ⓓ $500

2 How much money was in the account when Julia was 5 years old?

Ⓐ $500

Ⓑ $700

Ⓒ $900

Ⓓ $1000

3 How much money was in the savings account when Julia was 10 years old?

Ⓐ $1,000

Ⓑ $900

Ⓒ $800

Ⓓ $700

4 Which is the best estimate of how much the account grew from when Julia was 4 to when she was 8?

Ⓐ by $200

Ⓑ by $250

Ⓒ by $300

Ⓓ by $350

Use the equation to answer Questions 5 and 6.

The equation $P = 100W$ is used by librarians at Lincoln School. P stands for the number of pages and W stands for the weight in pounds.

5 How many pages are in a book that weighs 2 pounds?

Ⓐ 100 pages

Ⓑ 200 pages

Ⓒ 400 pages

Ⓓ 500 pages

6 If a book has 600 pages, how much does it weigh according to the formula?

Ⓐ 2 pounds

Ⓑ 3 pounds

Ⓒ 5 pounds

Ⓓ 6 pounds

7 Carla uses the equation below to determine the fee she makes for a babysitting job. In the equation F stands for her total fee, and h stands for the number of hours she works.

$$F = 5h + 4$$

How many hours will Carla have to work to make more than \$15 but less than \$20? (Answer is a whole number.) Explain.

____

____

____

____

____

____

Progress Check for Lessons 16–21

1 Use the distributive property:

$13(x + 7) = ?$

Ⓐ $13x + 13$

Ⓑ $13x + 7$

Ⓒ $13x + 91$

Ⓓ $x + 91$

2 Find the value of the expression below if $x = 3$ and $y = 1$.

$2xy + x + 1$

Ⓐ 10

Ⓑ 8

Ⓒ 7

Ⓓ 6

3 Which letter shows the point with coordinates (2,5)?

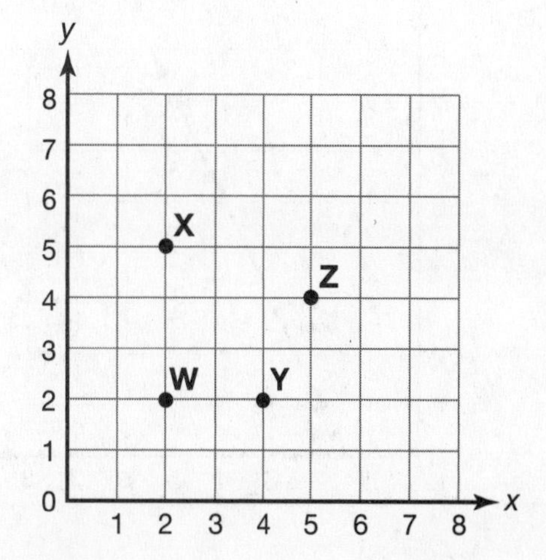

Ⓐ W

Ⓑ X

Ⓒ Y

Ⓓ Z

4 Which equation represents this sentence?

When a certain number is multiplied by 5, and then 2 is added, the result is 42.

Ⓐ $5x + 2 = 42$

Ⓑ $(x + 5) + 2 = 42$

Ⓒ $5x - 2 = 42$

Ⓓ $(5 + 2)x = 42$

5 For $x = 0, 1, 2,$ and 3, what are the y-values for the equation $y = 3x + 1$?

Ⓐ 0, 1, 2, and 3

Ⓑ 1, 4, 5, and 7

Ⓒ 1, 4, 7, and 10

Ⓓ 1, 4, 7, and 11

6 Which equation is graphed below?

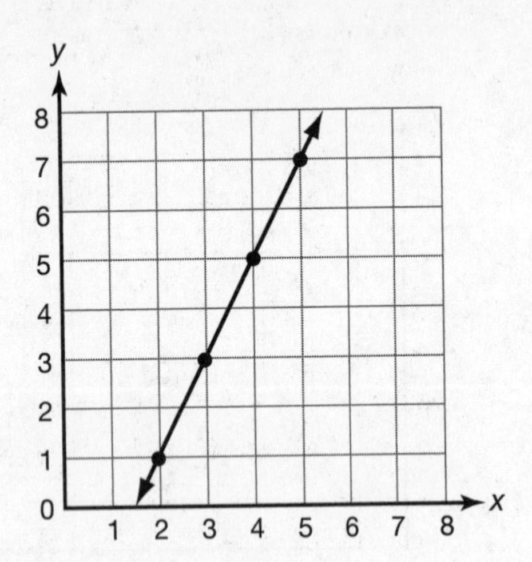

Ⓐ $y = 2x - 3$

Ⓑ $y = x + 1.5$

Ⓒ $y = 2x + 1.5$

Ⓓ $y = 3x - 2$

7 What is the length of the segment MN if $M = (12,3)$ and $N = (12,0)$?

Ⓐ 15

Ⓑ 9

Ⓒ 6

Ⓓ 3

8 The rate for a taxi from the airport to Mrs. Norton's hotel was \$1.25 for every mile. If the hotel is 9 miles from the airport, what did she pay for the ride, not including the tip?

Ⓐ \$9.25

Ⓑ \$10.25

Ⓒ \$11.25

Ⓓ \$11.75

Standard 3
Open-Ended Questions

1 a) Find four ordered pairs for this equation $y = x + 2$

b) Graph and label the ordered pairs you found. Then draw a line through the points.

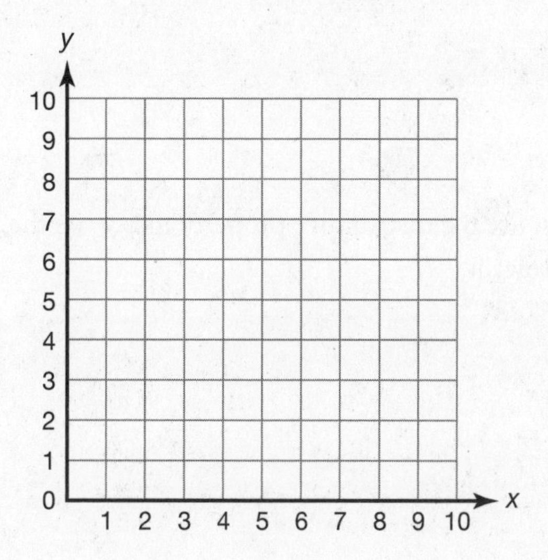

2 Find the value of xyz if $x = 20, y = 7.5$ and $z = \frac{1}{2}$. Show all your work.

3 Write a problem that fits the formula.

$T = \$5.00h + \$3.50$

4 Explain how you can use the distributive property to rewrite the expression so that you can use mental math to solve it.

12×198

Standard

4 Geometry

22 Properties of Segments, Lines, and Angles

5.4.1: Measure, identify and draw angles, perpendicular and parallel lines, rectangles, triangles and circles by using appropriate tools

You should know the following geometrical terms.

Lines and Segments

Parallel Two lines in the same plane that do not meet are parallel.

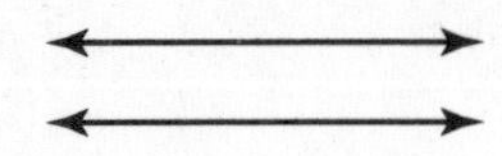

Intersect If two lines or segments meet, they intersect at a point.

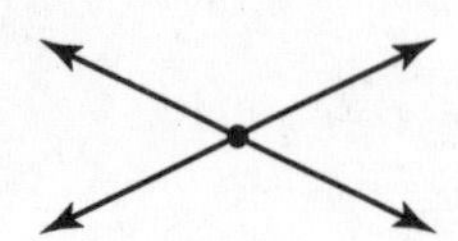

Perpendicular If two lines or segments intersect to make square corners (right angles), they are perpendicular.

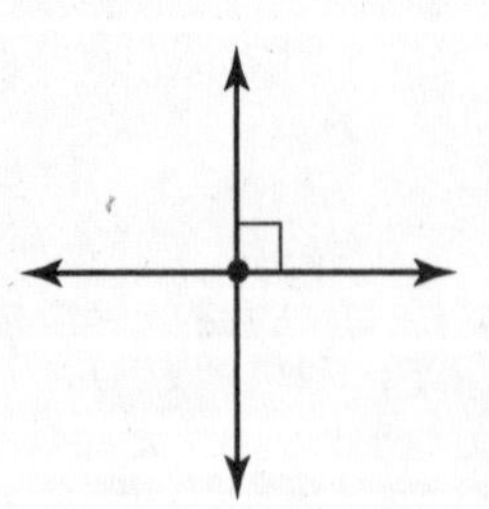

Angles

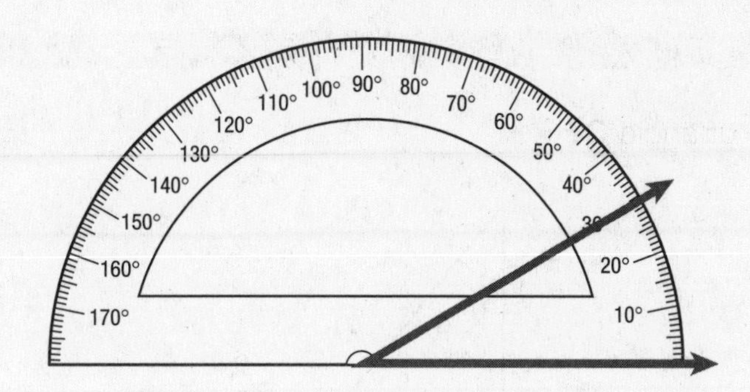

A protractor is a tool for measuring angles. The angle above measures 30 degrees (30°).

Right Angle An angle that measures 90° (a square angle)

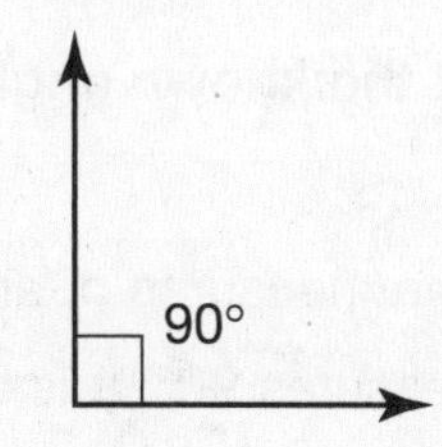

Acute Angle An angle that measures less than 90°

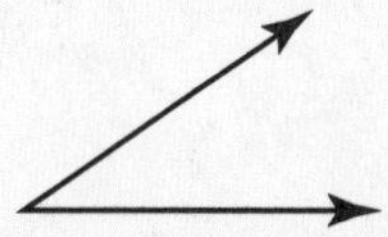

Obtuse Angle An angle that measures more than 90°

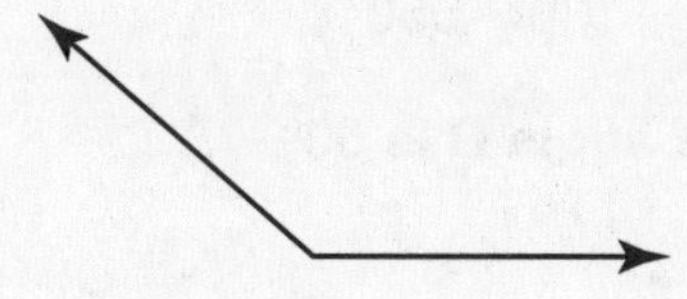

Straight Angle An angle that measures 180°

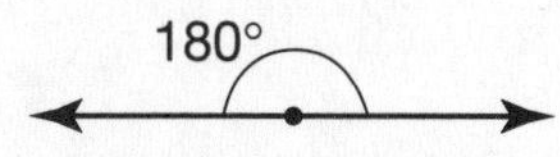

Sum of the Angles of a Triangle

The sum of the measures of the angles of any triangle is 180°.

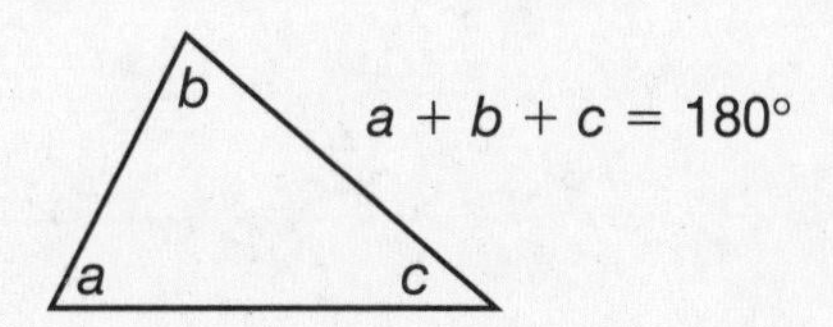

Example 1

What is the measure of angle C?

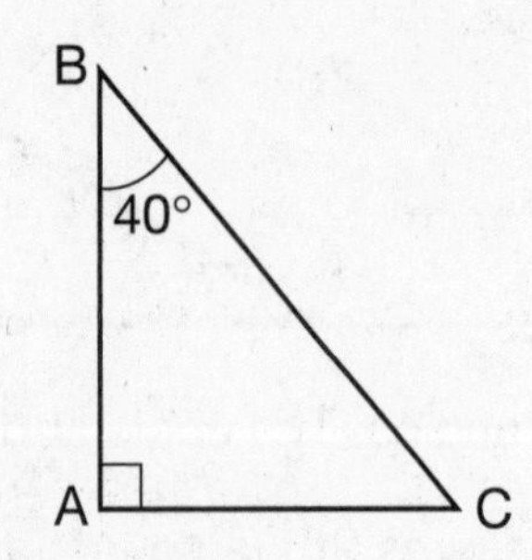

STRATEGY: **Add the measures of the known angles of the triangle. Then subtract the sum from 180°.**

STEP 1: What are the measures of angles A and B?

Angle A measures 90°. It is a right angle.

Angle B measures 40°.

STEP 2: Add the measures of angles A and B.

$$\begin{array}{r} 90° \\ +\ 40° \\ \hline 130° \end{array}$$

STEP 3: Subtract 130° from 180°.

$180° - 130° = 50°$

SOLUTION: **The measure of angle C is 50°.**

You can use a protractor to draw angles with given measures and a ruler to draw segments with given lengths.

Example 2

Draw a rectangle with sides of 5 in. and 3 in.

STRATEGY: **Use a protractor to make the right angles and a ruler to make the sides.**

STEP 1: Draw a ray to represent one side. A rectangle has four right angles. Use a protractor to draw right angle A.

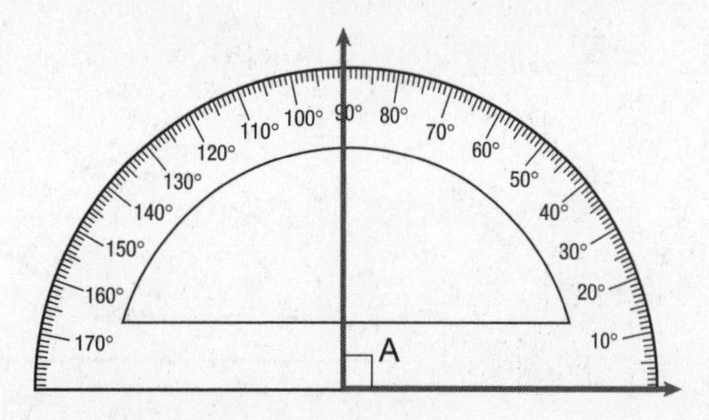

STEP 2: Mark off lengths of 5 in. and 3 in. on the sides of the angle. Label the points B and D.

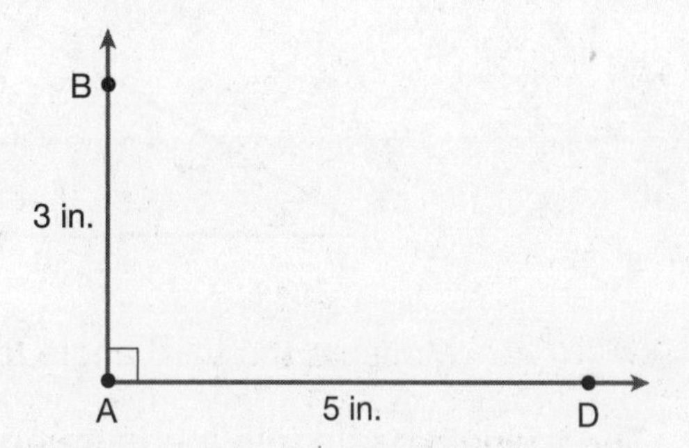

STEP 3: Use a protractor to make right angles with vertices at B and D. Label the point of intersection of the two rays C.

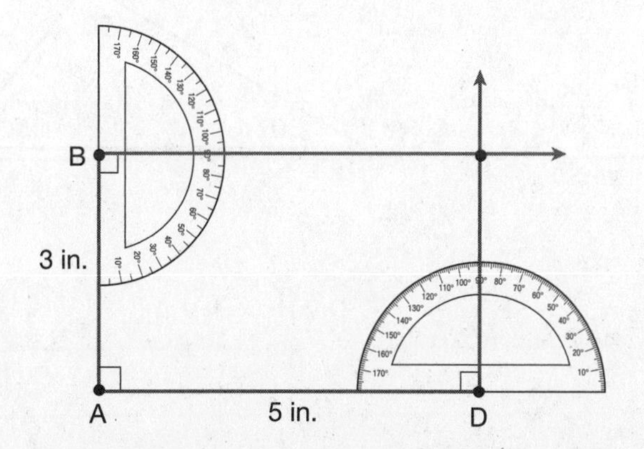

SOLUTION: **Step 3 shows a rectangle with sides measuring 5 in. and 3 in.**

You can use a protractor to draw a triangle with given angle measures.

Example 3

Draw a triangle with angles measuring 30°, 50°, and 100°.

STRATEGY: **There is no mention of side lengths, so use a protractor to draw the three angles.**

STEP 1: Draw a 30° angle.

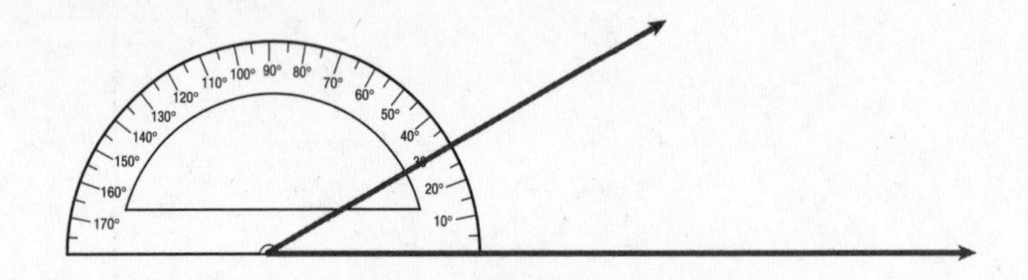

STEP 2: Draw a 50° angle along one side of the 30° angle.

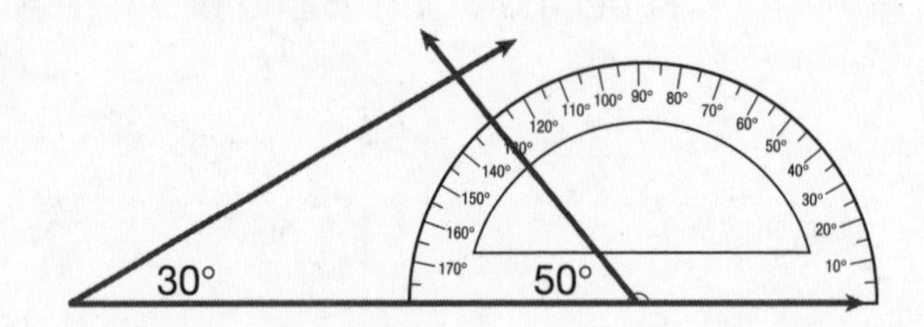

Measure the third angle formed. It measures 100°.

SOLUTION: **The triangle has angle measures of 30°, 50°, and 100°.**

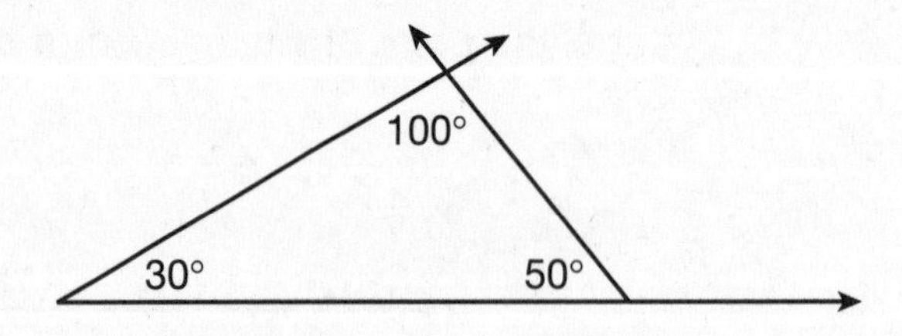

Sample Test Questions

1 Which angle is closest to 30°?

Ⓐ 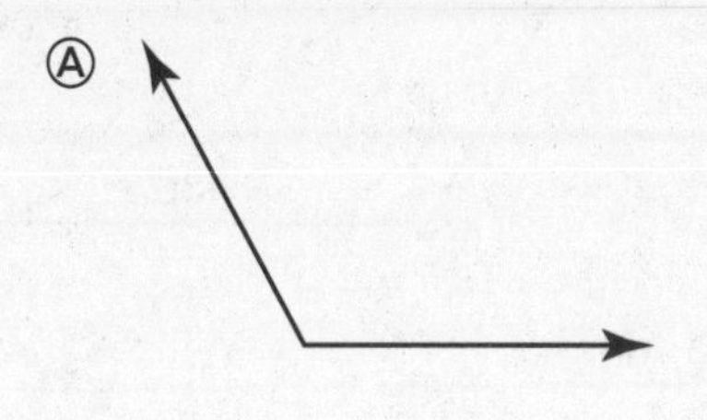

Ⓑ 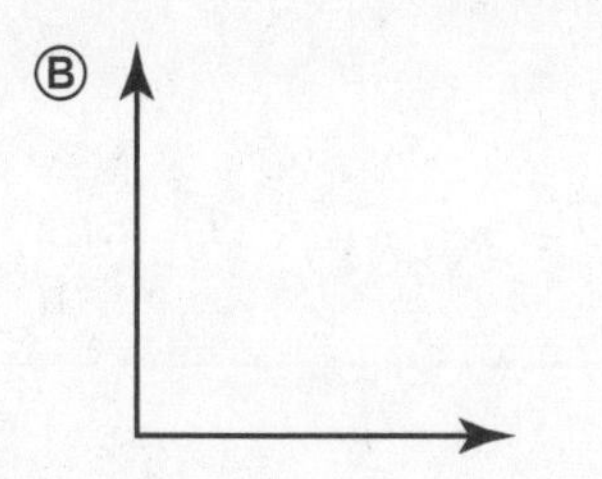

Ⓒ 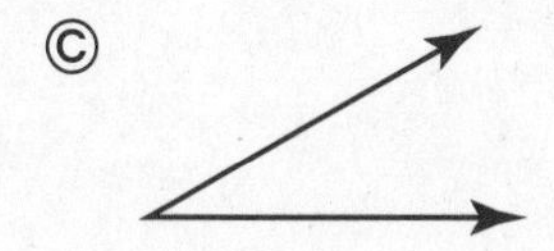

Ⓓ 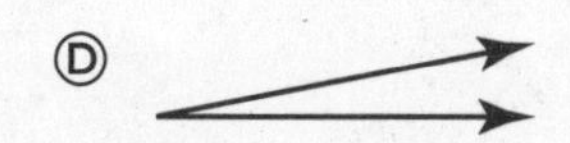

2 Which of these lines are perpendicular?

Ⓐ 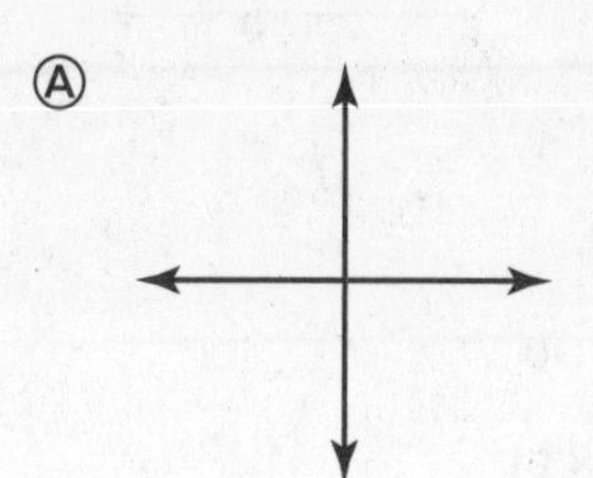

Ⓑ 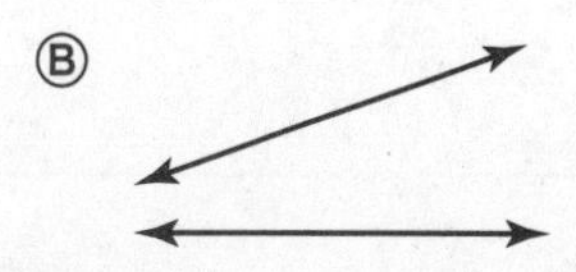

Ⓒ 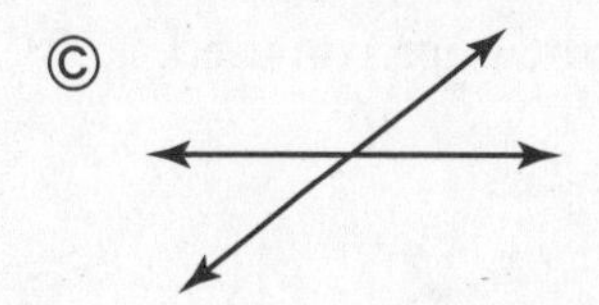

Ⓓ 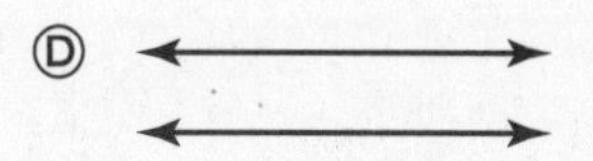

3 What kind of angle is this?

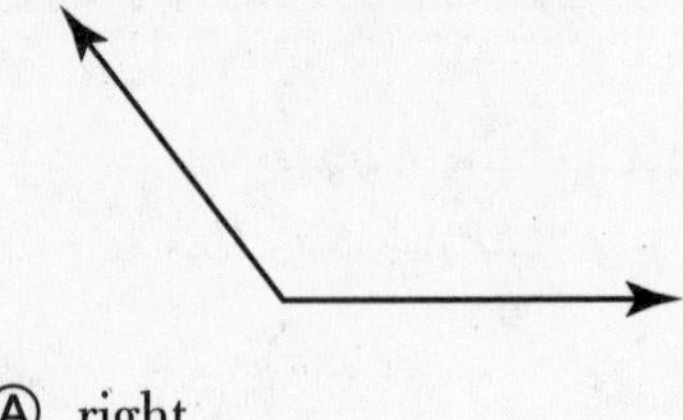

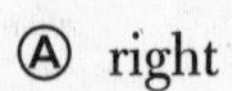

Ⓐ right

Ⓑ acute

Ⓒ obtuse

Ⓓ straight

4 What is the measure of angle Z?

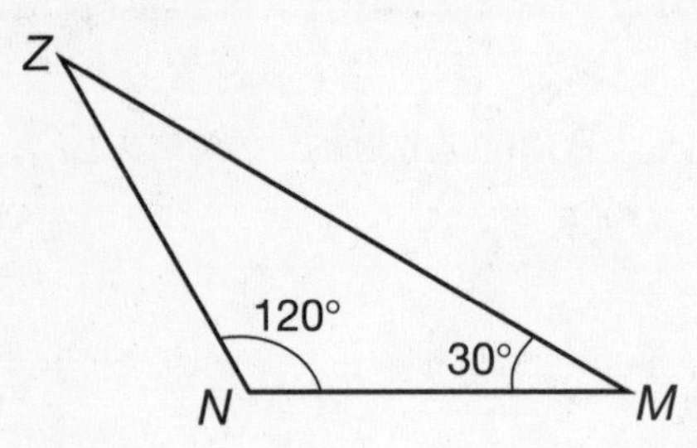

Ⓐ 90°

Ⓑ 50°

Ⓒ 40°

Ⓓ 30°

---

5 In the space below, draw a rectangle with sides 7 cm and 4 cm. Use a ruler and a protractor. Explain the steps you used.

23 Two-Dimensional Figures

5.4.4: Identify, describe, draw and classify polygons, such as pentagons and hexagons

Here are several geometric figures you should know.

Polygon A figure made up of line segments. The figure is closed—there are no gaps or openings in it.

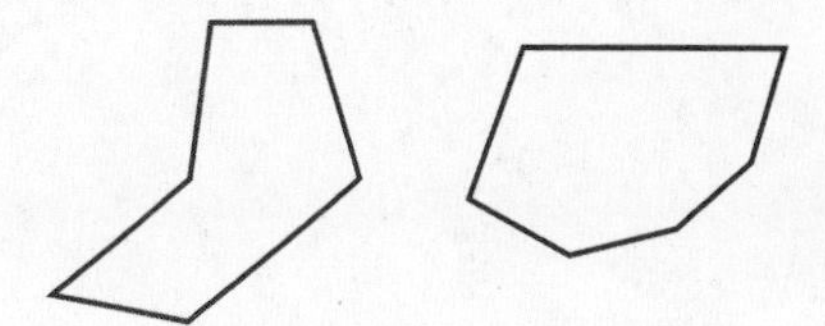

Triangle A polygon with three sides and three angles. All of these figures are triangles.

Rectangle A polygon with four sides and four square corners (four right angles).

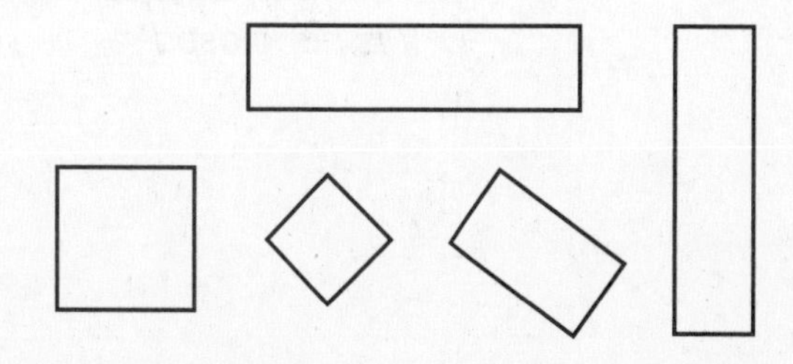

Square A rectangle with all sides of equal length.

Pentagon A polygon with 5 sides and 5 angles.

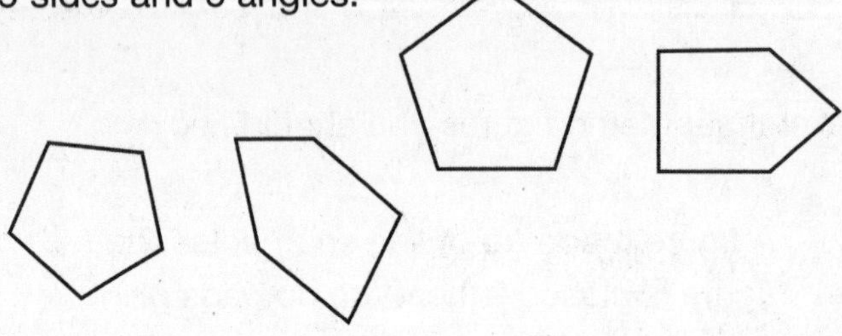

Hexagon A figure with 6 sides and 6 angles.

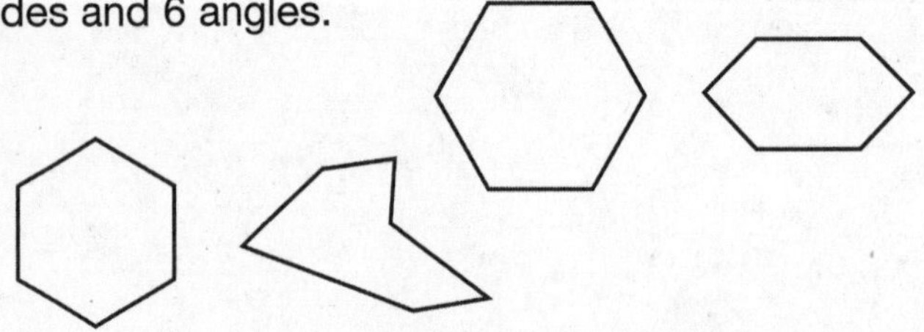

Not every figure is a polygon. Circles are not polygons. Neither are these.

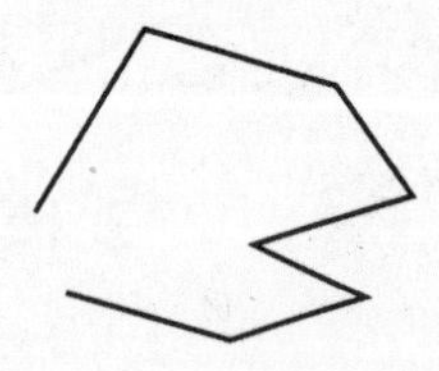

Not a polygon because it is not closed

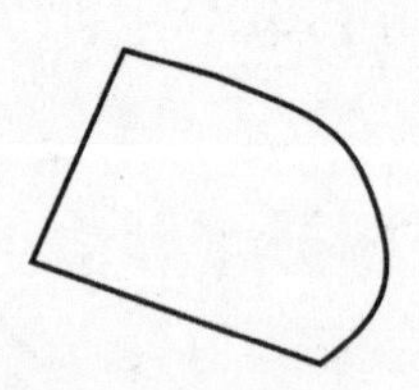

Not a polygon because one side isn't a line segment.

Sample Test Questions

1 Which of the following is NOT a polygon?

Ⓐ
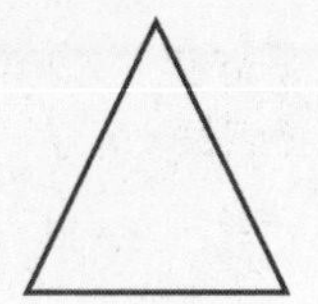

Ⓑ
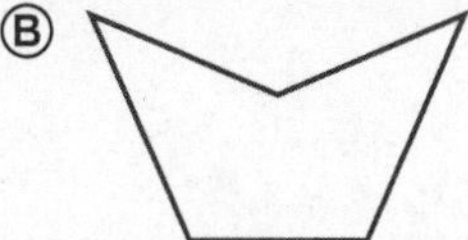

Ⓒ
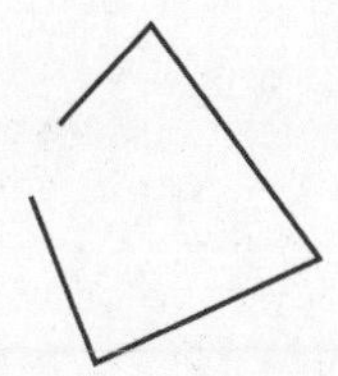

Ⓓ

2 Which figure has the most angles?

Ⓐ hexagon

Ⓑ square

Ⓒ pentagon

Ⓓ triangle

3 How can this figure best be classified?

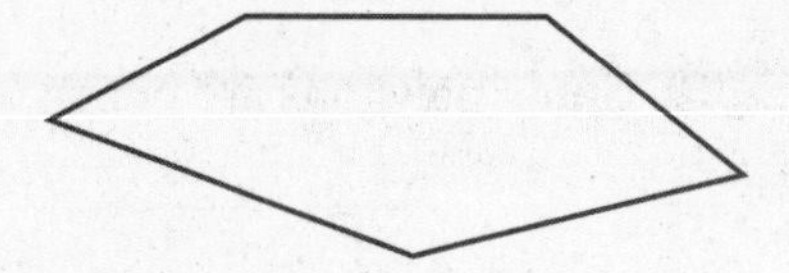

Ⓐ quadrilateral

Ⓑ pentagon

Ⓒ hexagon

Ⓓ rectangle

4 Which statement is NOT true?

Ⓐ All squares are rectangles.

Ⓑ Some rectangles are squares.

Ⓒ All triangles are polygons.

Ⓓ Some hexagons are not polygons.

5 What do the following figures have in common?

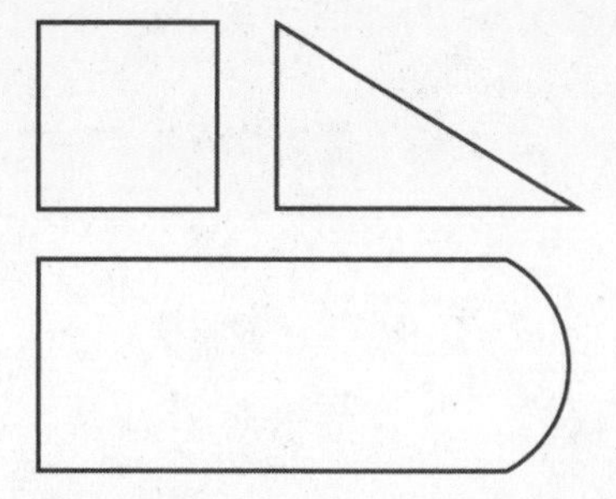

Ⓐ They are all polygons.

Ⓑ They all have at least one right angle.

Ⓒ They all have 1 line of symmetry.

Ⓓ They have nothing in common.

6 Which statement is NOT true?

Ⓐ Circles are not polygons.

Ⓑ All rectangles are squares.

Ⓒ Hexagons are polygons.

Ⓓ Some polygons are pentagons.

7 In the space below, draw an example a pentagon and an example of a hexagon. Explain why your drawings are correct.

24 Congruent Triangles

5.4.3: Identify congruent triangles and justify your decisions by referring to sides and angles

Two line segments are congruent if they have the same length.

Two angles are congruent if they have the same measure.

Two figures are congruent if they have the same shape and size.

Congruent Triangles

Example 1

Which triangles are congruent?

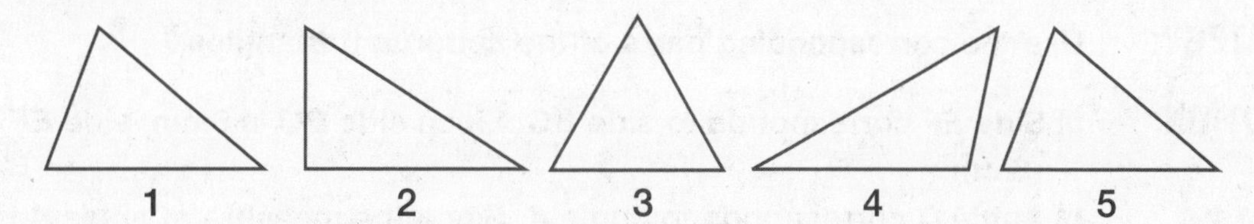

STRATEGY: **Look at the triangles. Imagine placing one exactly on top of another.**

SOLUTION: **Triangles 1 and 5 are congruent, since they have the same size and shape.**

NOTE: Two figures can be congruent even if they face different directions. For example, these two triangles are congruent, since they have the same size and shape.

If two triangles are congruent, then the corresponding angles are congruent and the corresponding sides are congruent. Tick marks can help you identify the congruent sides and angles in two congruent triangles.

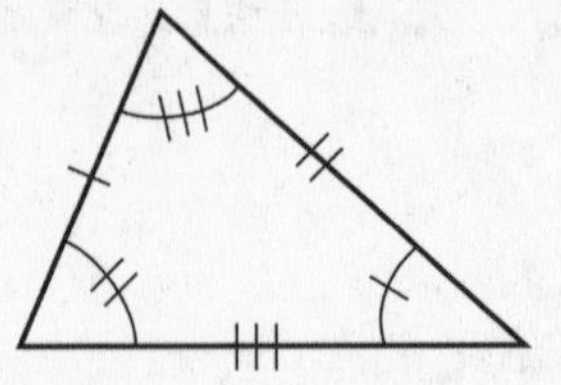

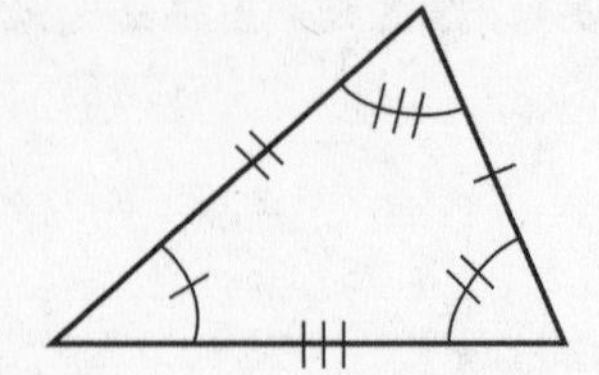

Example 2

Triangle *ABC* is congruent to triangle *DEF*.

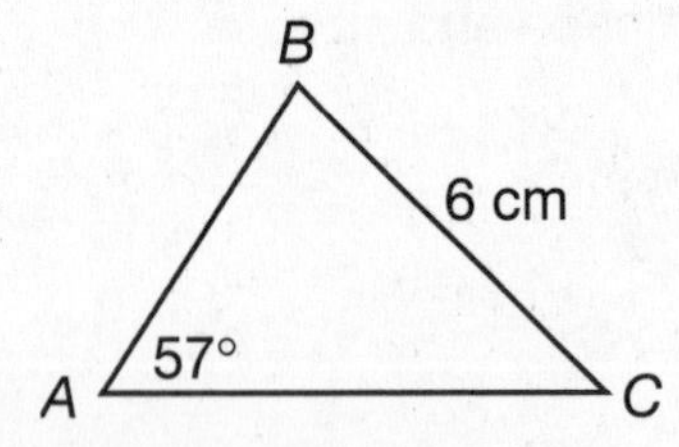

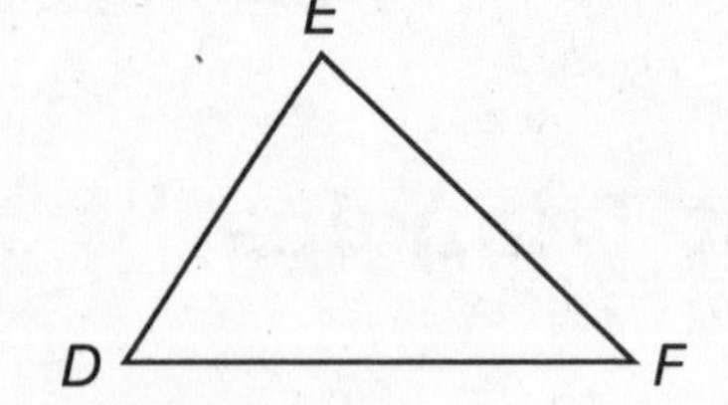

a) If the length of side *BC* is 6 cm, what is the length of side *EF*?

b) If the measure of angle *A* is 57°, what is the measure of angle *D*?

STRATEGY: **Use the corresponding parts of the congruent triangles.**

SOLUTION: **a) Side *EF* corresponds to side *BC*. Since side *BC* is 6 cm, side *EF* is 6 cm.**

b) Angle *D* corresponds to angle *A*. Since the measure of angle *A* is 57°, the measure of angle *D* is 57°.

Sample Test Questions

1 Which triangles are congruent?

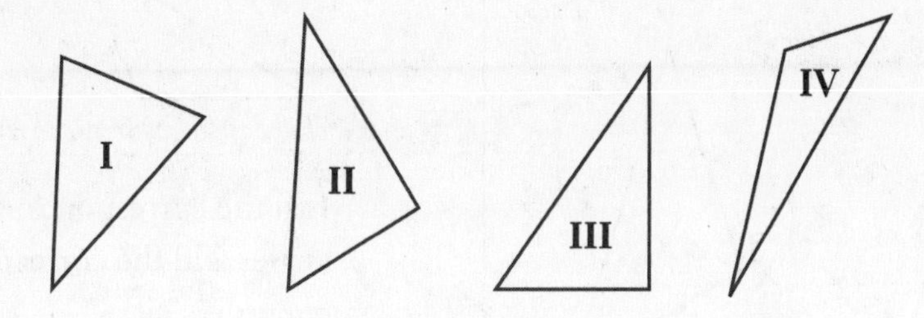

Ⓐ I and II

Ⓑ I and III

Ⓒ II and III

Ⓓ II and IV

2 Which triangle is not congruent to the others?

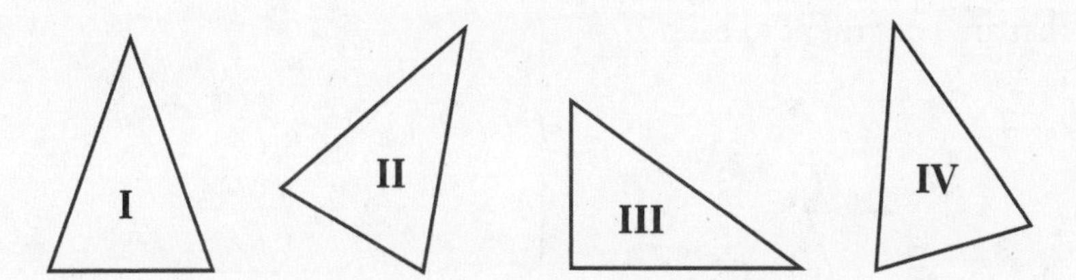

Ⓐ I

Ⓑ II

Ⓒ III

Ⓓ IV

3 Triangle *PQR* is congruent to triangle *XYZ*. Select the angles of the two triangles that are congruent to each other.

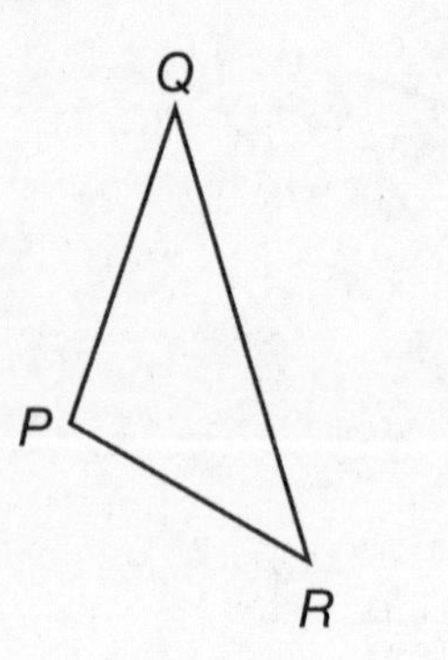

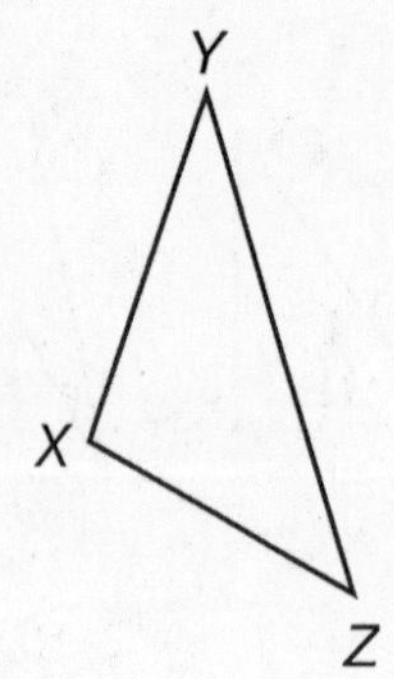

Ⓐ $\angle P$ and $\angle Y$

Ⓑ $\angle Q$ and $\angle Y$

Ⓒ $\angle P$ and $\angle Z$

Ⓓ $\angle R$ and $\angle X$

4 Triangle *DEF* is congruent to triangle *GHJ*. Select the sides of the two triangles that are congruent to each other.

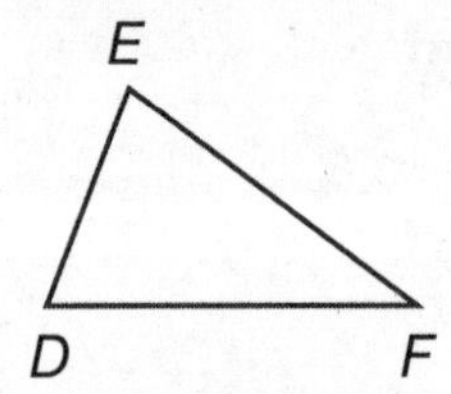

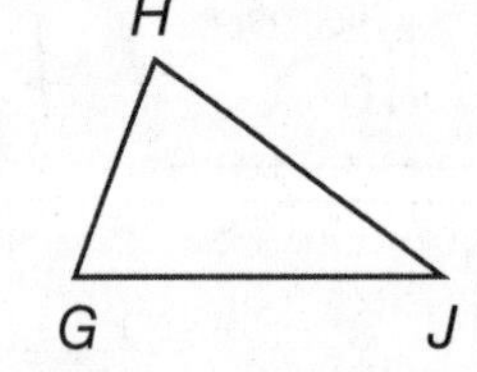

Ⓐ *DE* and *HJ*

Ⓑ *DE* and *GH*

Ⓒ *EF* and *GH*

Ⓓ *DF* and *GH*

5 Triangle *RST* is congruent to triangle *UVW*.

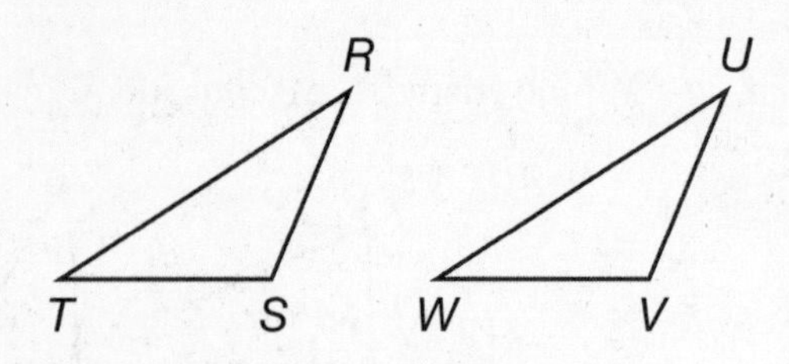

List the corresponding congruent angles and the corresponding congruent sides.

____

____

____

____

____

____

____

25 Special Triangles

5.4.2: Identify, describe, draw, and classify triangles as equilateral, isosceles, scalene, right, acute, obtuse, and equiangular

You can classify triangles by their angles.

A **right triangle** has a right angle.

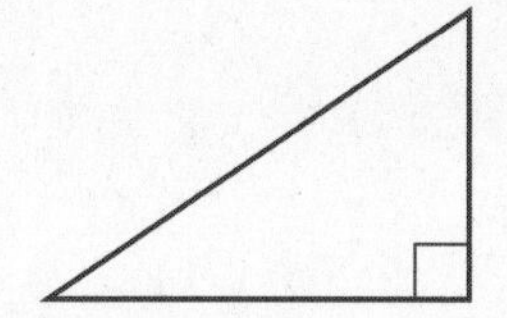

An **obtuse triangle** has an obtuse angle.

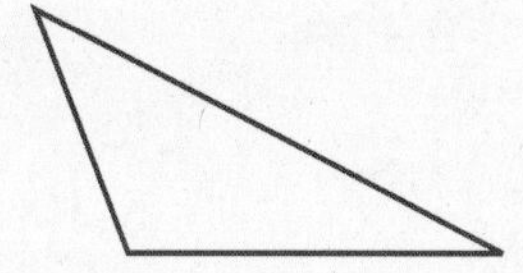

In an **acute triangle**, all three angles are acute.

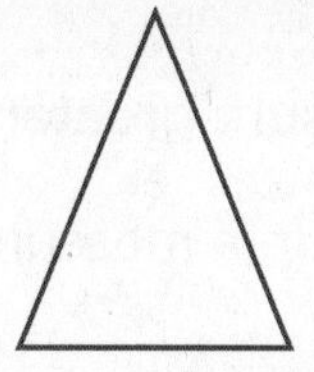

In an **equiangular triangle,** all three angles are congruent.

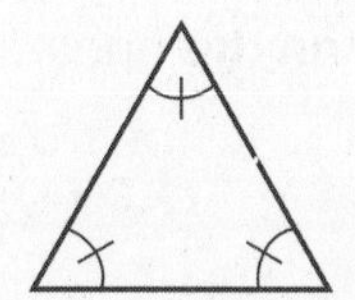

You can also classify triangles by their sides.

In an **equilateral triangle,** all three sides are congruent. (Lateral means side.)

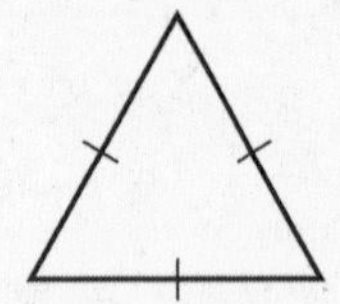

An equilateral triangle is also equiangular.

In an **isosceles triangle**, at least two of the sides are congruent.

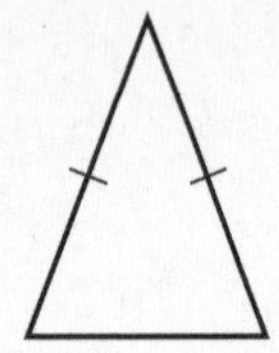

In a **scalene triangle**, none of the sides are congruent.

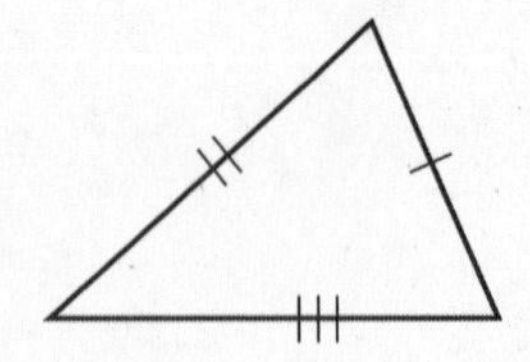

Example 1

What is the name of a triangle with an angle greater than 90°?

STRATEGY: **Recall the name for an angle with a measure greater than 90°.**

STEP 1: What is the name for an angle with a measure greater than 90°?

An angle with a measure greater than 90° is obtuse.

STEP 2: Look at the list of triangles classified by their angles.

The triangle has the same name as the angle.

SOLUTION: **The triangle is an obtuse triangle.**

Example 2

What is the measure of each angle of an equiangular triangle?

STRATEGY: **Recall that the sum of the measures of the angles of any triangle is 180°.**

An equiangular triangle has three congruent angles, so divide 180° by 3.

$180° \div 3 = 60°$

SOLUTION: **Each angle of an equiangular triangle has a measure of 60°.**

Example 3

What is the name for a triangle that has a right angle and two congruent sides?

STRATEGY: **Study the list of triangles.**

A triangle with a right angle is a right triangle.

A triangle with two congruent sides is isosceles.

SOLUTION: **A triangle with a right angle and two congruent sides is an isosceles right triangle.**

Sample Test Questions

1 What is the name of a triangle with no congruent sides?

Ⓐ scalene

Ⓑ isosceles

Ⓒ equilateral

Ⓓ unequal

2 Each angle of triangle *PQR* has a measure of 60°. What kind of triangle is *PQR*?

Ⓐ congruent

Ⓑ equilateral

Ⓒ scalene

Ⓓ obtuse

3 In triangle *WXY*, the measure of angle *Y* is 80°, and angle *W* is congruent to angle *X*. What is the measure of angle *W*?

Ⓐ 40°

Ⓑ 50°

Ⓒ 80°

Ⓓ 100°

4 In triangle *MNP*, angle *M* is a right angle. If angle *N* measures 30°, then what is the measure of angle *P*?

Ⓐ 20°

Ⓑ 50°

Ⓒ 60°

Ⓓ 70°

5 What is the greatest number of obtuse angles a triangle can have?

Ⓐ 0

Ⓑ 1

Ⓒ 2

Ⓓ 3

6 What is the greatest number of acute angles a triangle can have?

Ⓐ 0

Ⓑ 1

Ⓒ 2

Ⓓ 3

7 In triangle *DEF*, angle *D* is a right angle. What is true of the other two angles?

Ⓐ They are both obtuse angles.

Ⓑ They are both right angles.

Ⓒ One angle is obtuse and the other is acute.

Ⓓ They are both acute angles.

8 Look at the triangle below.

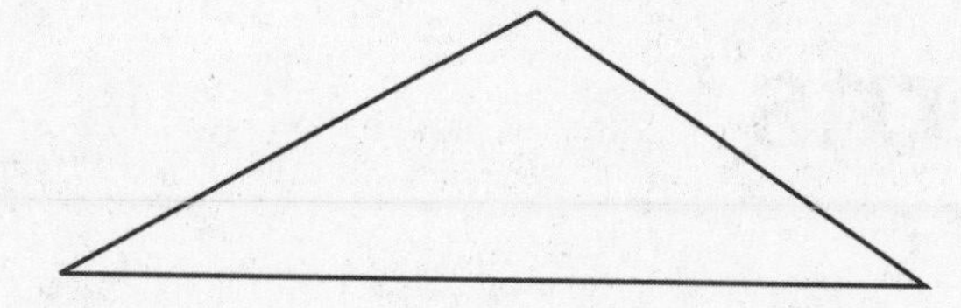

Identify the triangle as right, acute, or obtuse. Write your answer on the line below.

____

On the lines below, explain why you identified the triangle as right, acute, or obtuse.

____

____

____

____

____

26 Turns

5.4.7: Understand that 90°, 180°, 270°, and 360° are associated with quarter, half, three-quarters, and full turns respectively

A turn is a rotation of a figure around a point.

The figure shows a 90° clockwise turn of the letter T around the point. A 90° turn is also called a quarter turn.

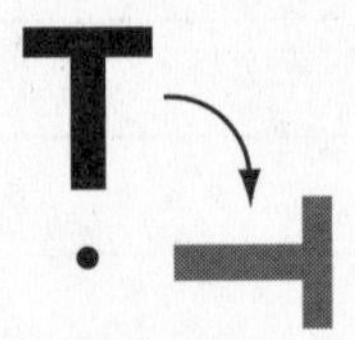

The figure shows a 180° clockwise turn of the letter T around the point. A 180° turn is also called a half turn.

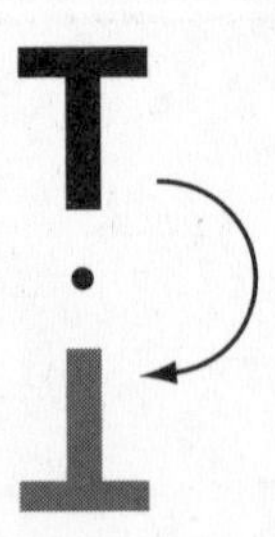

The figure shows a 270° clockwise turn of the letter T around the point. A 270° turn is also called a three-quarter turn.

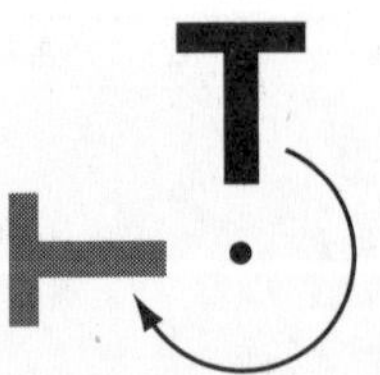

After a 360° turn, the letter T returns to its original position. A 360° turn is also called a full turn.

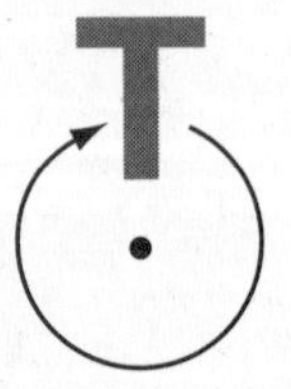

Quarter, half, three-quarter, and full turns can also be made in a counterclockwise direction.

Sample Test Questions

1 Which of these shows the letter after a half turn?

P

Ⓐ P

Ⓑ

Ⓒ

Ⓓ

2 What kind of turn is this?

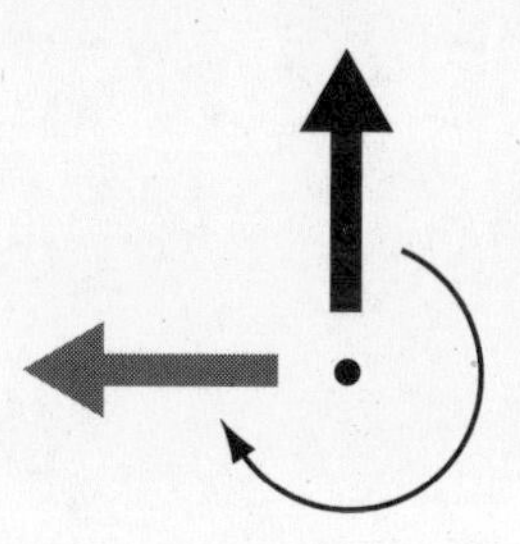

Ⓐ 360° clockwise turn

Ⓑ 270° counterclockwise turn

Ⓒ 270° clockwise turn

Ⓓ 90° clockwise turn

3 What kind of turn is this?

Ⓐ quarter turn clockwise

Ⓑ half turn clockwise

Ⓒ three-quarter turn counterclockwise

Ⓓ full turn clockwise

4 Which of the following is the same as a quarter turn in a clockwise direction?

Ⓐ quarter turn in a counterclockwise direction

Ⓑ half turn in a counterclockwise direction

Ⓒ three-quarter turn in a counterclockwise direction

Ⓓ three-quarter turn in a clockwise direction

5 The first grid shows the triangle after a quarter turn in a clockwise direction around point A. On the second grid, draw the triangle after a half turn around point A.

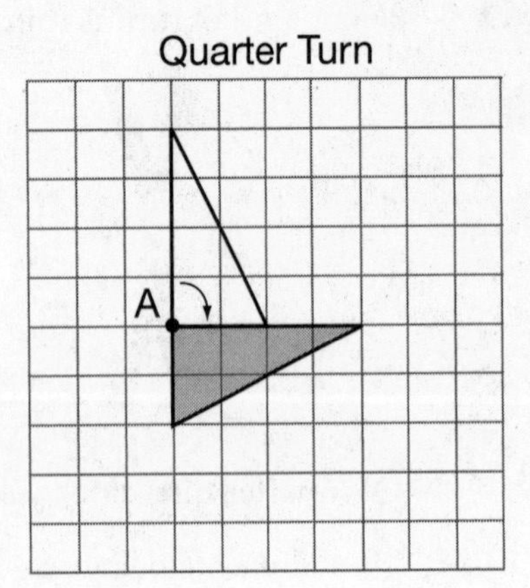

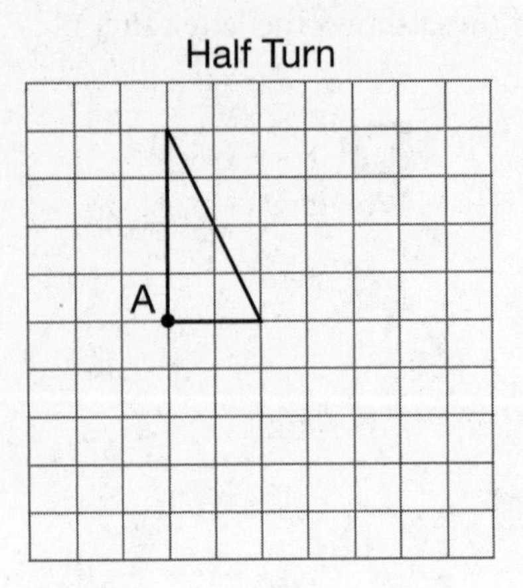

27 Symmetry

5.4.6: Identify shapes that have reflectional and rotational symmetry

This is a hexagon with all congruent sides.

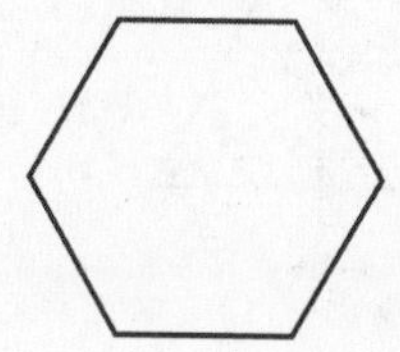

If you fold it in half along the dotted line, the two halves will match exactly. They are congruent.

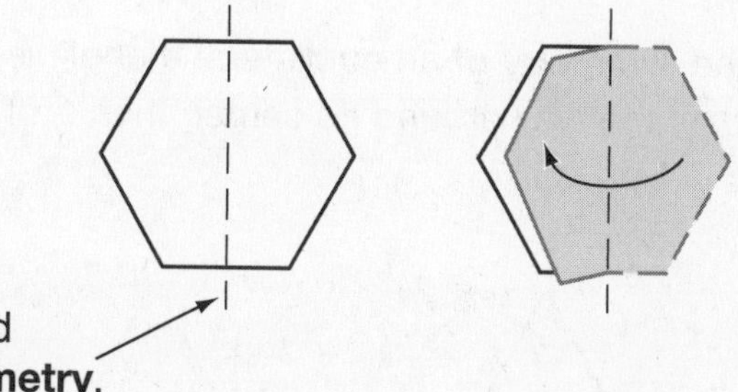

This line is called the **line of symmetry**.

This type of symmetry (involving a "flip" of half the figure) is sometimes called reflectional symmetry.

Example

The triangle is an equilateral triangle.

How many lines of symmetry does an equilateral triangle have?

STRATEGY: **Imagine folding the triangle exactly in half as many ways as you can.**

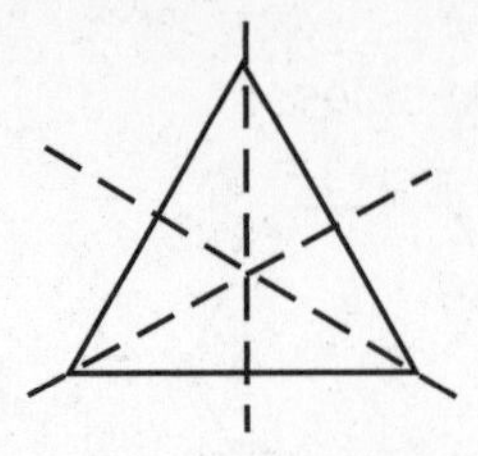

SOLUTION: **The dotted lines show that an equilateral triangle has 3 lines of symmetry.**

Another way to look at the symmetry of an equilateral triangle is to think of the triangle being turned clockwise $\frac{1}{3}$ of the way around its center, then $\frac{2}{3}$ of the way, and finally $\frac{3}{3}$ of the way.

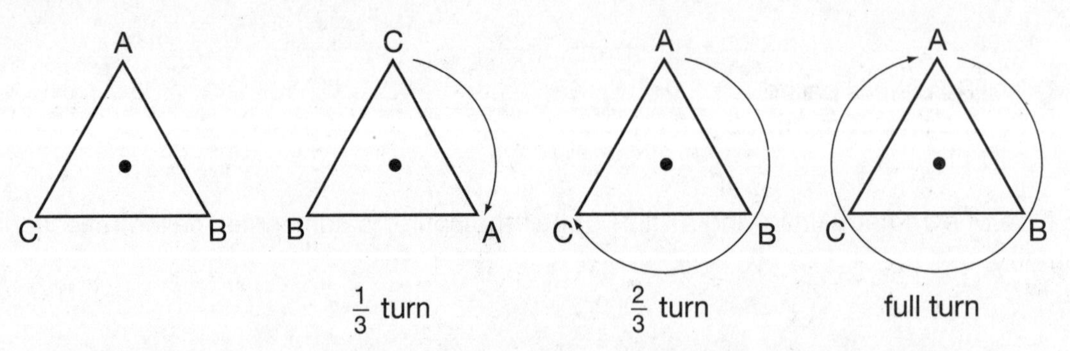

Notice that with each $\frac{1}{3}$ turn, the equilateral triangle fits exactly on top of itself. When a figure fits exactly on top of itself in a rotation less a full turn, the figure has rotational symmetry.

Sample Test Questions

1 Which of these figures does NOT have a line of symmetry?

Ⓐ 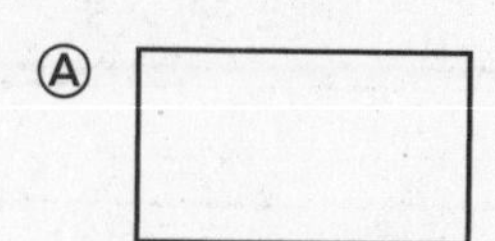

Ⓑ 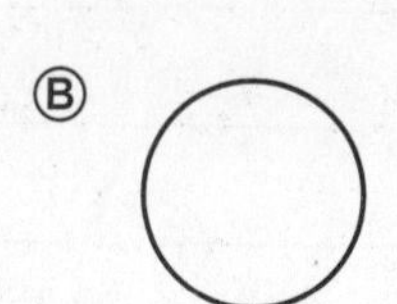

Ⓒ 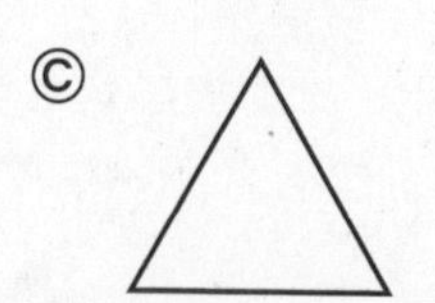

Ⓓ 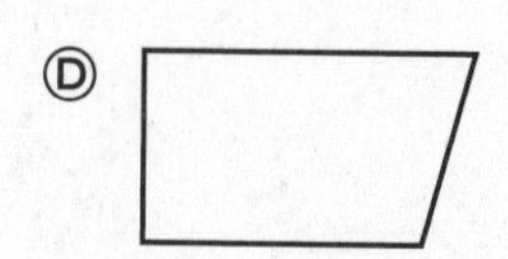

2 Which figure below has exactly two lines of symmetry?

Ⓐ 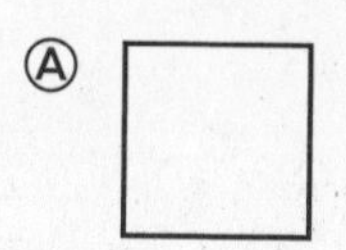

Ⓑ 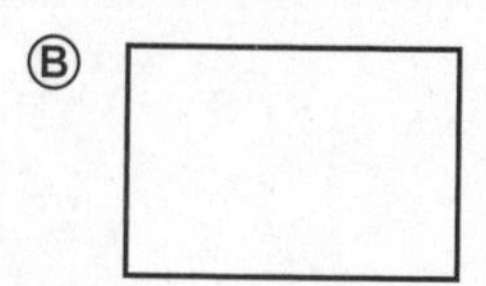

Ⓒ 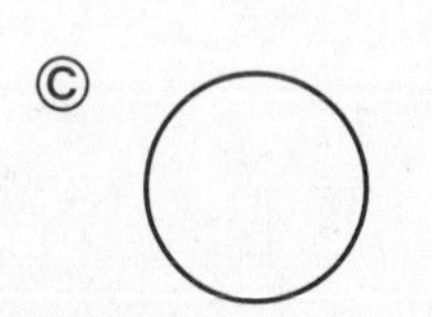

Ⓓ 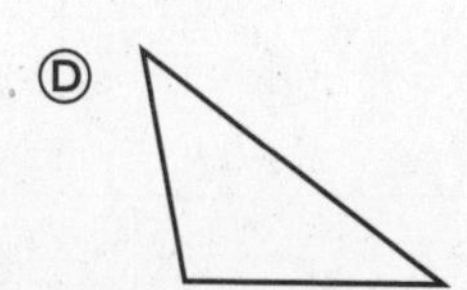

3 Which of these figures has only one line of symmetry?

Ⓐ 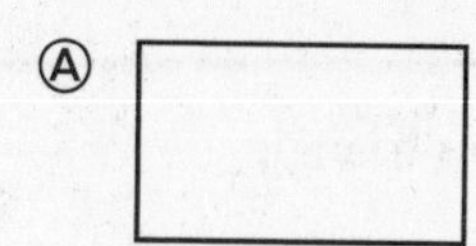

Ⓑ 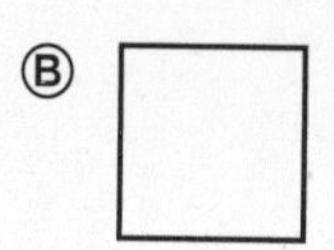

Ⓒ 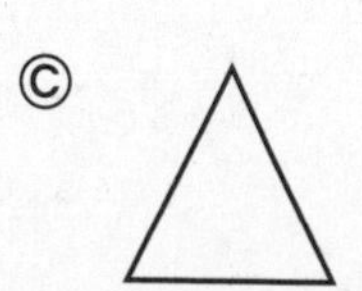

Ⓓ 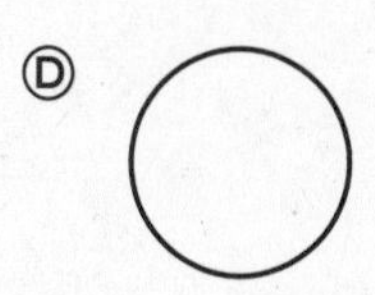

4 Which shape has exactly four lines of symmetry?

Ⓐ 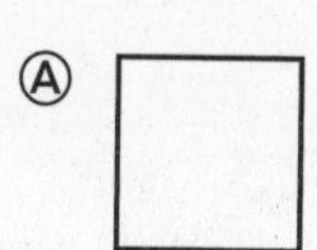

Ⓑ 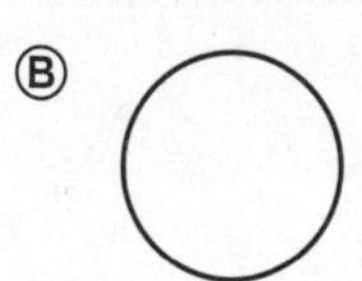

Ⓒ 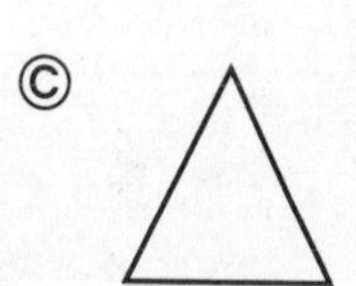

Ⓓ 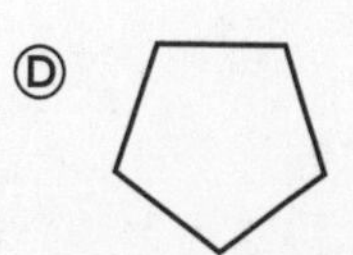

5 Which of these figures has rotational symmetry?

Ⓐ a scalene triangle

Ⓑ a right triangle

Ⓒ a square

Ⓓ an isosceles triangle

6 How many degrees are in a quarter turn? Explain how you know.

28 Circles

5.4.1: Measure, identify, and draw angles, perpendicular and parallel lines, rectangles, triangles, and circles by using appropriate tools
5.4.5: Identify and draw the radius and diameter of a circle and understand the relationship between the radius and diameter

A circle is a set of points in a plane that are all the same distance from a point called the center of the circle. The tool for drawing a circle is a compass. Place the point of the compass at the center point. The points of the circle are made by the pencil. Notice that all the points on the circle are the same distance from the center.

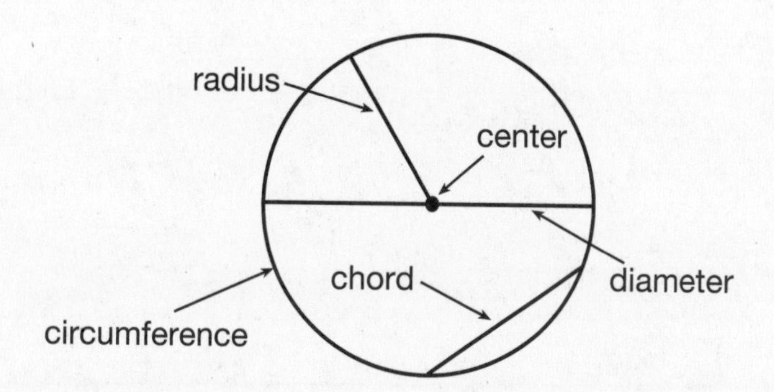

The circumference is the distance around the circle, its perimeter.

The diameter is the length of a line segment passing through the center of the circle, with endpoints on the circle.

The radius is the length of a line segment from the center of the circle to any point on the circle. The radius is equal to $\frac{1}{2}$ the diameter of the circle.

A chord is a line segment that connects any two points of the circle.

Example 1

In Circle A, what part of the circle is segment AB?

(A circle is often named by its center. In this case, the center is A.)

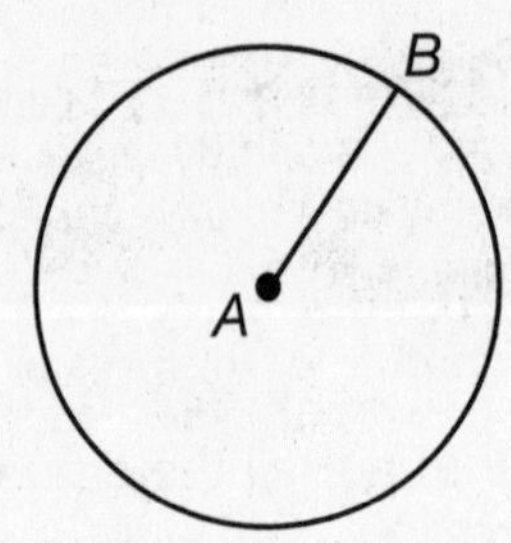

STRATEGY: **Look at the endpoints of the segment.**

One endpoint is at the center, and the other is on the circle.

SOLUTION: **Line segment *AB* is a radius.**

Sample Test Questions

Use the figure for Questions 1 and 2.

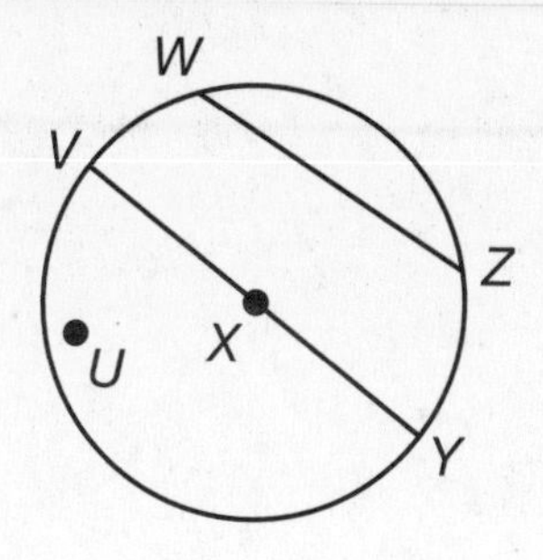

1 In Circle X, which of the following is an example of a chord?

Ⓐ $\overline{XY}$

Ⓑ $\overline{WZ}$

Ⓒ $\overline{UZ}$

Ⓓ $\overline{XZ}$

2 Which segment in circle X is a diameter?

Ⓐ segment WZ

Ⓑ segment XZ

Ⓒ segment XY

Ⓓ segment VY

3 Which of the following statements is true about Circle Q?

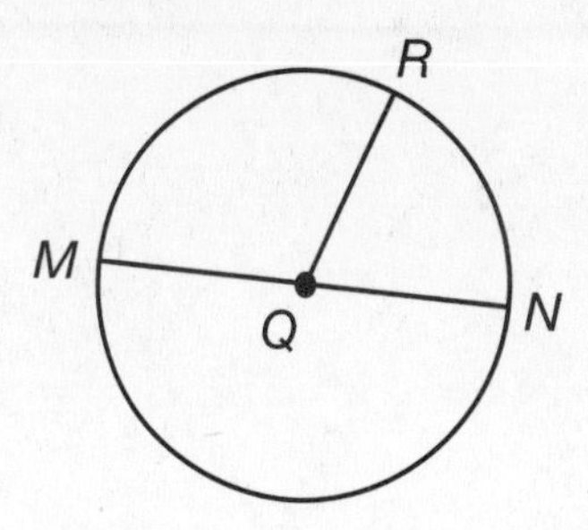

Ⓐ Line segment QM is longer than line segment QN.

Ⓑ Line segment QM is shorter than line segment QR.

Ⓒ Line segment MN is twice the length of line segment QR.

Ⓓ Line segment QR is twice the length of line segment MN.

4 The radius of a circle is always

Ⓐ shorter than the circumference.

Ⓑ longer than the diameter.

Ⓒ longer than the circumference.

Ⓓ shorter than any chord.

5 A certain circle has a radius with a length of 8 inches. What is the length of the diameter?

Ⓐ 4 inches

Ⓑ 8 inches

Ⓒ 16 inches

Ⓓ 25.12 inches

6 a) Draw and label a radius and a diameter on this circle. Explain how the radius and diameter are different.

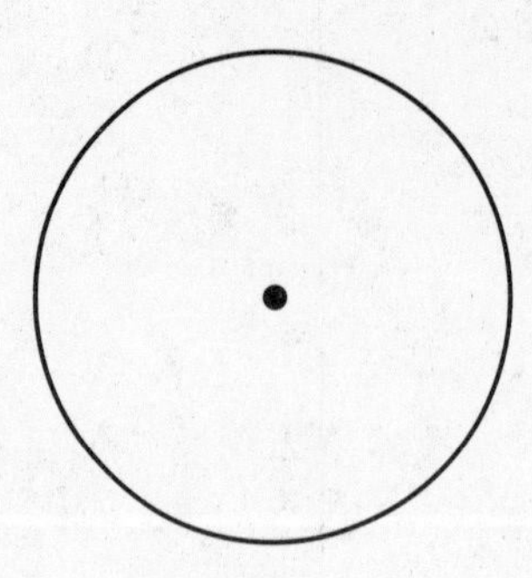

b) How many radii (plural of radius) does a circle have? Explain.

____

____

____

____

29 Models for Solids and Volume

5.4.8: Construct prisms and pyramids using appropriate materials
5.4.9: Given a picture of a three-dimensional object, build the object with blocks
5.5.4: Find the surface area and volume of rectangular solids using appropriate units

Volume is the amount of space occupied by a solid figure.

A common way to measure volume is to find the number of cubes in a solid figure.

Example 1

How many cubes are in this box?

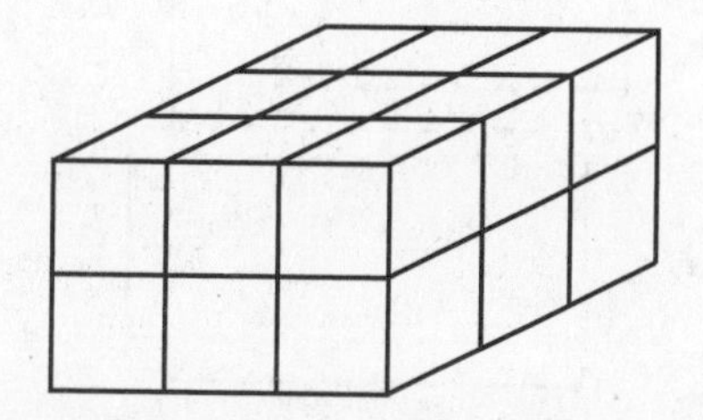

STRATEGY: **Count the number of cubes in each layer. Then add the layers.**

STEP 1: Find the number of cubes in the bottom layer.

The bottom layer has 3 rows of 3 cubes each. That makes 9 cubes.

STEP 2: Find the number of cubes in the second layer.

There are the same number of cubes in the second layer as in the first layer. So there are 9 cubes in the second layer.

STEP 3: Add.

$9 + 9 = 18$ cubes.

SOLUTION: **There are 18 cubes in the box. The volume of the figure is 18 cubic units. (Remember to measure area in square units and volume in cubic units.)**

HINT: First you found the area of one layer by using the formula $L \times W$. Then you multiplied this product by the height. A formula for volume is

$$V = L \times W \times H.$$

In this case, the length is 3, the width is 3, and the height is 2.

So $V = 3 \times 3 \times 2$

$V = 18$ cubic units—the same answer you got by counting the cubes.

You can use two-dimensional figures, called nets, to build three-dimensional figures such as prisms and pyramids.

Example 2

What solid figure can be made by folding this net along the dashed segments?

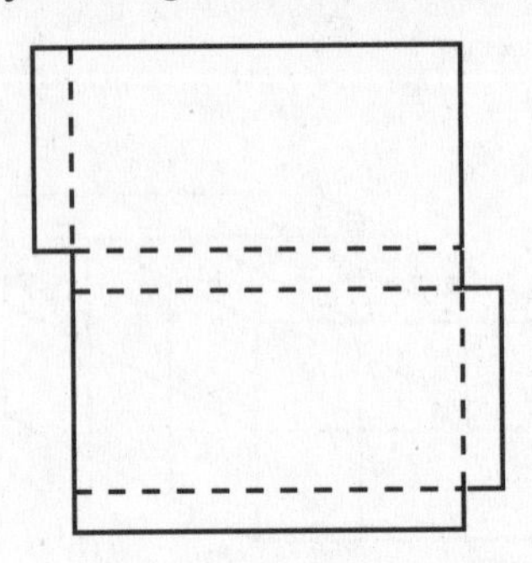

STRATEGY: **Examine the net and imagine folding it.**

STEP 1: Count the number of faces and identify the polygons.

There are 6 faces. They are all rectangles.

STEP 2: Which faces are congruent?

There are three pairs of congruent rectangles. These could be the opposite faces of a prism.

STEP 3: Imagine folding the net.

The folded net would look like this.

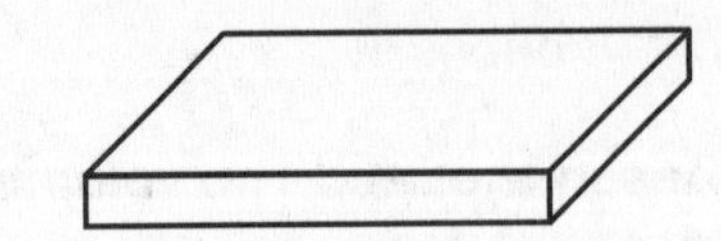

SOLUTION: **When folded, the net will be a rectangular prism.**

Sample Test Questions

1 How many cubes are in this figure?

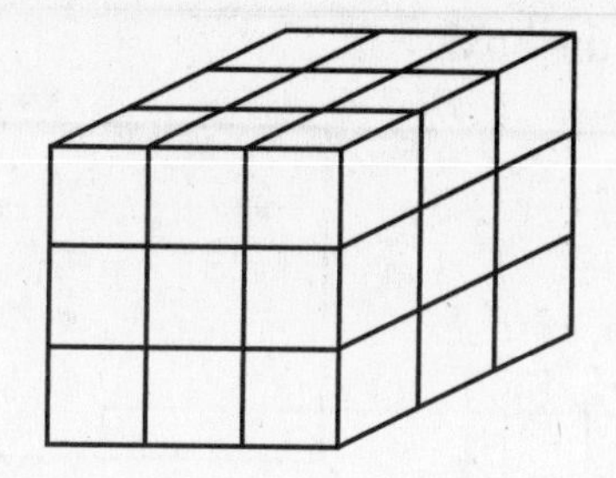

Ⓐ 9

Ⓑ 18

Ⓒ 27

Ⓓ 36

2 Which of the following figures has the greatest volume?

Ⓐ

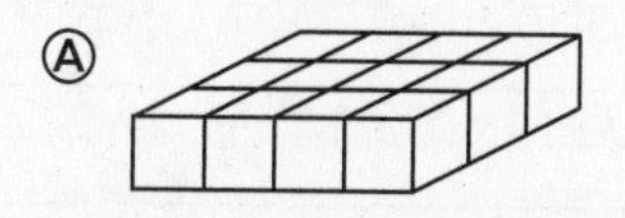

Ⓑ

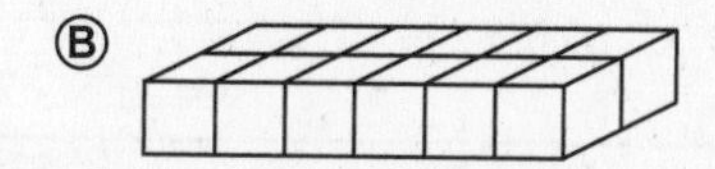

Ⓒ

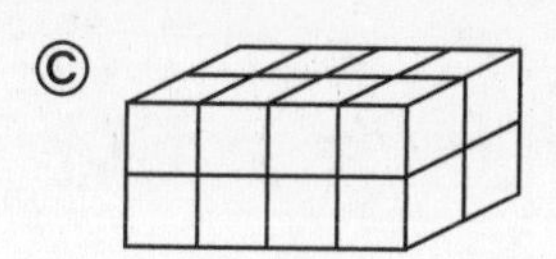

Ⓓ

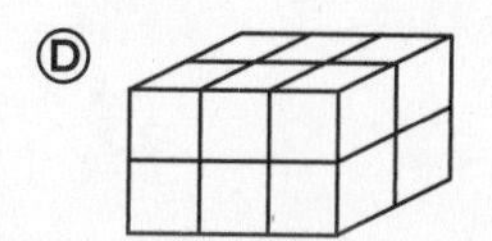

3 How many 1-centimeter cubes will fill the box below?

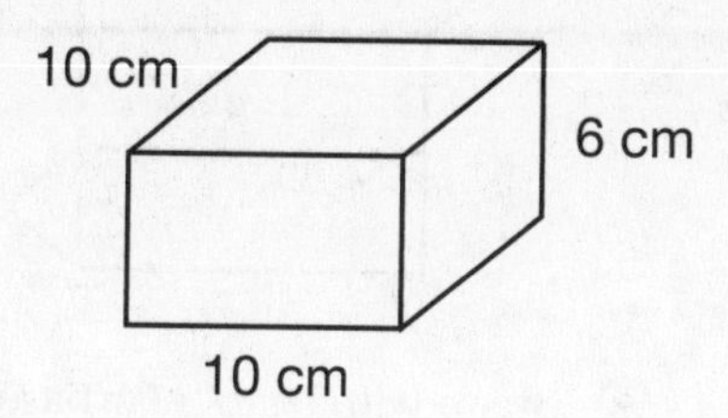

Ⓐ 25

Ⓑ 60

Ⓒ 500

Ⓓ 600

4 What is the volume of this box?

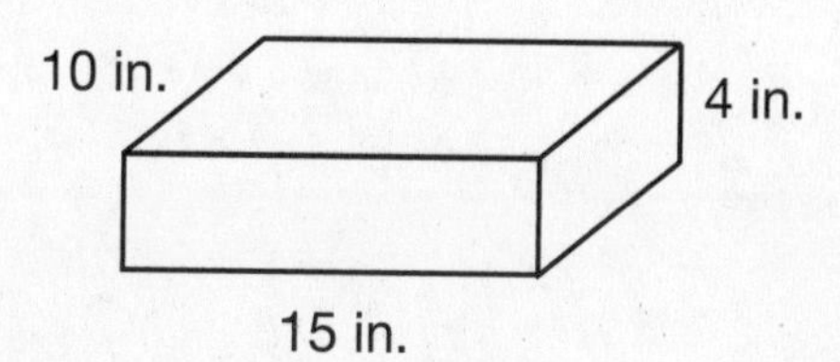

Ⓐ 600 cubic inches

Ⓑ 150 cubic inches

Ⓒ 29 cubic inches

Ⓓ 14 cubic inches

5 What solid figure can be made by folding this net along the dashed segments?

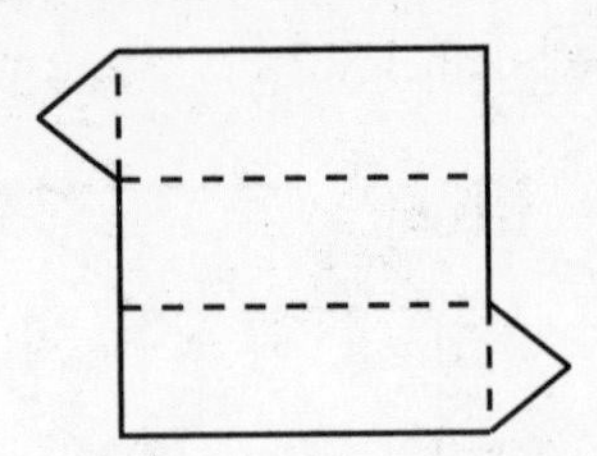

Ⓐ prism with triangular bases

Ⓑ pyramid with a square base

Ⓒ pyramid with a triangular base

Ⓓ cone

6 Cindy placed these 1-inch cubes along the length, width, and height of this plastic storage box. How many more cubes will she need to completely fill the box?

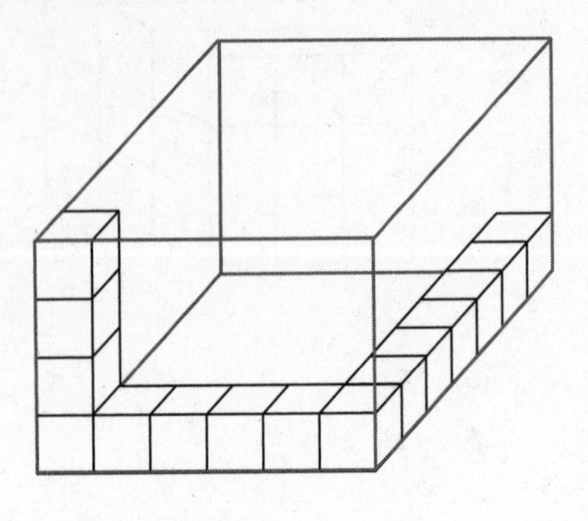

Explain your answer.

____

____

____

____

____

____

____

Progress Check for Lessons 22–29

1 Find the measure of angle C.

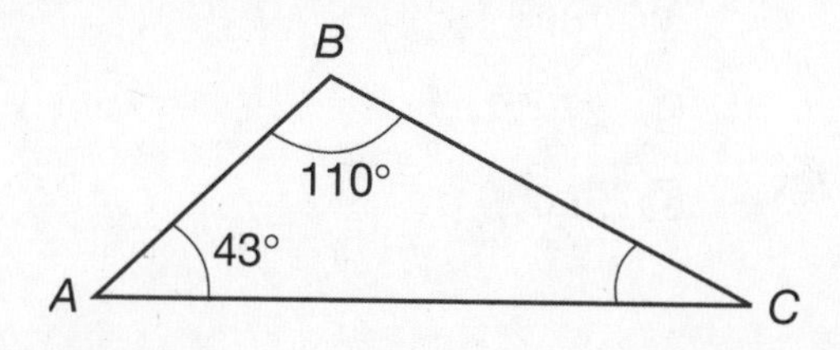

Ⓐ 27°

Ⓑ 127°

Ⓒ 207°

Ⓓ 217°

2 How many 1-centimeter cubes will fit in the box?

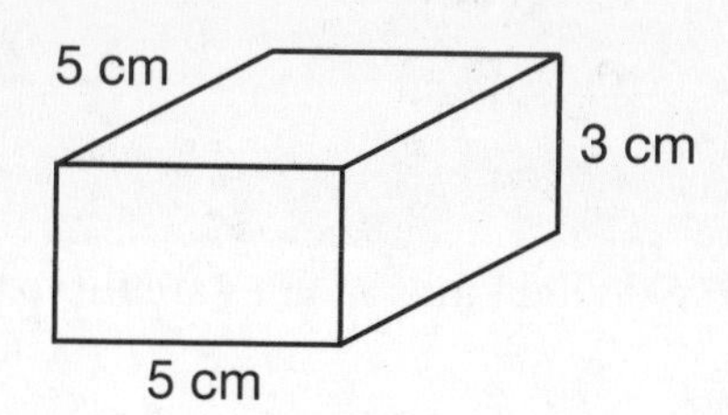

Ⓐ 13

Ⓑ 30

Ⓒ 70

Ⓓ 75

3 Which statement is true about the radius of a circle?

Ⓐ It is one-third the circumference.

Ⓑ It is half the circumference.

Ⓒ It is half the diameter.

Ⓓ It is a line segment that connects any two points on the circle.

4 How many lines of symmetry does a square have?

Ⓐ 4

Ⓑ 3

Ⓒ 2

Ⓓ 1

5 Which name describes these figures?

Ⓐ rectangles

Ⓑ squares

Ⓒ polygons

Ⓓ hexagons

6 What kinds of sides do rectangles have?

Ⓐ parallel segments and no perpendicular segments

Ⓑ perpendicular segments and no parallel segments

Ⓒ no parallel segments and no perpendicular segments

Ⓓ parallel segments and perpendicular segments

7 What kind of clockwise turn is shown below?

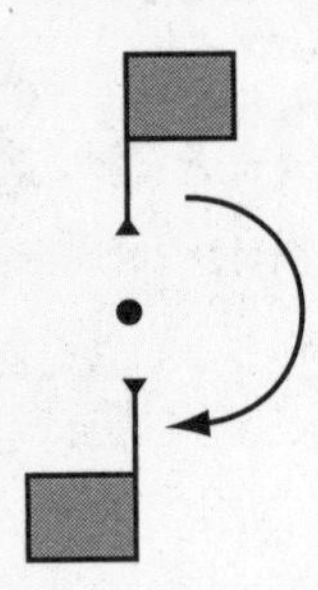

Ⓐ 90°

Ⓑ 180°

Ⓒ 270°

Ⓓ 360°

8 What kind of triangle is this?

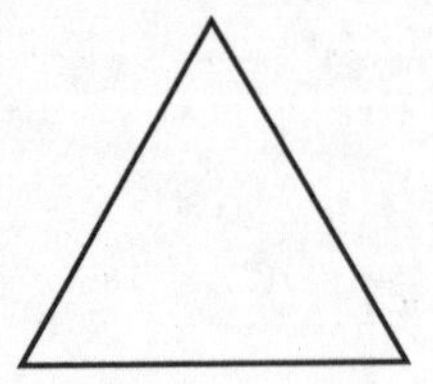

Ⓐ acute

Ⓑ right

Ⓒ obtuse

Ⓓ straight

9 What kinds of lines are these?

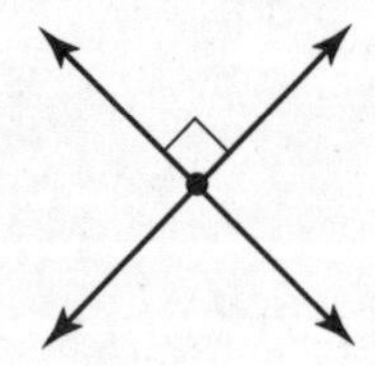

Ⓐ parallel

Ⓑ obtuse

Ⓒ perpendicular

Ⓓ segments

10 Which triangles are congruent?

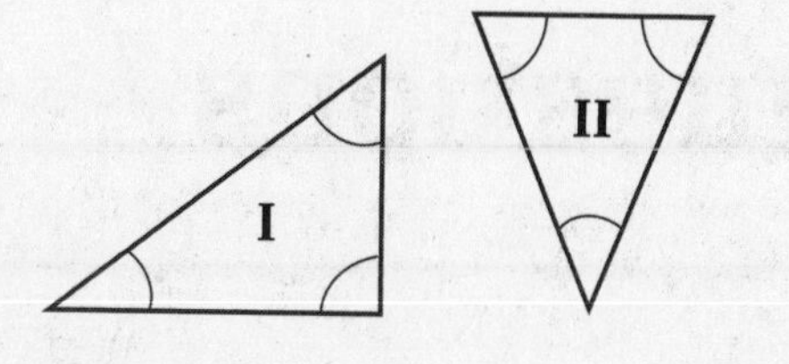
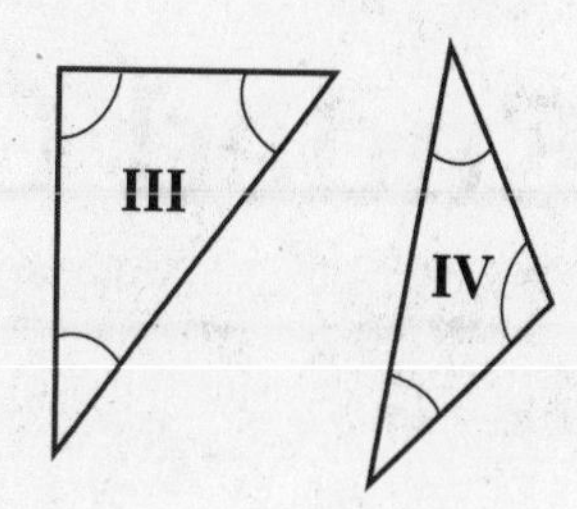

Ⓐ I and II

Ⓑ I, II, and III

Ⓒ I and III

Ⓓ II and IV

11 Which name describes the solid figure that can be made by folding this net along the dashed lines?

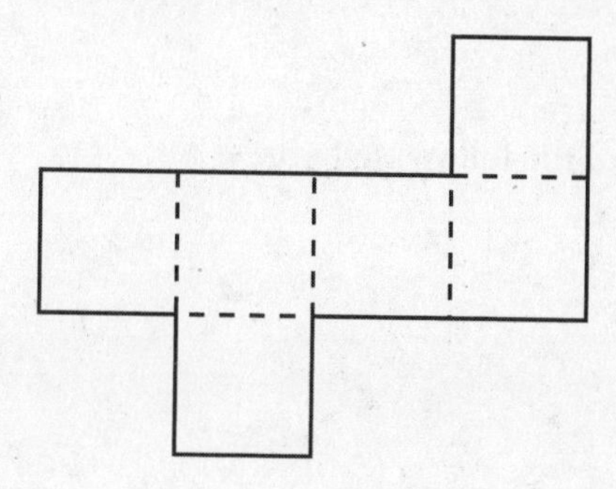

Ⓐ square pyramid

Ⓑ cube

Ⓒ rectangular pyramid

Ⓓ triangular prism

Standard 4
Open-Ended Questions

1 Show how the letter V would look after a half turn around point *Z*.

2 Draw an example of each of the following figures.

a) two parallel lines

b) one line perpendicular to a second line

c) an acute triangle

d) a figure with five angles

e) two congruent triangles

3 Trace this design on another sheet of paper. Cut out the figure along the outside border. Then fold along the dashed segments to make a three-dimensional figure.

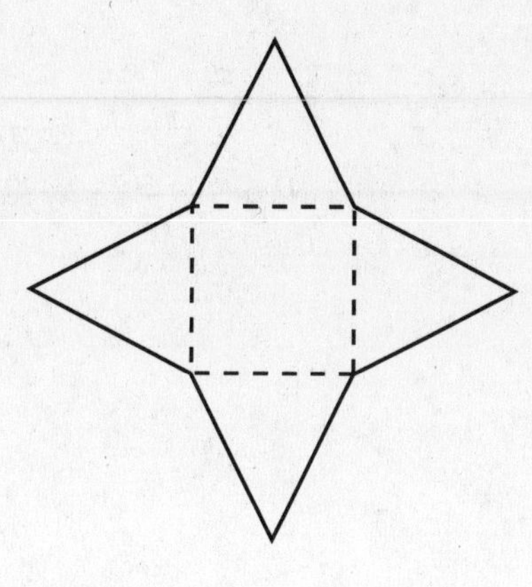

a) What is the name of this figure?

____

b) What are the two-dimensional figures (faces) that make up the three-dimensional figure?

____

4 Rotate the triangle 90° clockwise around point P. Draw the rotated triangle.

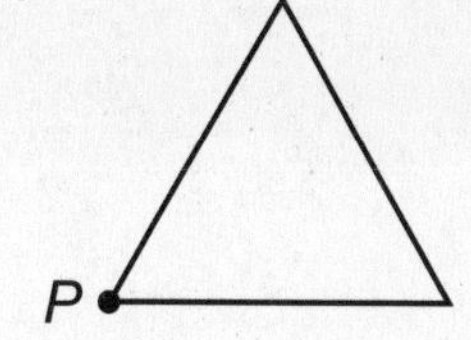

Standard

5

Measurement

30 Estimating and Measuring Weight

5.5.5: Understand and use the smaller and larger units for measuring weight (ounce, gram and ton) and their relationship to pounds and kilograms

Customary Units

Here are some customary units of weight.

ounce about the weight of 5 grapes

pound about the weight of a small book
1 pound = 16 ounces

ton 1 ton = 2,000 pounds
A car weighs about $1\frac{1}{2}$ tons.

Metric Units

Here are some metric units of weight.

gram about the weight of a raisin

kilogram 1 kilogram = 1,000 grams

How close are measures of metric weight to measures of customary weight?

1 gram is about 0.035 ounce.

1 kilogram is about 2.2 pounds.

Example 1

What is a REASONABLE weight for a floor lamp?

Ⓐ 40 grams
Ⓑ 400 grams
Ⓒ 4 kilograms
Ⓓ 400 kilograms

STRATEGY: **Look at each answer choice. Eliminate choices that do not make sense.**

STEP 1: Think about answer A.

40 grams would be the weight of about 40 raisins.

This is much too small.

STEP 2: Think about answer B.

400 grams would be about 400×0.035 ounce, or 14 ounces.

14 ounces is less than a pound, so this is too light to be the weight of a lamp.

STEP 3: Think about answer C.

4 kilograms is about 8.8 pounds. This answer seems about right, but check answer D anyway.

STEP 4: Think about answer D.

400 kilograms is about 8,800 pounds, much too heavy for a floor lamp.

SOLUTION: **The most reasonable weight for a floor lamp is 4 kilograms, answer C.**

Example 2

A recipe for potato salad calls for $2\frac{1}{2}$ pounds of potatoes. How many ounces is this?

STRATEGY: **Recall that 1 pound = 16 ounces.**

STEP 1: Write an expression to convert $2\frac{1}{2}$ pounds to ounces.

1 pound = 16 ounces

Since you are converting from larger units to smaller units, multiply.

$16 \times 2\frac{1}{2}$

STEP 2: Do the math.

$16 \times 2\frac{1}{2} = 16 \times \frac{5}{2} = 40$

SOLUTION: **The recipe calls for 40 ounces of potatoes.**

Sample Test Questions

1 Which is a REASONABLE weight for a textbook?

Ⓐ 1 ounce

Ⓑ 5 ounces

Ⓒ 2 pounds

Ⓓ 10 pounds

2 Which is a REASONABLE weight for a small truck?

Ⓐ 5 pounds

Ⓑ 50 pounds

Ⓒ 5 tons

Ⓓ 50 tons

3 Which is a REASONABLE weight for a small dog?

Ⓐ 7 g

Ⓑ 70 g

Ⓒ 7 kg

Ⓓ 70 kg

4 2,500 grams = ?

Ⓐ 250 kg

Ⓑ 25 kg

Ⓒ 2.5 kg

Ⓓ 0.25 kg

5 6,000 pounds = ?

Ⓐ 6 tons

Ⓑ 4 tons

Ⓒ 3 tons

Ⓓ 2 tons

6 48 ounces = ?

Ⓐ 2 pounds

Ⓑ 3 pounds

Ⓒ 4 pounds

Ⓓ 4.2 pounds

7 A supermarket scale indicated that the weight of a block of cheese was 42 ounces. How many pounds was this? Explain your answer.

____

____

____

____

____

____

31 Perimeter and Area of Polygons

5.5.1: Understand and apply the formulas for the area of a triangle, parallelogram, and trapezoid
5.5.2: Solve problems involving perimeters and areas of rectangles, triangles, parallelograms, and trapezoids, using appropriate units

Perimeter of a Polygon

A polygon is any closed figure formed by line segments. Examples of polygons are triangles, rectangles, pentagons, and hexagons (see Lesson 23).

The perimeter of a polygon is the distance around the polygon.

RULE: To find the perimeter of a polygon, you can add the lengths of the sides.

Here are some formulas for finding the perimeter (P) of polygons.

Rectangle

w

l

$P = 2l + 2w$ or $P = 2(l + w)$
(l = length and w = width)

Square

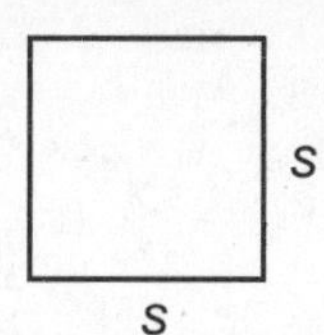

$P = 4s$ (s = length of a side)

Triangle

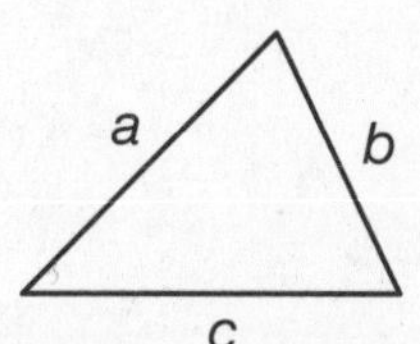

$P = a + b + c$

Area

The area of a figure is the number of square units needed to cover it.

Example 1

What is the area of this rectangle?
Each square covers 1 square unit.

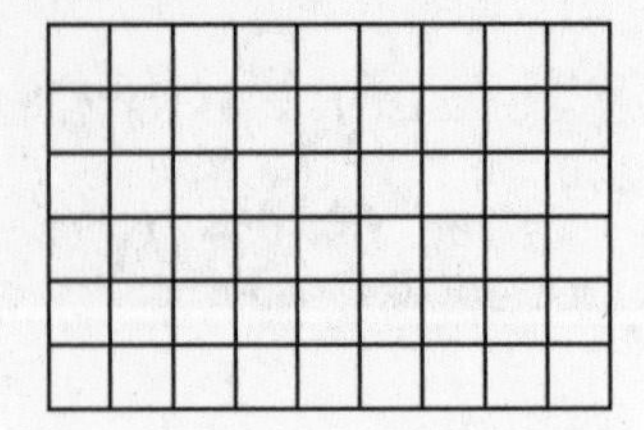

STRATEGY: **Calculate the number of square units in the square.**

STEP1: Count the number of rows.
There are 6 rows.

STEP 2: Count the number of columns.
There are 9 columns.

STEP 3: Multiply the rows by the columns.
$6 \times 9 = 54$ squares.

SOLUTION: **The rectangle's area is 54 square units.**

Here are some formulas for finding the area (A) of polygons.

Parallelogram

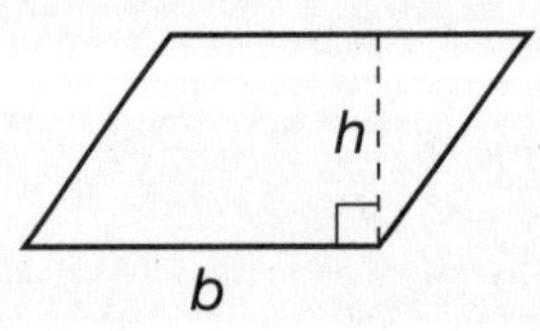

$A = bh$
(b = base and h = height)

Rectangle

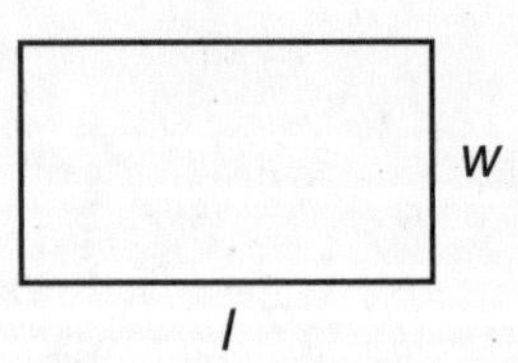

$A = lw$
(l = length and w = width)

Square

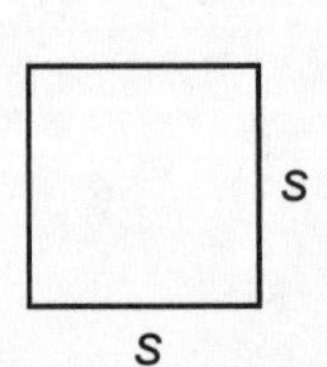

$A = s \times s = s^2$
(s = side)

Triangle

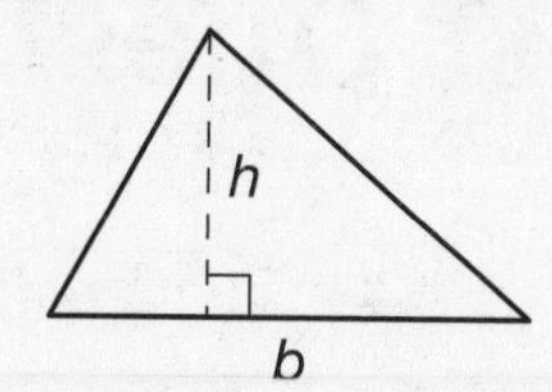

$A = \frac{1}{2}bh$
(b = base and h = height)

Trapezoid

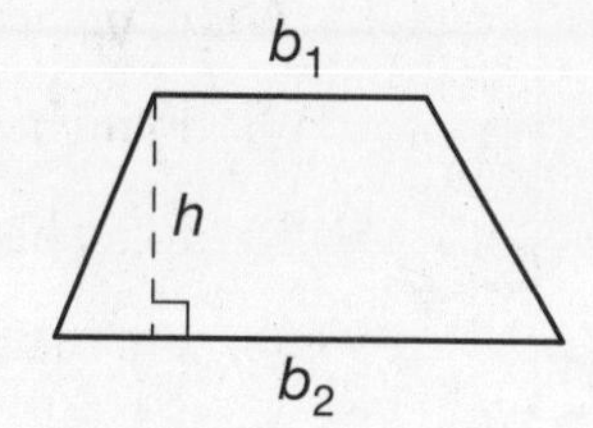

$A = \frac{1}{2}h(b_1 + b_2)$
(h = height, b_1 = one of the bases, and b_2 = the other base)

Example 2

A section of the roof of a house has the shape of a trapezoid. What is the area of the section of roof?

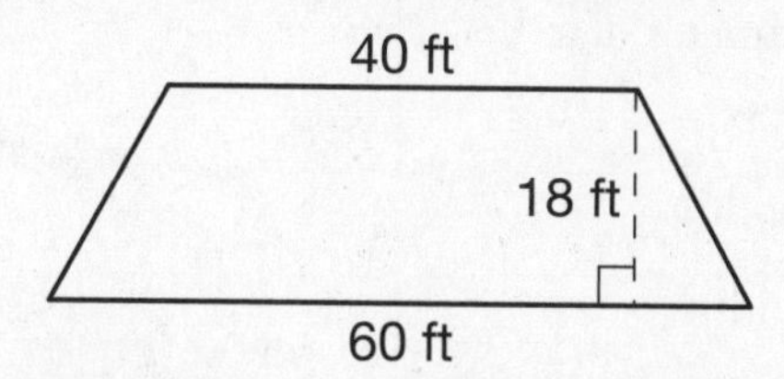

STRATEGY: **Use the formula for area of a trapezoid.**

STEP 1: Write the formula.

$A = \frac{1}{2}h(b_1 + b_2)$

STEP 2: Substitute values.

$A = \frac{1}{2} \times 18 \times (40 + 60)$

STEP 3: Do the math.

$A = \frac{1}{2} \times 18 \times (40 + 60)$

$= \frac{1}{2} \times 18 \times 100$

$= 9(100)$

$= 900$

SOLUTION: **The area of the section of roof is 900 square feet.**

Sample Test Questions

1 What is the perimeter of this figure?

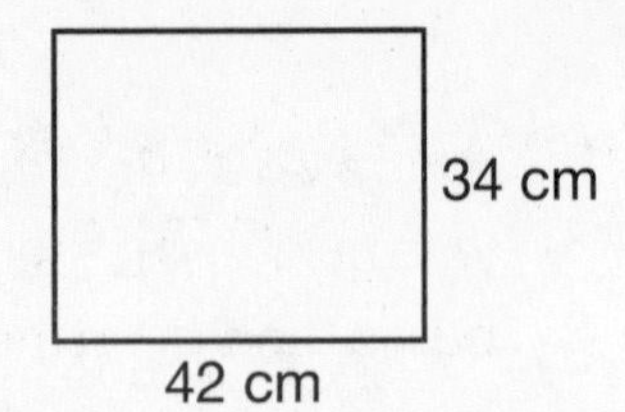

Ⓐ 1428 cm

Ⓑ 168 cm

Ⓒ 152 cm

Ⓓ 136 cm

2 How do you find the perimeter of a rectangle?

Ⓐ $P = 2 \times$ length + width

Ⓑ $P =$ length + $2 \times$ width

Ⓒ $P = 2 \times$ length + $2 \times$ width

Ⓓ $P =$ length $\times$ width

3 What is the area of the shaded section?

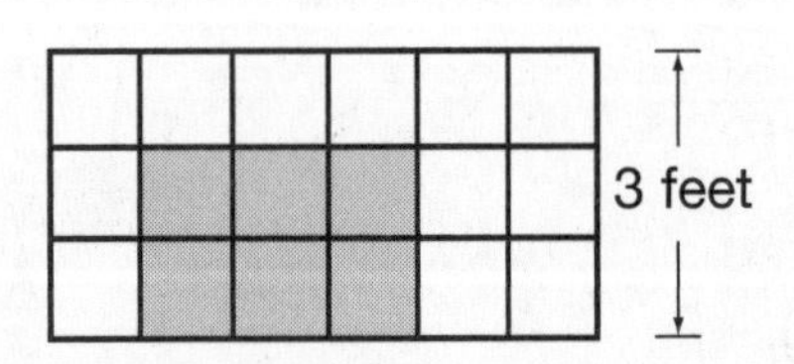

Ⓐ 3 square feet

Ⓑ 6 square feet

Ⓒ 9 square feet

Ⓓ 12 square feet

4 What is the perimeter of a square with sides measuring 14 inches?

Ⓐ 56 inches

Ⓑ 66 inches

Ⓒ 96 inches

Ⓓ 196 inches

5 What is the area of the shaded triangle?

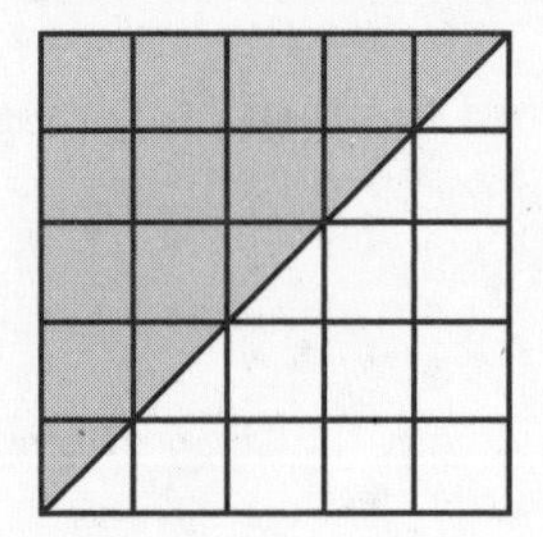

Ⓐ 10 square units

Ⓑ 12 square units

Ⓒ 12.5 square units

Ⓓ 15.5 square units

6 How many square-foot tiles would it take to cover the floor in this plan?

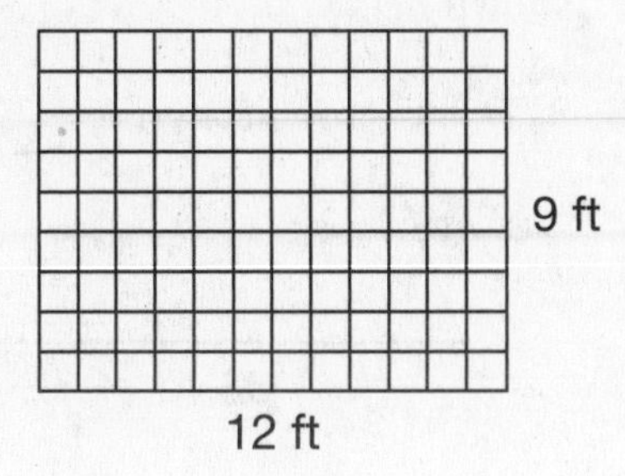

Ⓐ 54 tiles

Ⓑ 64 tiles

Ⓒ 81 tiles

Ⓓ 108 tiles

7 Shawn uses a desk that is 30 inches long and 25 inches wide. Taylor uses a desk that is twice as long and twice as wide. What is the perimeter of Taylor's desk, in inches?

Ⓐ 85

Ⓑ 110

Ⓒ 160

Ⓓ 220

8 What is the perimeter of a triangle whose sides are 7 cm, 8 cm, and 9 cm?

Ⓐ 15 cm

Ⓑ 23 cm

Ⓒ 24 cm

Ⓓ 33 cm

9 A section of Nelson's back yard has the shape of a parallelogram. How many square feet of sod will Nelson need to cover the parallelogram with sod?

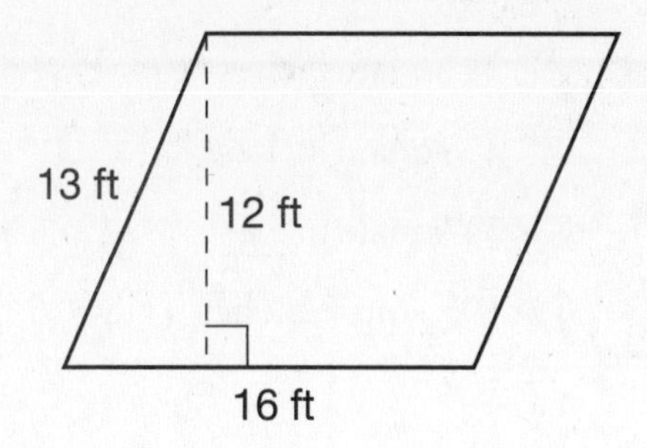

Ⓐ 156 square feet

Ⓑ 192 square feet

Ⓒ 200 square feet

Ⓓ 208 square feet

10 A square sheet of glass has sides that measure 12 inches. What is the area of the glass?

Ⓐ 24 square inches

Ⓑ 48 square inches

Ⓒ 72 square inches

Ⓓ 144 square inches

11 Lenny is making a pennant in the shape of a triangle whose base is 6 inches and whose height is 18 inches. How many square inches of fabric will the pennant have?

Ⓐ 24 square inches

Ⓑ 48 square inches

Ⓒ 54 square inches

Ⓓ 108 square inches

12 The rectangular rug in Tanya's bedroom measures 8 feet by 12 feet. What is the area of the rug?

Ⓐ 20 square feet

Ⓑ 40 square feet

Ⓒ 48 square feet

Ⓓ 96 square feet

13 The drawing below shows a reflecting pool in a park. What is the perimeter of the pool?

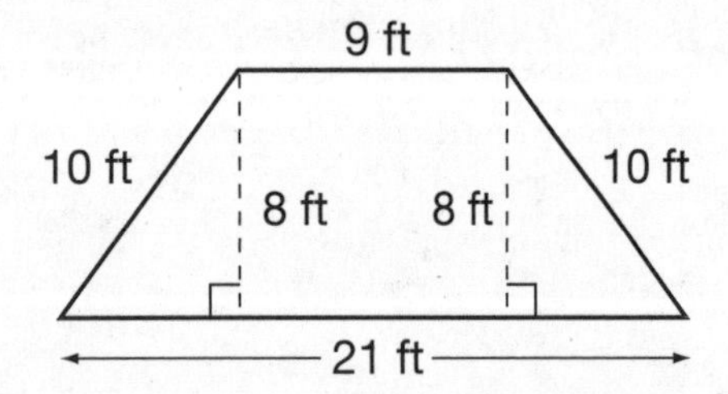

Ⓐ 50 feet

Ⓑ 60 feet

Ⓒ 66 feet

Ⓓ 120 feet

14 The Johnson family bought a piece of land. The land had the dimensions shown below.

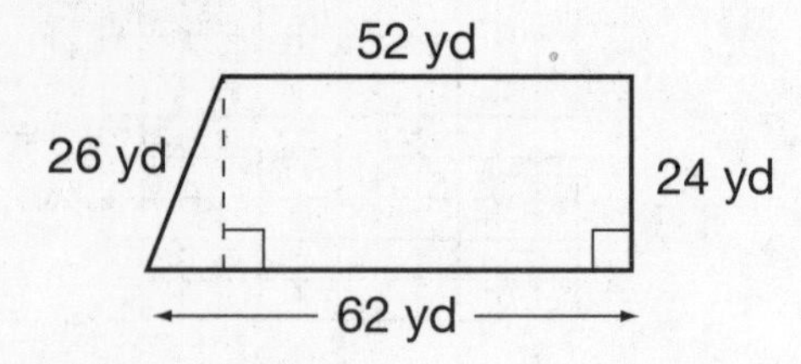

Find the area and perimeter of the land. Explain how you found each measure.

____

____

____

____

____

32 Computing Area of Complex Shapes

5.5.3: Use formulas for the areas of rectangles and triangles to find the area of complex shapes by dividing them into basic shapes

You can sometimes find the area of a complex shape by separating the shape into rectangles and triangles.

Example

This is the floor plan of a living room for a new house. How many square feet of carpeting will be needed to cover the floor of the living room?

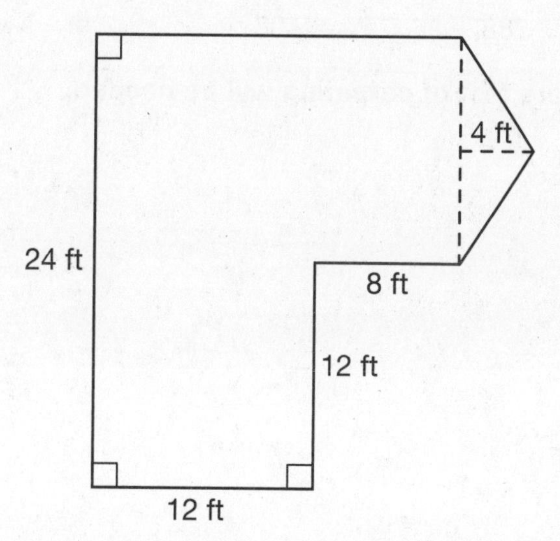

STRATEGY: **Divide the floor plan into shapes whose areas are easy to find.**

STEP 1: Divide the floor plan.

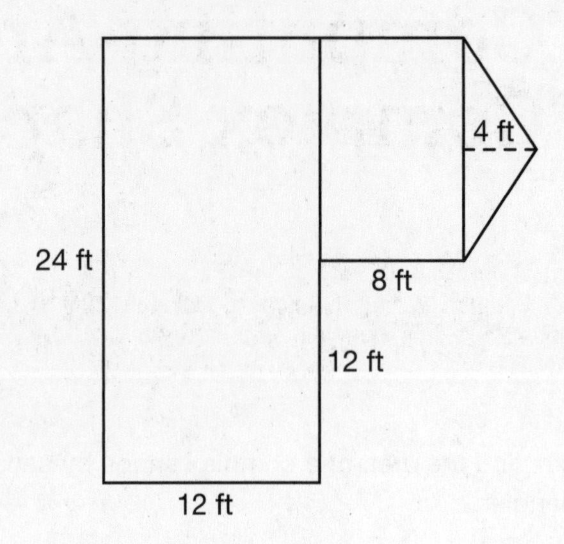

STEP 2: Find the area of each shape.

Area of large rectangle = $lw = 24 \times 12 = 288$ square feet

Area of small rectangle = $lw = 12 \times 8 = 96$ square feet

Area of triangle = $\frac{1}{2}bh = \frac{1}{2} \times 12 \times 4 = 24$ square feet

STEP 3: Add the areas.

$288 + 96 + 24 = 408$

SOLUTION: **408 square feet of carpeting will be needed.**

Sample Test Questions

1 What is the area of the figure?

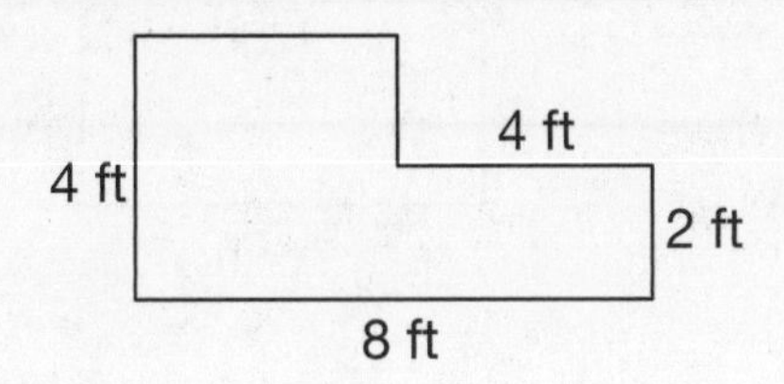

Ⓐ 20 square feet

Ⓑ 24 square feet

Ⓒ 30 square feet

Ⓓ 32 square feet

2 What is the area of the shaded region?

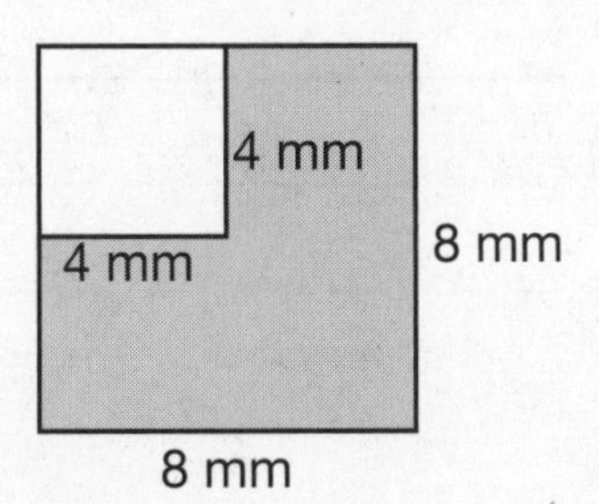

Ⓐ 16 square mm

Ⓑ 32 square mm

Ⓒ 48 square mm

Ⓓ 64 square mm

3 The sixth-grade class is going to paint a picture of the hexagonal school seal on a piece of poster paper. How many square feet of the paper will be painted?

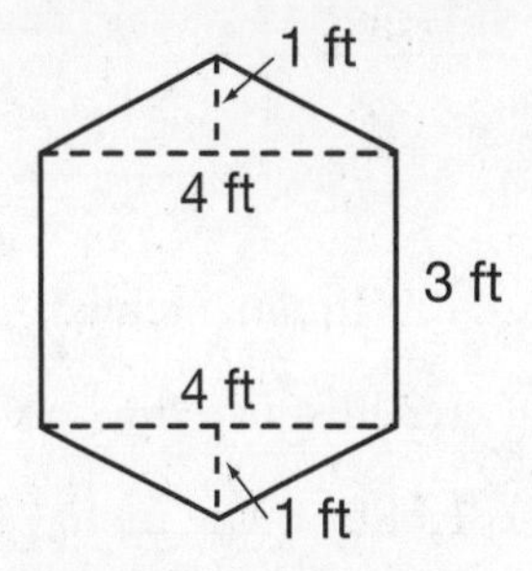

Ⓐ 14 square feet

Ⓑ 16 square feet

Ⓒ 18 square feet

Ⓓ 20 square feet

4 Mel is going to build a sidepiece to a staircase from a sheet of plywood. Each riser will be 8 inches and each tread will be 10 inches. How many square inches of plywood will he use?

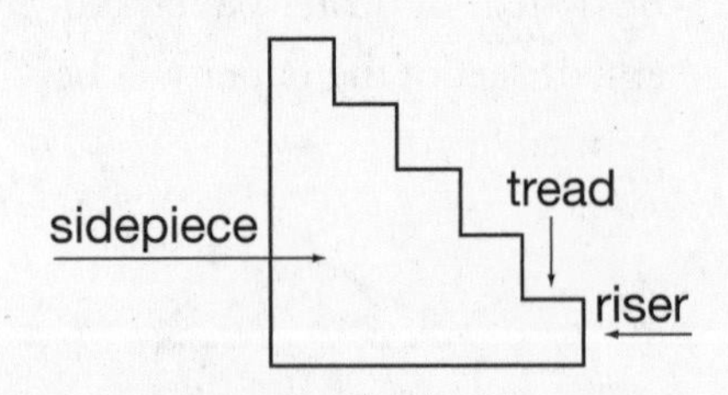

Ⓐ 400 square inches

Ⓑ 1,200 square inches

Ⓒ 1,600 square inches

Ⓓ 2,400 square inches

5 Find the area of this figure.

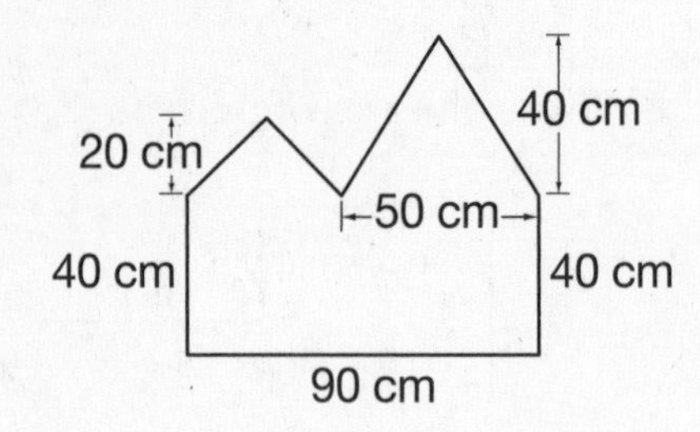

Explain how you found the area. Draw lines on the figure to show how you separated the complex shape into simpler shapes.

____

____

____

____

____

____

33 Temperature

5.5.6: Compare temperatures in Celsius and Fahrenheit

You should know some benchmark temperatures.

Customary Units		Metric Units
32° Fahrenheit (32°F)	water freezes	0° Celsius (0°C)
about 68° Fahrenheit (68°F)	comfortable room temperature	about 20° Celsius (20°C)
about 90° Fahrenheit (90°F)	hot day	about 32° Celsius (32°C)
212° Fahrenheit (212°F)	water boils	100° Celsius (100°C)

Example 1

At which temperature is it neither too hot nor too cold?

Ⓐ 10°C

Ⓑ 22°C

Ⓒ 34°C

Ⓓ 40°C

STRATEGY: **Look at the chart above.**

SOLUTION: **Since 20°C is a comfortable room temperature, then most people would consider 22° neither too hot or too cold. So the best answer is B.**

If you know a temperature in degrees Fahrenheit, you can use a formula to find the temperature in degrees Celsius.

$$C = \frac{5}{9}(F - 32)$$

If you know a temperature in degrees Celsius, you can use a formula to find the temperature in degrees Fahrenheit.

$$F = \frac{9}{5}C + 32$$

Example 2

What is the Fahrenheit equivalent of 40°C?

STRATEGY: **Use the formula for converting Celsius degrees to Fahrenheit degrees.**

STEP 1: Write the formula.

$$F = \frac{9}{5}C + 32$$

STEP 2: Substitute the Celsius temperature.

$$F = \frac{9}{5}C + 32$$
$$= \frac{9}{5} \times 40 + 32$$
$$= 72 + 32$$
$$= 104$$

SOLUTION: **The Fahrenheit equivalent of 40°C is 104°F.**

Example 3

What is the Celsius equivalent of 50°F?

STRATEGY: **Use the formula for converting Fahrenheit degrees to Celsius degrees.**

STEP 1: Write the formula.

$C = \frac{5}{9}(F - 32)$

STEP 2: Substitute the Fahrenheit temperature.

$$\begin{aligned} C &= \frac{5}{9}(F - 32) \\ &= \frac{5}{9}(50 - 32) \\ &= \frac{5}{9}(18) \\ &= 10 \end{aligned}$$

SOLUTION: **The Celsius equivalent of 50°F is 10°C.**

Sample Test Questions

1 Carla is working in her office. She feels that the temperature is comfortable without a sweater. About what temperature would her office be?

Ⓐ 10°C

Ⓑ 15°C

Ⓒ 20°C

Ⓓ 35°C

2 Ivan checked the temperature in his room. It was 75°F. How many degrees above the freezing point is this?

Ⓐ 25 degrees

Ⓑ 43 degrees

Ⓒ 53 degrees

Ⓓ 75 degrees

3 What is the Celsius equivalent of 77°F?

Ⓐ 25°C

Ⓑ 35°C

Ⓒ 45°C

Ⓓ 113°C

4 What is the Fahrenheit equivalent of 15°C?

Ⓐ 59°F

Ⓑ 37°F

Ⓒ 27°F

Ⓓ 15°F

5 The weather report predicted high and low temperatures of 10°C and 5°C.

What are the predicted high and low temperatures in degrees Fahrenheit? Explain your answer.

____

____

____

____

____

____

____

34 Surface Area and Volume of Rectangular Prisms

5.5.4: Find the surface area and volume of rectangular solids using appropriate units

The surface area of a three-dimensional figure is the area of the outside surface. To find the surface area, you need to know the number of different surfaces on the figure and their dimensions.

Rectangular Prism

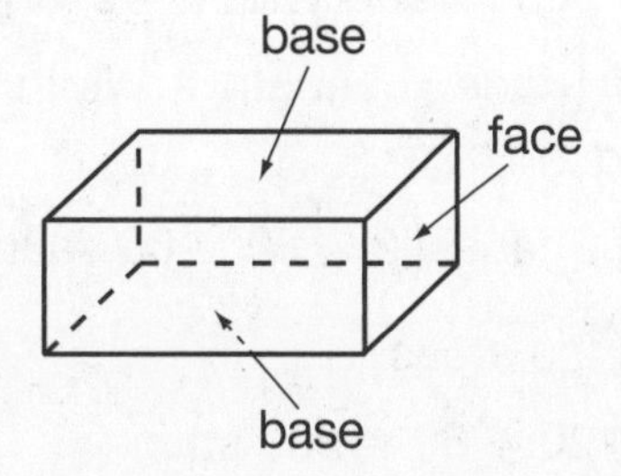

A rectangular prism has 6 faces, all rectangles. The top and bottom faces, called bases, are congruent. So are the front and back faces as well as the two end faces.

To find the surface area of a rectangular prism, add the areas of the 6 faces.

Example 1

Find the surface area of this rectangular prism.

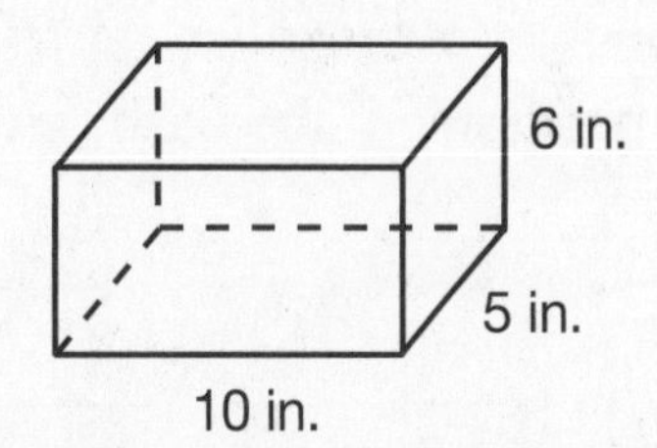

STRATEGY: **Add the areas of the 6 faces, using what you know about congruence.**

STEP1: Find the area of the top and bottom faces, the two bases.

Remember: Since the two faces are congruent, they have the same length and width.

Length = 10 in. and Width = 5 in.

Area of 1 base = Length $\times$ Width = $L \times W$ = 10×5 = 50 sq in.

Area of 2 bases: $2 \times 50 = 100$ sq in.

STEP 2: Find the area of the front and back faces.

Length = 10 in. and Width = 6 in.

Area of 1 face = Length $\times$ Width = $L \times W$ = 10×6 = 60 sq in.

Area of 2 faces: $2 \times 60 = 120$ sq in.

STEP 3: Find the area of the two end faces.

Length = 5 in. and Width = 6 in.

Area of 1 face = Length $\times$ Width = $L \times W$ = 5×6 = 30 sq in.

Area of 2 faces: $2 \times 30 = 60$ sq in.

STEP 4: Add all the areas.

$100 + 120 + 60 = 280$ sq in.

SOLUTION: **The surface area of the rectangular prism is 280 sq in.**

NOTE: A quick way to find the surface area of a rectangular prism is to use one of these two formulas:

Surface Area = $2LW + 2LH + 2WH$

Surface Area = $PH + 2LW$

where L = length of the base

W = width of the base

H = height of the prism

P = perimeter of the base

The volume of a three-dimensional figure is measured by the number of unit cubes that fit inside the figure. Unit cubes can be cubic centimeters, cubic inches, cubic meters, or cubic feet.

Volume of Rectangular Prisms

Example 2

Find the volume of this rectangular prism.

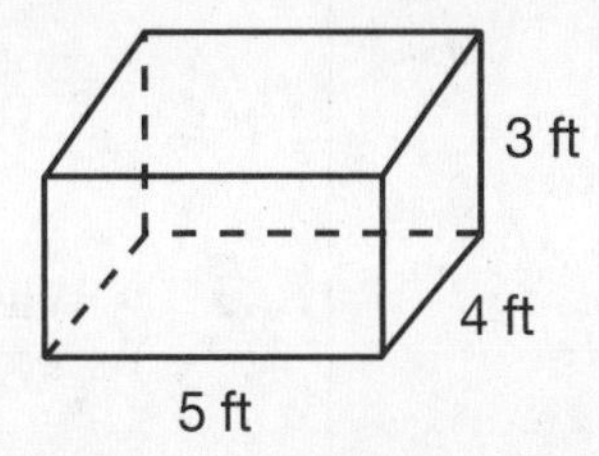

STRATEGY: **Count or calculate the number of cubic feet that fit inside the prism.**

STEP 1: How many cubes, each 1 cubic foot, fit on the bottom of the prism?

You can place 4 rows of 5 cubes each across the bottom of the prism. That makes a layer of 20 cubes or 20 cubic feet.

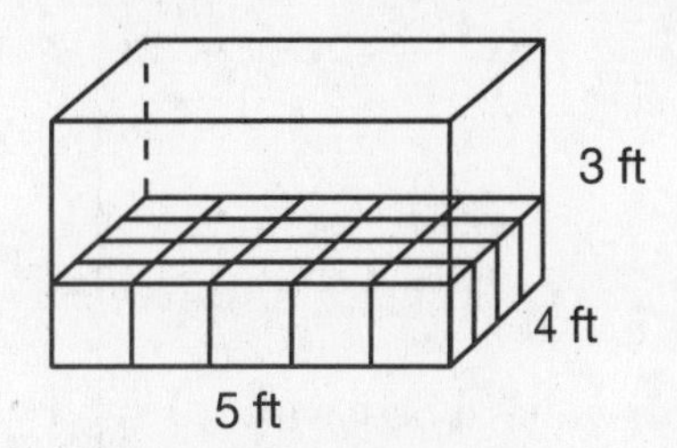

STEP 2: How many layers of cubes are there?

There are 3 layers.

STEP 3: How many cubic feet fit inside the prism?

3 layers of 20 cubic feet each $= 3 \times 20 = 60$ cubic feet

SOLUTION: **The volume of the prism is 60 cubic feet.**

Formula: A fast way to find the volume of a rectangular prism is by means of a formula.

$V = L \times W \times H$ where V stands for volume, L for length, W for width, and H for height

Sample Test Questions

1 Find the surface area of this rectangular prism.

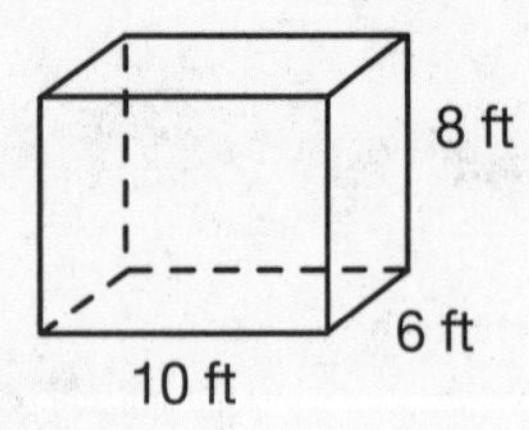

Ⓐ 480 sq ft

Ⓑ 376 sq ft

Ⓒ 316 sq ft

Ⓓ 256 sq ft

2 The surface area of a rectangular prism is 5,400 sq. cm. Find the height if the length is 60 cm and the width is 30 cm.

Ⓐ 10 cm

Ⓑ 20 cm

Ⓒ 30 cm

Ⓓ 40 cm

3 A rectangular prism has a base with length 40 inches and width 20 inches. If the height of the prism is 20 inches, what is the volume of the prism?

Ⓐ 8,000 cubic inches

Ⓑ 12,000 cubic inches

Ⓒ 14,000 cubic inches

Ⓓ 16,000 cubic inches

4 The base of a rectangular prism is 4 ft by 3 ft. If the volume of the prism is 84 cu. ft, what is the height of the prism?

Ⓐ 6 ft

Ⓑ 7 ft

Ⓒ 8 ft

Ⓓ 9 ft

5 Which measure of this cube has the greater number of units, the surface area or the volume? Explain.

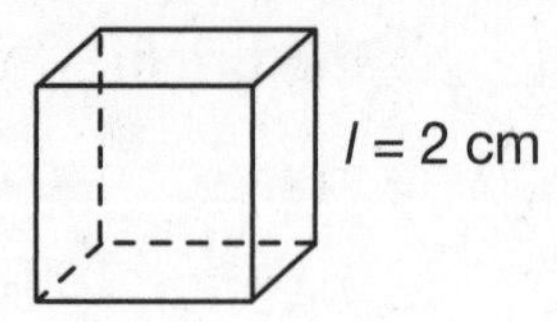

____

____

____

____

____

____

Progress Check for Lessons 30–34

1 What is the perimeter of this rectangular garden?

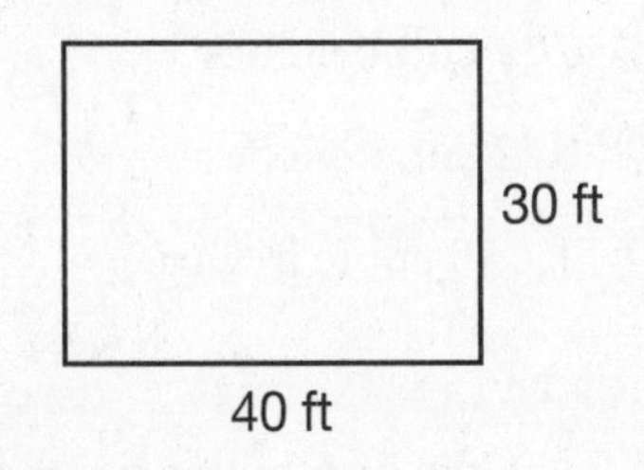

Ⓐ 70 ft

Ⓑ 100 ft

Ⓒ 120 ft

Ⓓ 140 ft

2 The perimeter of a square is 44 m. What is the length of each side?

Ⓐ 8 m

Ⓑ 10 m

Ⓒ 11 m

Ⓓ 121 m

3 What is the area of the shaded triangle?

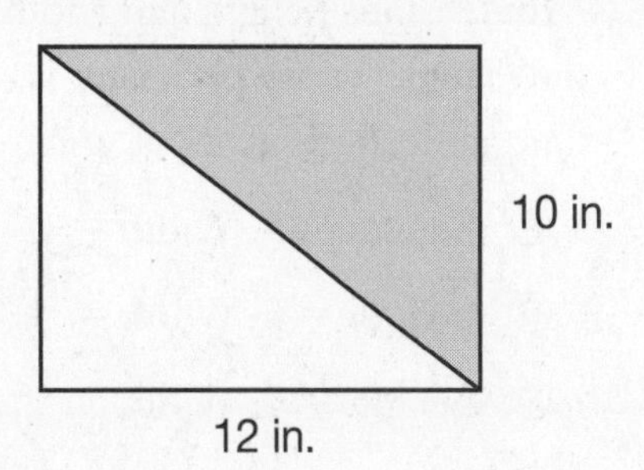

Ⓐ 60 square inches

Ⓑ 65 square inches

Ⓒ 70 square inches

Ⓓ 80 square inches

4 What is the area of this figure?

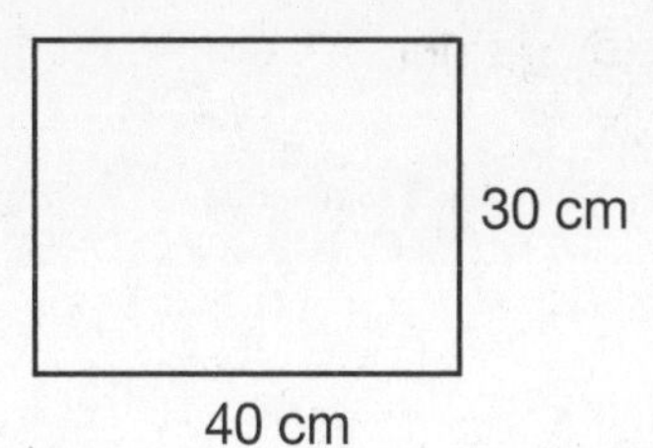

Ⓐ 70 square cm

Ⓑ 149 square cm

Ⓒ 1,200 square cm

Ⓓ 2,400 square cm

5 How do you find the perimeter of a square?

Ⓐ $P = 4 \times$ length of one side

Ⓑ $P = 3 \times$ length of one side

Ⓒ $P = 2 \times$ length of one side

Ⓓ $P =$ length of side $\times$ length of side

6 Which of the following are the dimensions (length and width) of a rectangle whose perimeter is numerically equal to its area?

Ⓐ Length = 5; Width = 2

Ⓑ Length = 6; Width = 3

Ⓒ Length = 7; Width = 3

Ⓓ Length = 8; Width = 2

7 How many grams are equivalent to 2.3 kilograms?

Ⓐ 23

Ⓑ 230

Ⓒ 2,300

Ⓓ 23,000

8 At what temperature does water boil?

Ⓐ 32°C

Ⓑ 100°F

Ⓒ 212°C

Ⓓ 212°F

9 What is the volume of a cube with edges measuring 9 inches?

Ⓐ 486 cubic inches

Ⓑ 729 cubic inches

Ⓒ 972 cubic inches

Ⓓ 1,458 cubic inches

10 What is the area of this figure?

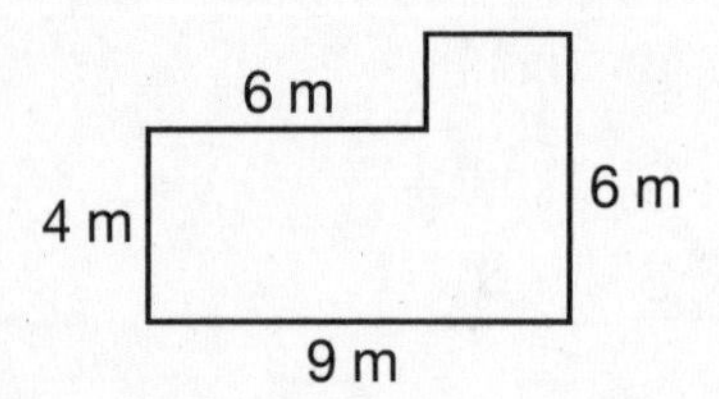

Ⓐ 42 square meters

Ⓑ 46 square meters

Ⓒ 48 square meters

Ⓓ 50 square meters

Standard 5
Open-Ended Questions

1 How many square inches are in a square foot? Explain your answer.

2 Show how two rectangles can have the same perimeter but different areas. Draw diagrams to help explain your answer.

3 An isosceles trapezoid is a trapezoid whose nonparallel sides are congruent. Find the area of this isosceles trapezoid. Explain how you found your answer.

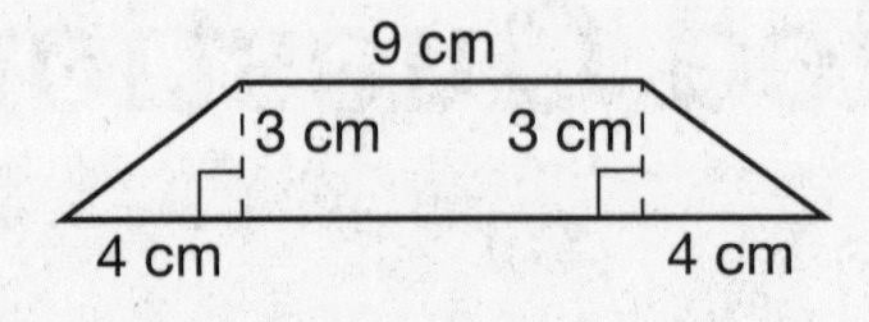

____

____

____

____

____

____

4 Michelle mailed packages weighing 12 ounces, 20 ounces, and 14 ounces. What was the total weight in pounds of the packages she mailed? Explain how you found your answer.

____

____

____

____

____

____

Standard

6

Data Analysis and Probability

35 Interpreting Information From Graphs

5.6.1: Explain which types of displays are appropriate for various sets of data

A graph is a way to show and compare numerical information. There are four kinds of graphs you should know about.

Pictographs

Pictographs are graphs that use pictures.

Example 1

The pictograph shows how many of Kora's roses bloomed each month. How many roses bloomed in June?

Number of Roses that Bloomed

April	❋ ❋ ❋ ❋ ❋ ❋ ❋
May	❋ ❋ ❋ ❋ ❋ ❋ ❋ ❋ ❋
June	❋ ❋ ❋ ❋ ❋ ❋ ❋ ❋ ❋ ❋
KEY: ❋ equals 2 roses	

STRATEGY: **Count the flowers in June. Then use the key.**

STEP 1: Find June on the graph. Then count the flowers.

There are 10 flowers.

STEP 2: Look at the key.

Each picture of a flower represents 2 roses.

STEP 3: Multiply to find the total number of roses that bloomed in June.

$10 \times 2 = 20$

SOLUTION: **20 roses bloomed in June.**

Bar Graphs

Bar graphs use bars of different heights to compare data.

Example 2

The graph shows how many books were read by four children. Who read the most books, and how many did that person read?

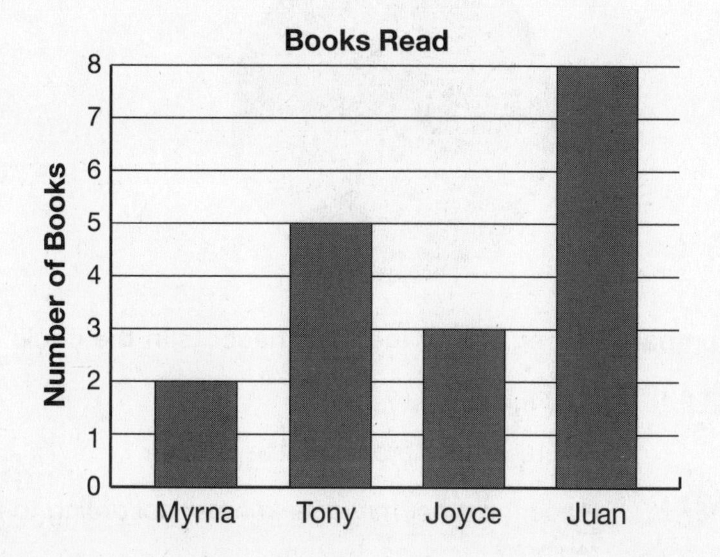

STRATEGY: **Find the highest bar. Then read the number on the scale to the left.**

STEP 1: Look at all the bars.

The highest bar is the one for Juan.

STEP 2: From the top of the highest bar, follow a line to the number on the left.

It tells you the number of books Juan read.

STEP 3: The top of Juan's bar is at 8.

SOLUTION: **Juan read 8 books.**

Circle Graphs

A circle graph divides a circle into regions. Each region represents a part of a whole.

Example 3

Students in Mrs. Johnson's class voted for a school mascot. She showed the results in a circle graph.

List the four mascots in order from the most popular to the least popular.

School Mascot Preferences

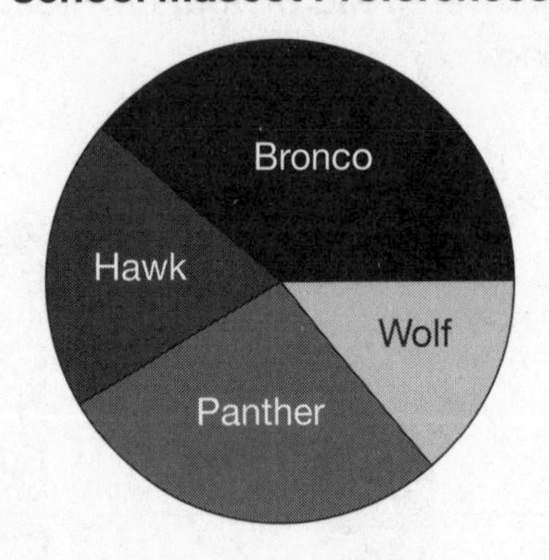

STRATEGY: **Compare the regions of the four mascots in the circle graph.**

STEP 1: Find the largest region.

The region for bronco is the largest.

STEP 2: Place the other mascots in order according to the size of their regions.

Panther, Hawk, and Wolf.

SOLUTION: **The most popular mascot is the Bronco, then the Panther, then the Hawk, and finally the Wolf.**

Line Graphs

In a line graph, a line shows a change in data over time.

Example 4

The graph shows the number of hours Kirsti practiced piano over 5 weeks.

How many more hours did Kirsti practice during week 5 than during week 2?

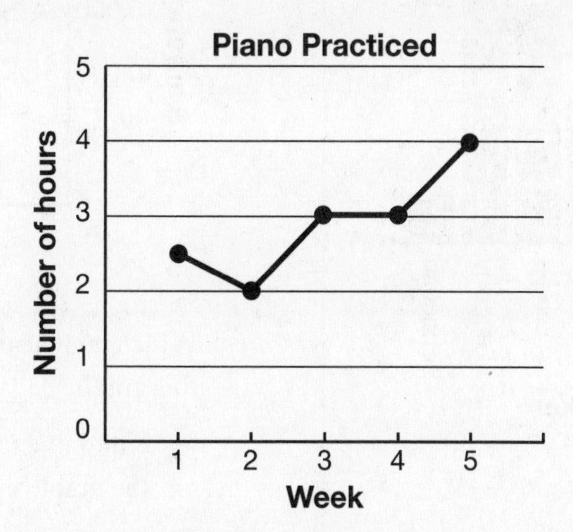

STRATEGY: **Compare the number of hours for the two weeks and find the difference.**

STEP 1: Find Week 2 and move up to the data line.

STEP 2: Move left and read the number on the scale.

The number is 2 hours.

STEP 3: Repeat Steps 1 and 2 for Week 5.

The number is 4 hours.

STEP 4: Subtract. $4 - 2 = 2$

SOLUTION: **Kirsti practiced 2 more hours during week 5 than during week 2.**

Sample Test Questions

1 What type of graph is shown here?

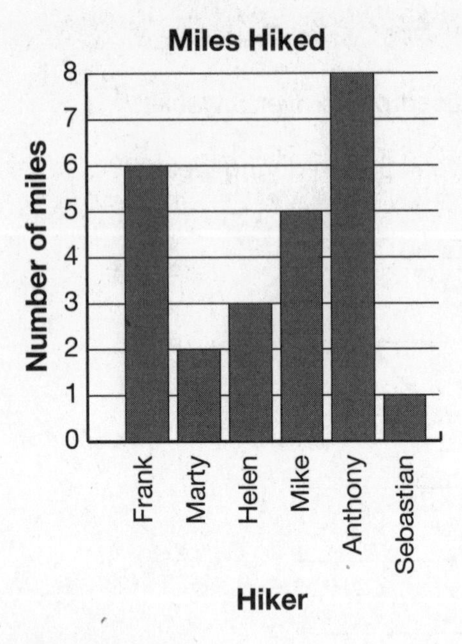

Ⓐ line graph

Ⓑ bar graph

Ⓒ circle graph

Ⓓ pictograph

2 This graph shows the value of a car over the first five years after it was purchased.

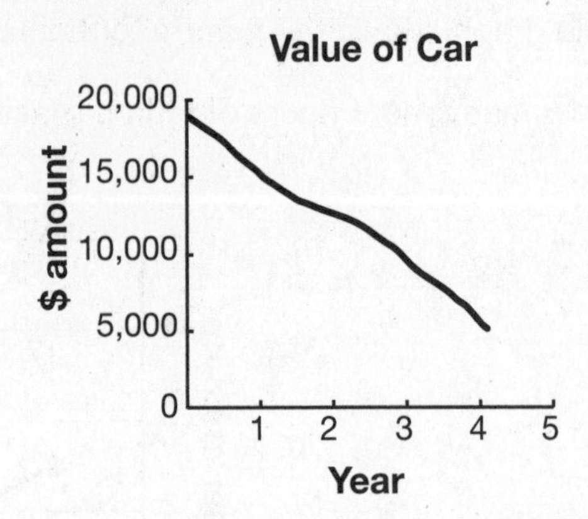

Which conclusion can you draw from this graph?

Ⓐ The value of the car increased in the first five years.

Ⓑ The value of a car remained roughly the same for the first five years.

Ⓒ The value of a car decreased in the first five years.

Ⓓ The value of a car increased and decreases several times over the first five years.

3 How many students attend School D?

Students' Attendance

School A	
School B	
School C	
School D	
School E	
= 1,000 students	

Ⓐ 500

Ⓑ 1,500

Ⓒ 1,500

Ⓓ 2,500

4 Last month, Darryl saw 10 movies, Bart saw 8 movies, Willie saw 7 movies, and Hadassah saw 6 movies. In the graph below, which bar shows the number of movies Willie saw?

Ⓐ I

Ⓑ II

Ⓒ III

Ⓓ IV

5 Manny made a graph showing how he spent his money last year.

Money Spent Last Year

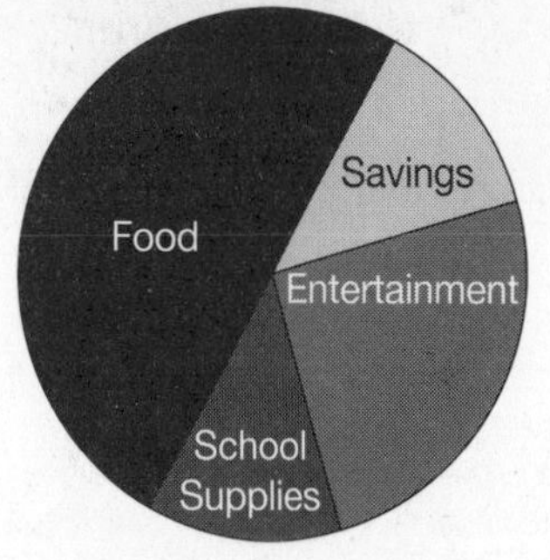

How did he spend $\frac{1}{2}$ of his money?

Ⓐ food

Ⓑ savings and entertainment

Ⓒ entertainment

Ⓓ school supplies and savings

6 You want to show how the number of students in your school has increased or decreased over the past five years. What kind of graph would be the best way to show this trend?

Ⓐ bar graph

Ⓑ pictograph

Ⓒ line graph

Ⓓ circle graph

7 You have taken a survey to find your fellow students' favorite school subjects. You want to graph the data to see how the number of students who voted for math compares with the total number of students surveyed. Which kind of graph would be best for displaying the data?

Ⓐ line graph

Ⓑ bar graph

Ⓒ circle graph

Ⓓ pictograph

8 You have recorded the number of votes received by the four candidates running for class president. You want to graph the data so that the display compares the number of votes each student received. What kind of graph would be best for displaying the data?

Ⓐ circle graph

Ⓑ bar graph or pictograph

Ⓒ line graph

Ⓓ line graph or pictograph

9 Rick collected these data on his classmates' favorite recreational activities.

Watch television	12
Play sports	10
Play video games	6
Hobbies	4

What would be a good graph for Rick to use to display his data? Explain your choice.

____

____

____

____

____

36 Range, Median, Mode, and Mean

5.6.2: Find the mean, median, mode, and range of a set of data

Range

The range of a set of numbers is the difference between the greatest and the least number in the set.

Example 1

The students at the Claridge School voted on their next field trip. The results are shown in the table.

Votes on Next Field Trip

Type of Trip	Votes
Art Museum	38
TV Studio	97
Zoo	51
Space Museum	65

What is the range of the number of votes?

STRATEGY: **Use the definition of range.**

STEP 1: Find the greatest number of votes.

The greatest number was for the TV Studio—97 votes.

STEP 2: Find the least number of votes.

The least number was for the Art Museum—38 votes.

STEP 3: Subtract the least from the greatest.

$97 - 38 = 59$

SOLUTION: **The range of the number of the votes is 59.**

The median, mode, and mean are called measures of central tendency. Measures of central tendency give information about a set of data.

Median

When a set of numbers is ordered from least to greatest, the middle number is the median.

Example 2

What is the median weight of Johnny's friends?

Weights of Johnny's Friends

Name	Weight (lb)
Holly	68
Max	72
Mabel	62
Jane	70
Violetta	58
Keith	66
Lynne	61

STRATEGY: **Use the definition of median.**

STEP 1: Order the weights from least to greatest.

58, 61, 62, 66, 68, 70, 72

STEP 2: Find the weight in the middle.

The middle weight is 66.

SOLUTION: **The median weight is 66 lb.**

NOTE: If there is an even number of data, then you have to do arithmetic to find the median: Add the two middle numbers and divide by 2.

Mode

The mode of a set of numbers is the number that appears most often.

Example 3

The table shows the number of goals made by the top scorers in the after-school lacrosse league at Tom's school.

Top Scorers

Name	Number of Goals
Greg	4
Doug	3
Stan	4
Marty	2
Jason	6
Shawn	4
Al	5

What is the mode of the goal data?

STRATEGY: **Use the definition of mode.**

Find the number of goals that appears most frequently in the table above.

The number 4 appears three times.

SOLUTION: **The mode is 4 goals.**

NOTE: It is possible for a set of numbers to have no mode or more than one mode.

Mean

You are already familiar one measure of central tendency: the average, or mean. To calculate the mean of the goal data on the previous page, simply add all the scores (28) and divide the total by the number of scorers (7). In this case, the mean number of goals scored is 4.

Sometimes, one measure of central tendency may describe a set of data better than another.

Example 4

Which measure of central tendency is best for describing this set of hourly wages for people who work in the same office?

$7, $7, $9, $20, $27

STRATEGY: **Find each measure of central tendency and compare it with the whole set of data.**

STEP 1: Find the mode.

The mode is the number that appears most often: $7.

STEP 2: Find the median.

The median is the middle number: $9.

STEP 3: Find the mean.

The mean is the sum of the numbers divided by the number of numbers:

($7 + $7 + $9 + $ 20 + $27) ÷ 5 = $14

STEP 4: Compare each measure with the data.

The mode is the least number in the set, so it is not the best measure for describing the set.

The median is close to the mode, so it may not be the best measure.

The mean is a good measure of the center of the data.

SOLUTION: **The best measure of central tendency for describing the data is the mean.**

Sample Test Questions

The table shows the number of books that students read in the last 3 months.

Use the table to answer Questions 1 and 2.

Books Read in Last Three Months

Student	Books
Scott	7
Dorothy	12
Boris	20
Monica	12
Ozzie	4

1 What is the range of the number of books read in the last 3 months?

Ⓐ 7

Ⓑ 11

Ⓒ 16

Ⓓ 20

2 What is the mean number of books read by the students?

Ⓐ 8

Ⓑ 9

Ⓒ 10

Ⓓ 11

Use the table to answer Questions 3–5.

Test Grades of Fifth-Grade Science Class

Number of Students	Grade
4	50
2	60
7	70
2	80
5	90
1	100

3 What is the range of grades on the science test?

Ⓐ 100

Ⓑ 70

Ⓒ 50

Ⓓ 40

4 What is the median of the grades on the science test?

Ⓐ 70

Ⓑ 65

Ⓒ 60

Ⓓ 55

5 What is the mode of the grades on the science test?

Ⓐ 60

Ⓑ 70

Ⓒ 80

Ⓓ 90

6 The range of prices of television sets at the B & Q Electronics Store is $500. If the lowest price is $350, what is the highest price?

Ⓐ $850

Ⓑ $500

Ⓒ $400

Ⓓ $350

7 If the median of the number of runs a baseball team got in the last 7 games is 5, what conclusion could you make?

Ⓐ This team never scored 10 runs in a game.

Ⓑ This team never scored 3 runs in a game.

Ⓒ This team scored 7 runs in 2 games.

Ⓓ The team scored 5 runs at least once.

8 Half of Diego's class received 80 on the first science quiz, one quarter of the class received 70, and one quarter received 90. What is the mode of the class scores?

Ⓐ 70

Ⓑ 80

Ⓒ 85

Ⓓ 90

9 After five tests, Whitney's average test score was 79. After she scored 85 on the sixth test, what was her new average?

Ⓐ 80

Ⓑ 81

Ⓒ 82

Ⓓ 83

10 Which is the best measure of central tendency for describing the number of volunteer hours of seven students during the month of November?

Students' Volunteer Hours in November

5	6	9	10	11	13	14

Ⓐ the mode and the mean

Ⓑ the median and the mean

Ⓒ the mode and the median

Ⓓ the range

11 Tyler recorded his math quiz scores for the first marking period.

74 84 84 88 89 91

His teacher says that he can use the mean, median, or mode for the period. Which should he choose? Explain.

____

____

____

____

____

____

37 Probability

5.6.3: Understand that probability can take any value between 0 and 1
5.6.4: Express outcomes of experimental probability situations verbally and numerically

To find out how likely an event is, compare the outcomes for the event with the total number of outcomes.

Example 1

If you spin this spinner once, on what color is it most likely to stop?

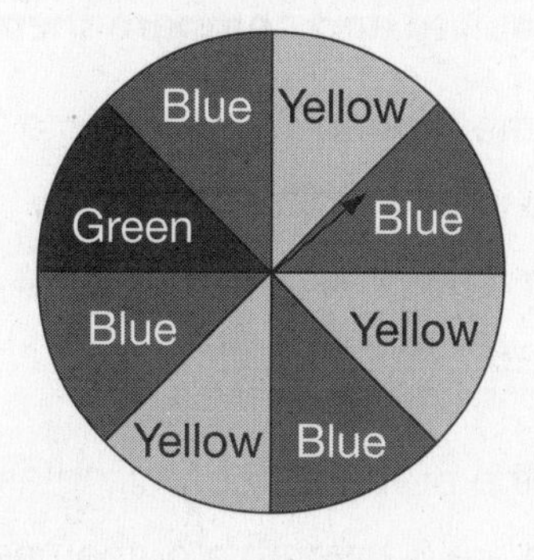

STRATEGY: **Follow these steps.**

STEP 1: Note the total number of outcomes.

There are 8 outcomes.

STEP 2: Count the number of outcomes for each color.

Yellow	3 outcomes
Blue	4 outcomes
Green	1 outcome

STEP 3: Note the color with the most outcomes. Blue has the most outcomes.

SOLUTION: **The spinner will most likely stop on blue.**

Probability is the chance that an event will occur. The probability of an event can be expressed as a fraction.

$$\frac{\text{the number of favorable outcomes}}{\text{the number of possible outcomes}}$$

To find the probability of getting tails when you toss a coin, write the number of favorable outcomes (1, because a coin has only 1 tail) over the number of possible outcomes (2, because there are 2 possible outcomes when you toss a coin: heads and tails).

$P(\text{tails}) = \frac{1}{2}$

An event that cannot happen has a probability of 0.
An event that is certain to happen has a probability of 1.
The more likely the event, the greater the probability of the event.

Example 2

Which event has the greater probability, rolling a 3 on a number cube numbered 1–6 or rolling an even number?

STRATEGY: **Find each probability and compare them.**

STEP 1: Find the probability of rolling a 3.

There is 1 favorable outcome.

There are 6 possible outcomes.

$$\frac{\text{favorable outcomes}}{\text{possible outcomes}} = \frac{1}{6}$$

STEP 2: Find the probability of rolling an even number.

There are 3 favorable outcomes for rolling an even number: 2, 4, and 6.

There are 6 possible outcomes.

Form a fraction with the favorable outcomes over the possible outcomes:

$$\frac{\text{favorable outcomes}}{\text{possible outcomes}} = \frac{3}{6} = \frac{1}{2}.$$

STEP 3: Compare the probabilities.

$\frac{1}{2} > \frac{1}{6}$

SOLUTION: **The probability of rolling an even number is greater than the probability of rolling a 3.**

Sample Test Questions

1 Karl has ten colored cubes in a box. Two cubes are green, four cubes are red, three cubes are yellow, and one cube is blue. Which color would he most likely choose if he picked a cube without looking?

Ⓐ green
Ⓑ red
Ⓒ yellow
Ⓓ blue

2 If you spin the spinner, on which number is it most likely to stop?

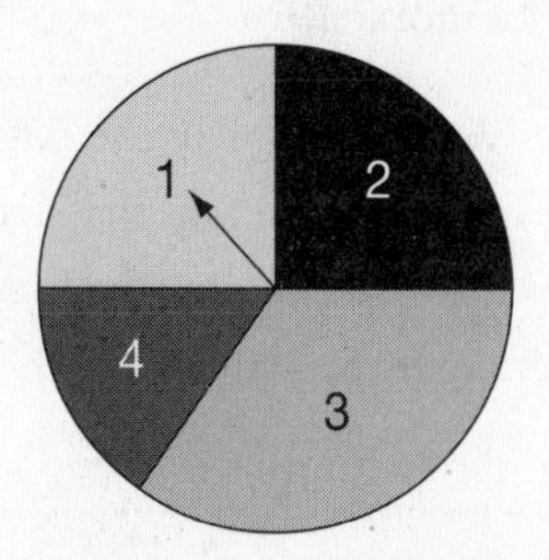

Ⓐ 1
Ⓑ 2
Ⓒ 3
Ⓓ 4

3 This spinner has 6 equal sections. If you spin the spinner once, what is the probability of spinning Blue?

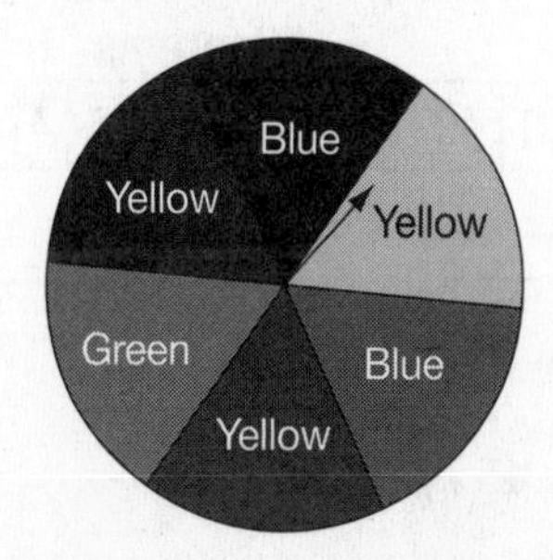

Ⓐ $\frac{1}{6}$
Ⓑ $\frac{1}{3}$
Ⓒ $\frac{1}{4}$
Ⓓ $\frac{1}{2}$

4 If you close your eyes and pick one of these figures, which figure are you least likely to pick?

Ⓐ circle
Ⓑ rectangle
Ⓒ square
Ⓓ triangle

5 Kim placed 7 red, 4 yellow, and 3 green cubes in a box. If she picks a cube without looking, what is the probability it will be green?

Ⓐ 3 out of 7
Ⓑ 3 out of 11
Ⓒ 3 out of 14
Ⓓ 3 out of 15

6 What is the probability of rolling a sum of 1 when you roll two number cubes, each with the numbers 1 to 6 on their faces? Explain your answer.

____

____

____

____

____

Progress Check for Lessons 35–37

1 Beth recorded the number of attendees at the school science fair for 5 consecutive years.

Year 1: 250

Year 2: 300

Year 3: 275

Year 4: 325

Year 5: 400

She wants to display the data so that people can see how attendance changed over the 5-year period. Which graph would be BEST to use?

Ⓐ circle graph

Ⓑ bar graph

Ⓒ line graph

Ⓓ pictograph

2 Tim recorded the percent of students in each grade at the local high school.

Freshmen: 31%

Sophomores: 28%

Juniors: 22%

Seniors: 19%

He wants to display the data so that people can compare the size of each grade as part of the whole school . Which graph would be BEST to use?

Ⓐ circle graph

Ⓑ bar graph

Ⓒ line graph

Ⓓ pictograph

3 What is the median weight of these weights, expressed in kilograms?

Kilograms

40	42	47	38	39	35	47	49	45

Ⓐ 49 kg

Ⓑ 47 kg

Ⓒ 45 kg

Ⓓ 42 kg

4 Which measure cannot be found for these data?

35 42 68 72 83

Ⓐ mean

Ⓑ median

Ⓒ mode

Ⓓ range

5 There are 20 tiles in a bag. Twelve are red, 6 are blue, and 2 are green. What is the probability of reaching into the bag without looking and drawing a red tile?

Ⓐ $\frac{1}{12}$

Ⓑ $\frac{1}{7}$

Ⓒ $\frac{3}{5}$

Ⓓ $\frac{6}{7}$

6 The probability of drawing a pair of black socks from a drawer is $\frac{1}{5}$. If there are 30 pairs of socks in the drawer, what is the number of pairs of black socks in the drawer?

Ⓐ 5

Ⓑ 6

Ⓒ 24

Ⓓ 25

7 Playing cards with the following numbers are mixed up and placed face down. Which number card would you most likely pick?

4 3 2 1 4

Ⓐ card with a 1

Ⓑ card with a 2

Ⓒ card with a 3

Ⓓ card with a 4

8 Thirteen students each have different weights. If the median weight of the group is 72 pounds, how many students weigh less than 72 pounds?

Ⓐ 5

Ⓑ 6

Ⓒ 7

Ⓓ 8

Standard 6
Open-Ended Questions

1 Mike and Dan took a survey of 100 students in the sixth grade of the Burlington Elementary School to find out what their favorite sports were. The table shows the results of the survey.

Sport	Votes
Football	25
Basketball	35
Soccer	10
Other	30

a) Draw a graph to show the results of this survey.

b) Explain your choice of graph.

____

____

____

2 The probability of choosing a red sock from a drawer is $\frac{1}{6}$. If there are 60 socks in the drawer, about how many red socks are in the drawer? Explain your answer.

3 The range of the 23 grades on the last math test in Shawn's class was 20. The median was 80.

a) What is the highest score possible, and what is the lowest score possible? Explain your answer.

b) How many students scored 80 or above? Explain.

c) How many students scored 80 or below? Explain.

4 Billie Joe has 2 cubes. One is called the left cube, the other is called the right cube. The faces of both cubes are marked with the numbers 1 through 6. When he rolls both cubes, he forms a 2-digit number by placing the cubes this way:

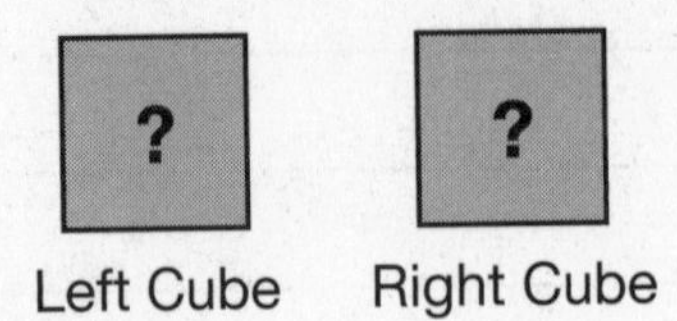

He says that the probability of getting a 2-digit even number this way is the same as getting a 2-digit odd number. Is he right? Explain.

____

____

____

____

____

5 These data show the amounts of money earned by seven students who participated in a charity walk.

$85 $90 $98 $10 $85 $97 $95

a) Find the mean, median, and mode for the data.

b) Which measure or measures (mean, median, or mode) best describe the data? Explain.

____

____

____

____

Standard

7

Problem Solving

38 Understanding the Language of Problems

5.7.4: Express solutions clearly and logically by using the appropriate mathematical terms and notation
5.7.7: Make precise calculations and check the validity of the results in the context of the problem

You need to be able to translate words into mathematical language.

Example 1

Julie ran around a track 4 times. The distance around the track is 440 yards. To find how far she ran, Julie added: 440 + 440 + 440 + 440. What is another way to find how far she ran?

STRATEGY: **Read the problem again.**

SOLUTION: **Since she ran the same distance 4 times, another way to solve this problem is to multiply: 4 × 440.**

Writing a number sentence is often a good way to solve word problems.

Example 2

A van from the mall costs $2 for the first mile and $0.75 for each additional mile. How can you figure out how much it will cost to travel 6 miles?

A $6 \times \$0.75 = \square$

B $\$2 + 5 \times \$0.75 = \square$

C $\$2 + 6 \times \$0.75 = \square$

D $5 \times \$0.75 = \square$

STRATEGY: **Think of the cost in two parts, $2 and $0.75.**

The first mile costs $2, and the other 5 miles cost $0.75 each.

So, the total cost is $2 + the cost of the 5 miles.

SOLUTION: **The answer is $\$2 + 5 \times \$0.75 = \square$, Answer B.**

Example 3

An electrician charges a fixed fee of $20 to come to a house and an hourly rate of $30 for each hour spent making repairs. The Spencers budgeted $225 for electrical repairs. The electrician spent $6\frac{1}{2}$ hours making a repair at their house. Will the repair be within their budget?

STRATEGY: **Compute the charges for $6\frac{1}{2}$ hours and add $20. Compare the result with $225.**

STEP 1: Find the charge for $6\frac{1}{2}$ hours.

The hourly charge is $30, so $6\frac{1}{2} \times 30 = \$195$.

STEP 2: Add the fixed fee for coming to the house.

$195 + 20 = 215$

STEP 3: Compare the total charge with the Spencer's budget.

$\$215 < \$225$

SOLUTION: **Since $\$215 < \$225$, the repair is within their budget.**

Sample Test Questions

1 Melanie charges $4 an hour to babysit. Which of the following shows a way of finding how many hours she must work to earn $64?

Ⓐ $64 \div 4$

Ⓑ 64×4

Ⓒ $64 - 4$

Ⓓ $64 \div (2 + 4)$

2 Gwen waits 15 minutes each day for her ride. How long does she wait in 5 days altogether? To find out how long she waited, Gwen multiplied 5×15. What is another way to find how long she waited?

Ⓐ $15 \div 5$

Ⓑ $5 + 15$

Ⓒ $15 + 15 + 15 + 15 + 15$

Ⓓ $15 + 15 + 15$

3 The cost of a special ice cream at the mall is $2.25. Kathy's father paid for 3 special ice creams. Kathy figured that the cost was $5.75. Was she correct?

Ⓐ No, 2 × $2.25 = $4.50

Ⓑ No, 3 × $2.25 = $6.75

Ⓒ Yes, $8.00 − $2.25 = $5.75

Ⓓ Yes, 3 + $2.75 = $5.75

4 It will take Dan 3 hours and 10 minutes to drive from home to the airport. It will take him another 40 minutes to get to the gate. He figures he needs $3\frac{1}{2}$ hours altogether to get from his home to the gate. Is he right?

Ⓐ No, because 3 hours and 10 minutes + 40 minutes is more than 4 hours.

Ⓑ Yes, because 3 hours and 10 minutes + 40 minutes is less than $3\frac{1}{2}$ hours.

Ⓒ Yes, because 3 hours and 10 minutes + 40 minutes is $3\frac{1}{2}$ hours.

Ⓓ No, because 3 hours and 10 minutes + 40 minutes is more than $3\frac{1}{2}$ hours.

5 Kim is 5 feet 4 inches tall. Her brother is 4 feet 6 inches tall. How much taller is Kim than her brother?

Ⓐ 6 inches

Ⓑ 8 inches

Ⓒ 10 inches

Ⓓ 12 inches

6 Letters from A to F are worth 3 points; letters from G to M are worth 4 points; letters from N to S are worth 5 points; and letters from T to Z are worth 2 points. What is the value of the word "loyalty"?

Ⓐ 25 points

Ⓑ 22 points

Ⓒ 21 points

Ⓓ 20 points

7 Kelly gets 5 cents for each empty bottle she returns to the supermarket. How many bottles must she return to earn $5.50?

Ⓐ 90 bottles

Ⓑ 100 bottles

Ⓒ 105 bottles

Ⓓ 110 bottles

8 Karl spent $16 for a model airplane. Jeff spent half as much for a model boat. How much did they spend all together?

Ⓐ $24

Ⓑ $20

Ⓒ $16

Ⓓ $8

9 The rates for ABC Cab Company are $4 for the first mile and $2.50 for each mile after the first mile. Which computation shows a way to find the cost of a 10-mile ride?

Ⓐ 10 × $2.50

Ⓑ $2.50 + 9 × 4

Ⓒ 4 + 9 × $2.50

Ⓓ 10 × 4

10 Books at the Wholesale Book Shop sell for $5 each for the first 10 books. After the tenth book, the cost becomes $4 for each book. If a customer buys 12 books, how much will it cost?

Ⓐ $40

Ⓑ $50

Ⓒ $58

Ⓓ $60

11 A recipe calls for $\frac{3}{8}$ cup of corn syrup. You plan to triple the recipe. You know that you have 1 cup of corn syrup in the house. Do you have enough corn syrup? Explain.

____

____

____

____

____

39 Strategies for Problem Solving

5.7.3: Apply strategies and results from simpler problems to solve more complex problems
5.7.8: Decide whether a solution is reasonable in the context of the original situation

You should know these strategies for solving problems.

Strategies

1. Act it out
2. Make a model
3. Draw a picture
4. Make a chart or graph
5. Look for a pattern
6. Make a simpler problem
7. Use logic
8. Work backwards
9. Guess and check
10. Break into parts

Example

Carlos lives 6 miles from Henry, and Henry lives 4 miles from Georgia. Which of the following is NOT a possible distance between Carlos and Georgia?

Ⓐ 2 miles

Ⓑ 4 miles

Ⓒ 10 miles

Ⓓ 12 miles

STRATEGY: **Choose the strategy that best fits this problem.**

STEP 1: Reread the problem several times and look at the list of strategies on the previous page. Which strategy would help you solve this problem?

One of the best strategies for this type of problem is "Draw a picture." You will see the possible locations on paper.

You will have to draw several pictures since there is more than one way that the houses can be set up.

STEP 2: Draw a picture.

Here is one picture of the three places in the problem.

Picture 1

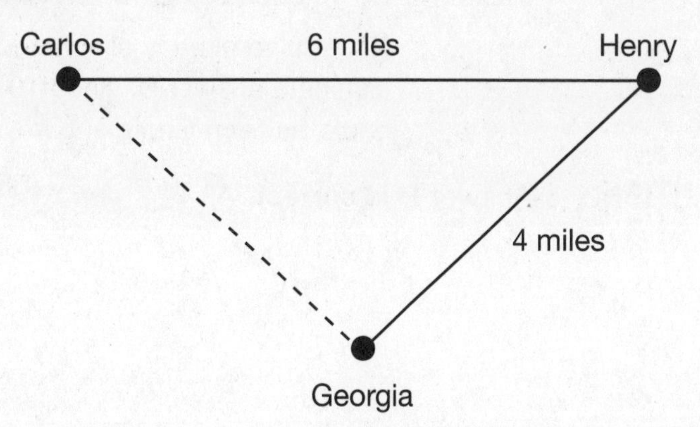

From Picture 1, you can see that the distance from Carlos to Georgia could be 4 miles. So Answer B is possible.

STEP 3: Draw another picture of the three places.

Picture 2

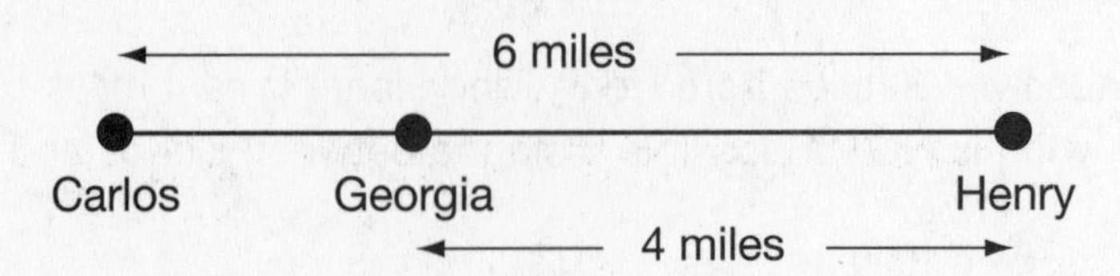

Picture 2 shows us that the 3 places can be on the same line. Here, Georgia lives 2 miles from Carlos (6 – 4 = 2).

Answer A is possible.

STEP 4: Draw another picture.

Picture 3

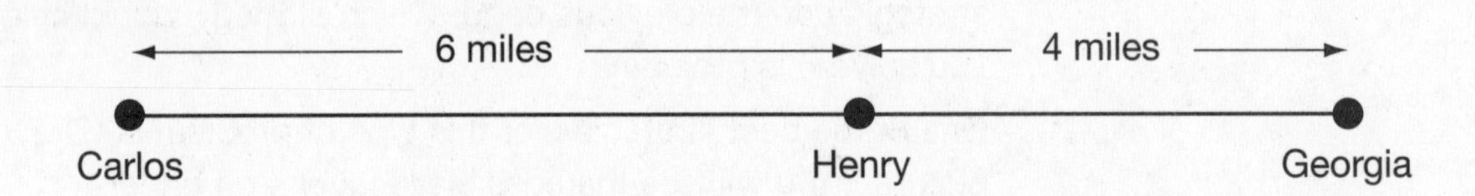

Picture 3 shows us another way that the locations can be on the same line. In this case, the distance between Georgia and Carlos is 10 miles. Answer C is possible.

This is also the farthest Carlos can be from Georgia.

STEP 5: Do you need to draw any more pictures?

No. You've already eliminated answers A, B, and C. You can't eliminate answer D, since 10 miles was the farthest Carlos could be from Georgia.

SOLUTION: **Answer D is correct.**

Sample Test Questions

1 Michelle is trying to find the next number in this sequence:

1, 7, 13, 19, 25, 31, ...

Which of the following would most help Michelle to solve this problem?

Ⓐ Make a model

Ⓑ Draw a picture

Ⓒ Break into parts

Ⓓ Look for a pattern

2 Harold asked his friend George whether he knew how many diagonals a regular polygon with 10 sides (called a decagon) has. Which of the following would help George the most in solving this problem?

Ⓐ Act it out

Ⓑ Guess and check

Ⓒ Work backwards

Ⓓ Draw a picture

3 Mrs. Jones asked 6 children to figure out how many hand shakes there would be if each child shakes hands with all the others. Which of the following would help most to solve this problem?

Ⓐ Act it out

Ⓑ Make a chart or graph

Ⓒ Work backwards

Ⓓ Guess and check

4 What is the area of the region enclosed by the figure below?

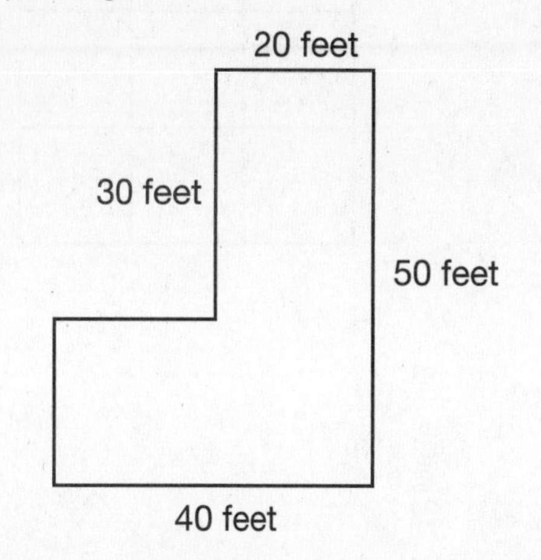

Ⓐ 1,040 square feet

Ⓑ 1,200 square feet

Ⓒ 1,400 square feet

Ⓓ 1,600 square feet

5 Samantha saves money every day. On Monday she saved \$1, on Tuesday she saved \$2, on Wednesday she saved \$4, on Thursday she saved \$8, and on Friday she saved \$16. If she continues in the same way, how much money will she save on Saturday?

Ⓐ \$20

Ⓑ \$24

Ⓒ \$32

Ⓓ \$36

6 How many squares are there in this grid?

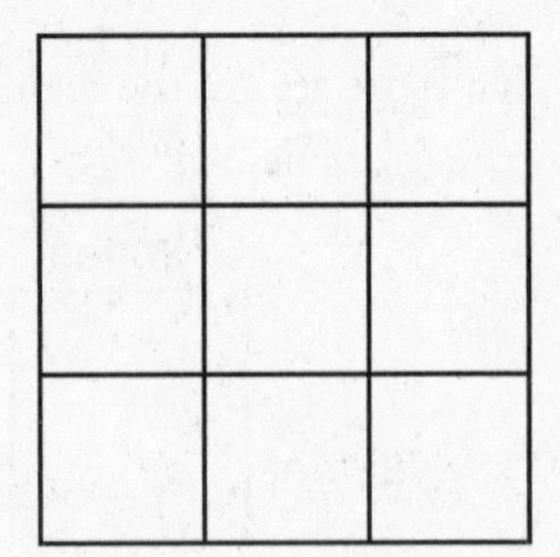

Ⓐ 16

Ⓑ 14

Ⓒ 10

Ⓓ 9

7 Clarence received 3 coins in change from a purchase. The cashier had only quarters, dimes, and nickels in the cash register. Which of the following would NOT be a reasonable amount for the change Clarence received?

Ⓐ 55

Ⓑ 45

Ⓒ 35

Ⓓ 10

8 Rosa found the probability of spinning a shaded area of this spinner and the probability of spinning a non-shaded area.

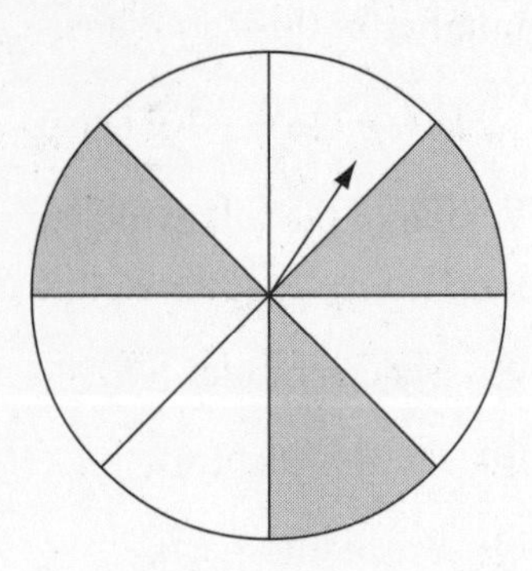

How can Rosa check her work by adding the probabilities?

____

____

____

____

____

40 Estimating to Solve Problems

5.7.5: Recognize the relative advantages of exact and approximate solutions to problems
5.7.6: Know and apply appropriate methods for estimating results of rational number computations

An estimate is an approximation of the exact answer. You can save time by estimating.

Example

Luz spent $39.99 for a pair of shoes, $26.95 for a dress, and $4.15 on a bottle of shampoo. What is a good estimate of how much she spent?

STRATEGY: **Use rounding.**

STEP 1: Round each amount to the nearest dollar.

$39.90 rounds to $40.

$26.95 rounds to $27.

$4.15 rounds to $4.

STEP 2: Add the rounded amounts:

$$\begin{array}{r} \$40 \\ 27 \\ +\ 4 \\ \hline \$71 \end{array}$$

SOLUTION: **Luz spent about $71.**

Sample Test Questions

1 On his vacation, Stan drove 873 miles on the first day and 624 miles on the second day. Estimate how many miles he drove altogether.

Ⓐ 1,400

Ⓑ 1,450

Ⓒ 1,500

Ⓓ 1,600

2 One route from Rafael's house to work is 29.5 miles long. Another route is 21.6 miles long. Estimate how much longer the first is.

Ⓐ 9 miles

Ⓑ 8 miles

Ⓒ 7 miles

Ⓓ 6 miles

3 Julia worked 185 hours in July, 172 hours in August, and 159 hours in September. Estimate how many hours she worked in the 3 months.

Ⓐ 420

Ⓑ 490

Ⓒ 510

Ⓓ 520

4 Ella drove for 8 hours from Atlanta to Indianapolis. Her average speed was 47 miles per hour. Which is the best estimate of the number of miles she drove?

Ⓐ 200 miles

Ⓑ 300 miles

Ⓒ 400 miles

Ⓓ 500 miles

5 Billy has to distribute 203 concert tickets among 19 students. Which is the best estimate of how many tickets each student will get?

Ⓐ 2

Ⓑ 10

Ⓒ 20

Ⓓ 30

6 Donna bought a sandwich at her neighborhood deli for $3.08. Estimate how much change she got from a $20 bill.

Ⓐ $17

Ⓑ $17.50

Ⓒ $18

Ⓓ $23

7 Gabriel weighs 98 pounds. He gained 21 pounds during the last year. Estimate how many pounds he weighed a year ago.

Ⓐ 60

Ⓑ 70

Ⓒ 80

Ⓓ 90

8 Kaitlyn spends between $\frac{1}{2}$ hour and 1 hour each day doing homework. Which is the best estimate of the amount of time she spends on homework in 1 week?

Ⓐ 1–3 hours

Ⓑ 3–7 hours

Ⓒ 7–10 hours

Ⓓ 10–20 hours

9 You are building scenery for a school show. One of your tasks is to cover rectangular wooden frames with canvas that will be painted to look like the walls of a room. How accurately should you measure and calculate the amount of canvas needed to cover the frames: to the nearest square yard, the nearest square foot, or the nearest square inch? Explain.

____

____

____

____

____

____

41 Different Ways to Solve Problems

5.7.2: Decide when and how to break a problem into simpler parts
5.7.9: Note the method of finding the solution and show a conceptual understanding of the method by solving similar problems

To solve some problems, you have to use a combination of skills

Example 1

The students in Carmen's class made a record of the vehicles parked in the school parking lot.

Motorcycles	Cars	Vans	Pickup Trucks
||	~~||||~~ ||	||||	~~||||~~ |

How many vans and pickup trucks were in the parking lot?

Ⓐ 7
Ⓑ 8
Ⓒ 9
Ⓓ 10

STRATEGY: **Follow these steps.**

STEP 1: Read the question carefully. Make sure you find the numbers for vans and pickup trucks.

STEP 2: Find the number of vans.

Four tally marks mean that there were 4 vans.

STEP 3: Find the number of pickup trucks.

There are 6 pickup trucks. ~~||||~~ means 5—four tally marks and one diagonal mark.

STEP 4: Add the number of vans and the number of pickup trucks.

$4 + 6 = 10$

SOLUTION: **The answer is D. There were 10 vans and pickup trucks.**

When you buy several of the same items, you can calculate what each one costs, or the unit price. The word "unit" is often used in place of "one."

How to Find the Unit Price

To find the unit price for a set of items, divide the total cost by the number of items.

Example 2

Jenny spent $3.20 for 8 chocolate donuts. What is the unit price for these donuts?

STRATEGY: **Use the method above.**

STEP 1: What is the total cost of the donuts?

The total cost is $3.20

STEP 2: How many donuts did Jenny buy?

She bought 8 donuts.

STEP 3: Divide.

Rewrite the $3.20 as cents.

$3.20 is the same as 320 cents.

$$\begin{array}{r} 40 \\ 8\overline{)320} \\ -\ 32 \\ \hline 00 \\ -\ 00 \\ \hline 0 \end{array}$$

$320 \div 8 = 40$ cents

SOLUTION: **The unit price is 40 cents.**

Sample Test Questions

1 Salvador placed these shapes in a row: triangle, square, hexagon, triangle, square, and hexagon. If he continues to place shapes in this pattern, what shape will be in the 12th place?

Ⓐ triangle

Ⓑ square

Ⓒ hexagon

Ⓓ rectangle

2 Kristen bought a 6-ounce can of tuna for $2.40. What is the unit price?

Ⓐ 30 cents per ounce

Ⓑ 40 cents per ounce

Ⓒ 50 cents per ounce

Ⓓ 60 cents per ounce

3 Alex spent 75 cents for a packet of 5 sports cards. What is the unit price per card?

Ⓐ 10 cents

Ⓑ 12 cents

Ⓒ 15 cents

Ⓓ 18 cents

4 Ten notebooks cost $4.99. Using the unit price for a notebook, about how much would you expect to spend for 3 notebooks?

Ⓐ $0.40

Ⓑ $0.50

Ⓒ $1.40

Ⓓ $1.50

5 Name a strategy to find the area of the living room.

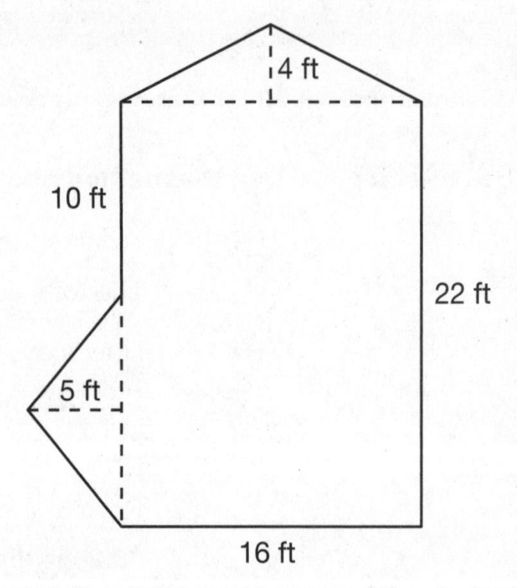

Use your strategy to find the area of the living room. Explain your steps.

____

____

____

____

____

42 Missing Information and Too Much Information

5.7.1: Analyze problems by identifying relationships, telling relevant from irrelevant information

When solving problems, it is important to know what information you need and what you don't need.

This lesson deals with two types of problems:

- Problems that are missing information.
- Problems with too much information—information that you don't need.

Missing Information

Example 1

The soccer team wants to raise $500, so the team members are selling raffle tickets. So far, they have sold 50 tickets. How many more tickets does the team have to sell to reach $500?

What additional information do you need to solve this problem?

STRATEGY: **Reread the problem.**

STEP 1: Make sure you know what the problem asks for.

The problem asks how many more tickets have to be sold.

STEP 2: Determine what you already know.

You know the number of tickets sold already—50 tickets.

And you know the amount of money the team wants to raise—$500.

STEP 3: Think about what is missing.

SOLUTION: **The missing information is the price of each ticket.**

For example, if each ticket costs $2, then the team would have $100 (50 × $2) and would need $400 more and would need to sell 200 more tickets.

Too Much Information

Example 2

Holly spent $56 last week on new shoes. This week she shopped at the supermarket and spent $48.63 on food. At the supermarket, how much change did she get if she paid with a $100 bill?

What information is NOT needed to solve this problem?

STRATEGY: **Find the information you need to solve the problem. What's left is information you don't need—extra information.**

SOLUTION: **The information not needed is the amount Holly spent on new shoes.**

Sample Test Questions

1 Nicki spent 3 hours 45 minutes traveling to her grandparents' house. At what time did she get there?

What additional information do you need to know to solve this problem?

- Ⓐ length of time she spent with her grandparents
- Ⓑ time she left her house
- Ⓒ time she returned home
- Ⓓ city where her grandparents live

2 Kathy is 11 years old. Her birthday is on September 25. Cindy is twice as old as Kathy. Rosa is two years older than Cindy. How old is Rosa?

What information is NOT needed to solve this problem?

- Ⓐ Kathy's age
- Ⓑ Kathy's birthday
- Ⓒ Cindy is twice as old as Kathy.
- Ⓓ Rosa is two years older than Cindy.

3 Red pencils cost 3 for 40 cents, blue pencils cost 15 cents each, and yellow pencils cost 2 for 25 cents. What is the cost of 6 red pencils and 6 yellow pencils?

- Ⓐ $1.25
- Ⓑ $1.55
- Ⓒ $1.65
- Ⓓ $1.75

4 The table shows the rates charged by a high school car wash.

Car	$7.00
Van	$10.00
Utility Vehicle	$12.00

Rashan says that 40 vehicles were washed last Saturday. How much money did the high school make?

What additional information is needed to solve this problem?

- Ⓐ how many vans were washed
- Ⓑ how many cars were washed
- Ⓒ how many utility vehicles were washed
- Ⓓ how many of each vehicle were washed

5 Jewell sent two packages by an express mail service. The rate for packages under 10 pounds is $15 anywhere in the United States. Her packages weighed 5 pounds and 7 pounds. One package was going to Japan and another package was going to New York. How much did she pay for the two packages?

Ⓐ $30

Ⓑ $45

Ⓒ You cannot solve the problem because you do not know the price of a package over 10 pounds.

Ⓓ You cannot solve the problem because you do not know the rate for sending a package to Japan.

6 Laurent saved 1,456 pennies and 378 dimes. How many more pennies must he save in order to have 2,500 pennies?

Ⓐ 1,044

Ⓑ 1,134

Ⓒ 1,144

Ⓓ 1,156

7 Harold earns an hourly wage for the first 40 hours he works in 1 week, and $1\frac{1}{2}$ times his hourly wage for each hour over 40 hours. Last week, he worked 45 hours. How much money did he earn?

a) What information is missing from this problem?

____

____

b) Create the missing information and solve the problem. Explain your choice of missing information and the steps you followed to solve the problem.

____

____

____

____

____

Standard 7
Open-Ended Questions

1 A spelling bee awards 3 points for spelling difficult words correctly and 1 point for easy words. Rhonda was given 11 words to spell and got 23 points. What combinations of 1 and 3 points could she have made? Show your work.

2 Harry has 7 coins in his pocket. Each coin has a value less than a quarter. He has 42 cents. What are the coins?

3 a) Natalie estimates that it takes 1 hour to drive to the airport and park her car. It takes 15 minutes to walk from the parking lot to the main terminal. She expects it will take half an hour to check in and walk to the gate. Her flight leaves at 12:00 noon. At what time should she leave her house so that she will have an extra 20 minutes at the airport?

b) Draw a time line to show how you should solve this problem. Divide the line into intervals 15 minutes apart.

4 a) Find the surface area of this box. Show your work, including computations.

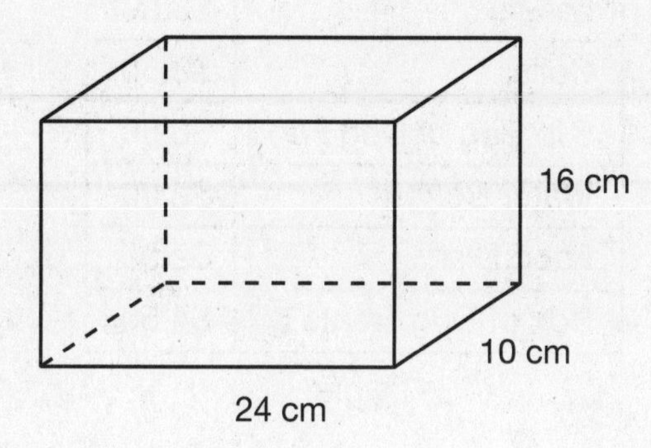

b) When would an accurate measurement of the volume of a box be important?

c) For what kinds of boxes are appropriate measurements satisfactory? (Hint: Think about what you might put in the box.)

5 Below are the costs of items at Leah's Puppy Palace.

Leash	$8.00
Collar	$3.50
5 lb Bag of Dog Food	$6.50
Water Bowl	$2.00
Food Dish	$2.50
Box of Dog Treats	$4.50

a) David has a $20 bill. He wants to buy three 5-lb bags of dog food. Does he have enough money? Explain why or why not.

b) Sonia wants to spend exactly $10 and buy three different items. What items can she buy? Show your work.

Take-Home Math Activities

NAME ______________________

Anna & Zeke's
Table of Contents

For the Student:

The *Take-Home Math Activities* contains mathematical terms, definitions, and examples in alphabetical order. Each page will contain at least one **Do I Understand?** question for you to determine if you understand a key idea. At the end of the book there is a Glossary, a list of abbreviations, units of time, math symbols, and formulas.

From,

Anna & Zeke

Addition

An operation on two or more numbers to find a sum.

Parts of Addition

These are the parts of an addition problem.

236	←	**addend**
+ 421	←	**addend**
657	←	**sum**

Whole Numbers

Add the digits from right to left. **Regroup** if necessary.

$$\begin{array}{r} {\scriptstyle 11} \\ 985 \\ +\ 627 \\ \hline 1{,}612 \end{array}$$

Decimals and Money

Decimal and money amounts are also added from right to left.

$$\begin{array}{r} {\scriptstyle 1\,1\,1\,1} \\ \$2{,}782.62 \\ +\ 1{,}837.54 \\ \hline \$4{,}620.16 \end{array}$$

Remember to place the decimal point in the sum. If it is a money amount, insert the dollar sign ($).

Fractions with Like Denominators

Add the numerators. The denominator remains the same. Write the sum in simplest form if possible.

$$\frac{3}{8} + \frac{7}{8} = \frac{3+7}{8} = \frac{10}{8} = 1\frac{2}{8} = 1\frac{1}{4}$$

Mixed Numbers with Like Denominators

Add the fraction part, the whole-number part, and then add the sums. Write the sum in simplest form.

$$2\frac{7}{10} + 3\frac{1}{10} = \left(\frac{7}{10} + \frac{1}{10}\right) + (2 + 3) =$$

$$\frac{8}{10} + 5 = 5\frac{8}{10} = 5\frac{4}{5}$$

Fractions with Unlike Denominators

Add $\frac{3}{5} + \frac{1}{4}$.

Write equivalent fractions using the LCD.

$$\frac{3}{5} = \frac{12}{20} \qquad \frac{1}{4} = \frac{5}{20}$$

Add the numerators. Simplify if possible.

$$\frac{12}{20} + \frac{5}{20} = \frac{17}{20}$$

Mixed Numbers with Unlike Denominators

Follow the same steps as you would with fractions, but remember to add the whole-number part.

$$3\frac{1}{2} + 4\frac{2}{5} = 3\frac{5}{10} + 4\frac{4}{10} =$$

$$\left(\frac{5}{10} + \frac{4}{10}\right) + (3 + 4) = \frac{9}{10} + 7 = 7\frac{9}{10}$$

Do I Understand?

Add. Write the answer in simplest form for problem 2.

1. $\begin{array}{r} \$283.76 \\ +\ 472.48 \\ \hline \end{array}$

2. $3\frac{1}{3} + 5\frac{7}{12}$ ____________

ANSWERS: 1. $756.24 **2.** $8\frac{11}{12}$

Angles

An angle is formed when two rays or line segments meet at the same endpoint.

Parts of an Angle

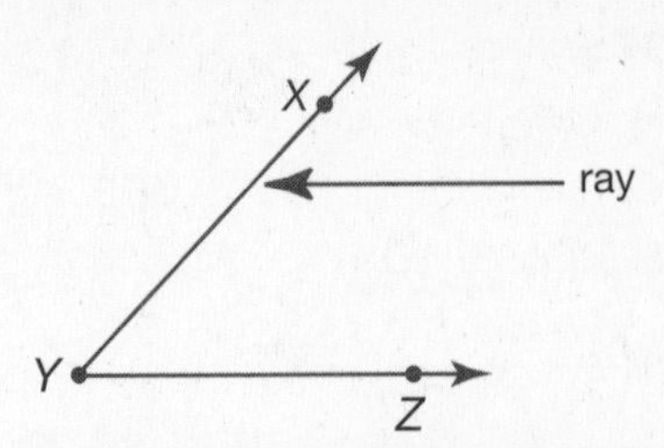

An **angle** can be named in three ways. The letter for the vertex is always in the middle.

This angle can be named $\angle XYZ$, $\angle ZYX$, or $\angle X$.

Classification of Angles

There are four types of angles. Angles are measured in **degrees (°)**.

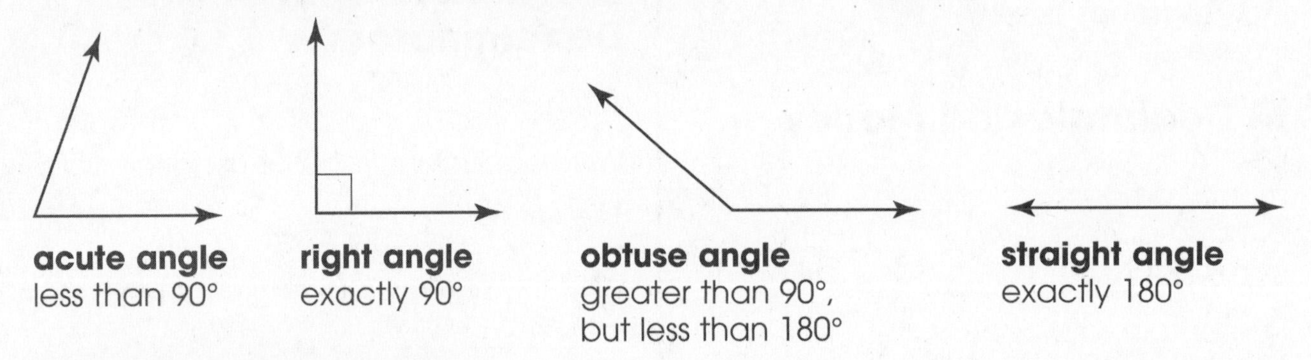

acute angle
less than 90°

right angle
exactly 90°

obtuse angle
greater than 90°, but less than 180°

straight angle
exactly 180°

Measuring Angles

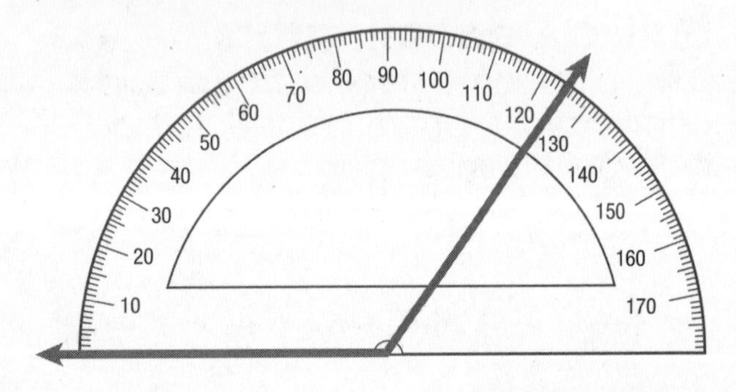

A **protractor** is used to measure angles. To use a protractor, align the center of the protractor with the vertex of the angle.

This angle measures 125°.

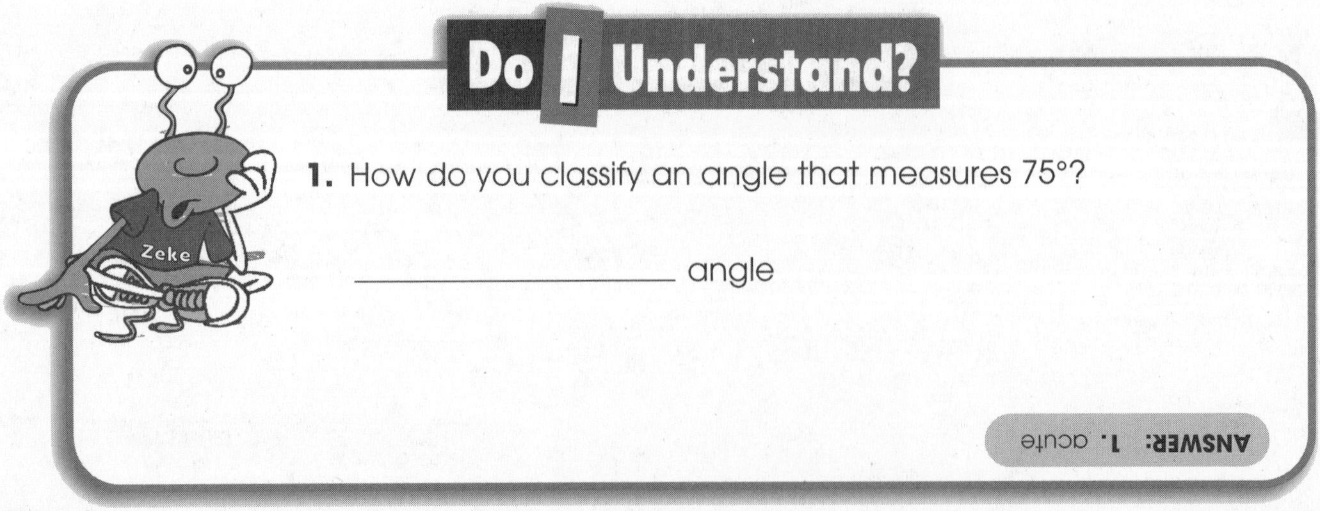

Do I Understand?

1. How do you classify an angle that measures 75°?

____________________ angle

ANSWER: 1. acute

Area

The number of square units needed to cover a region.

Square Units

Area is expressed in **square units (units²)**. A square unit is a square, one of whose sides is a given unit of length. Square units can be in inches, feet, centimeters, meters, or other units.

Rectangles and Squares

The formula for the area of a rectangle is Area = length × width, or $A = lw$.

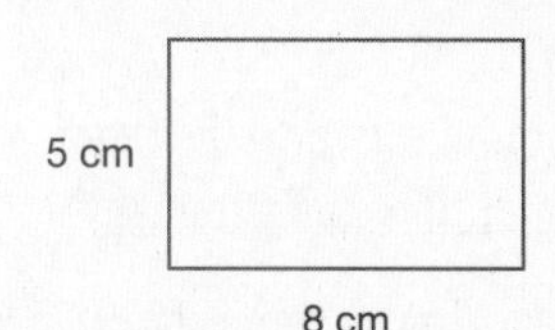

$A = 8\text{ cm} \times 5\text{ cm}$

$A = 40\text{ cm}^2$

The area of the rectangle is 40 cm².

Since a square has 4 equal sides, multiply the length of one of the sides by itself to find its area. To find the area of a square, use the formula $A = s^2$.

Parallelogram

The formula for the area of a parallelogram is Area = base × height or $A = bh$.

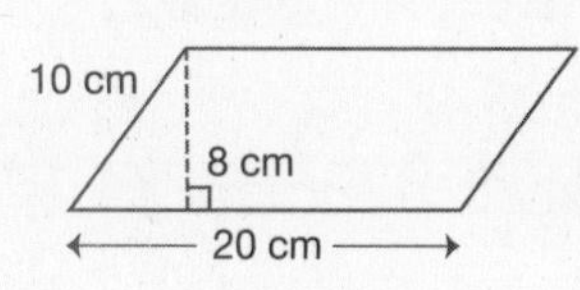

$A = 20\text{ cm} \times 8\text{ cm}$

$A = 160\text{ cm}^2$

The area of the parallelogram is

Triangle

The formula for the area of a triangle is Area $= \frac{1}{2} \times$ **base** $\times$ height or $A = \frac{1}{2}bh$.

Find the area of this triangle.

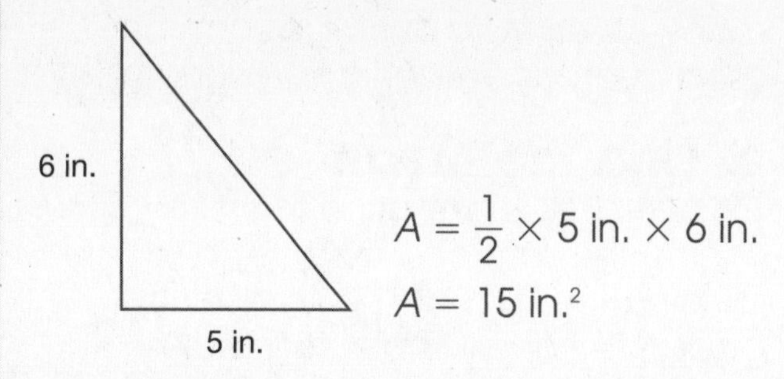

$A = \frac{1}{2} \times 5\text{ in.} \times 6\text{ in.}$

$A = 15\text{ in.}^2$

The area of the triangle is 15 in.².

Circle

The formula for the area of a circle is Area = $\pi \times$ radius² or $A = \pi r^2$. Let 3.14 represent π.

Find the area of this circle.

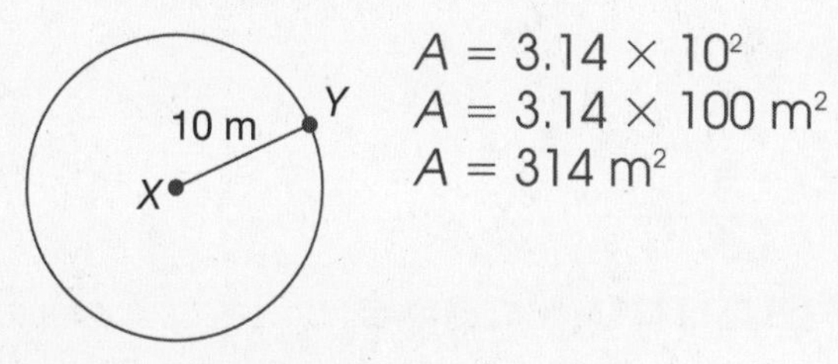

$A = 3.14 \times 10^2$

$A = 3.14 \times 100\text{ m}^2$

$A = 314\text{ m}^2$

The area of the circle is 314 m².

Do I Understand?

1. What is the area of a triangle with a base of 8 inches and a height of 6 inches?

________ in.²

2. What is the area of a circle with a radius of 6 centimeters?

________ cm²

ANSWERS: 1. 24 **2.** 113.04

Average

The sum of a set of numbers divided by the number of addends.

Averages in the Real World

Examples of **average** include miles **per** hour, cost per unit, points per game, and population density. There are many other ways averages can be used, such as determining your grades.

Find the Mean

An average, or **mean**, is found by finding the sum of a **data** set and then dividing the sum by the number of addends. For example, the table shows the temperature in degrees Fahrenheit at 12 noon last week.

Sun.	Mon.	Tue.	Wed.	Thu.	Fri.	Sat.
72	68	76	80	76	78	82

Find the sum of the numbers.
$72 + 68 + 76 + 80 + 76 + 78 + 82 = 532$

Divide the sum by the number of addends.
$532 \div 7 = 76$

The mean is 76°F.

Find the Range

The **range** is the difference between the greatest number and the least number in a data set. To find the range of the data set above, subtract $82 - 68 = 14$. The range is 14°F.

Find the Median

The **median** is the middle number of a data set when the numbers are ordered.

Order the numbers on the left from least to greatest.

68, 72, 76, **76**, 78, 80, 82

The middle number is 76, so the median is 76°F.

If there is an even number of data, find the mean of the two middle numbers.

For example, in the set 26, 27, 30, 32, 35, 40, the two middle numbers are 30 and 32. To find the mean of the two middle numbers, find the sum of $30 + 32 = 62$ and divide by 2: $62 \div 2 = 31$. The median is 31.

Find the Mode

The **mode** is the number or numbers that occur most often in a data set. If all of the numbers occur only once, then there is no mode.

Use this data set to find the mode.

44, 36, **52**, 40, **44**, **52**, 35, 38

The numbers 44 and 52 occur the most. The mode is 44 *and* 52.

Do I Understand?

Use this data set, 73, 68, 90, 73, 92, 87, to find the following:

1. mean ________ **2.** range ________ **3.** median ________ **4.** mode ________

ANSWERS: 1. 80.5 **2.** 24 **3.** 80 **4.** 73

Circles

A plane figure having all points the same distance from a fixed point called the center.

Parts of a Circle

Here are the parts of a **circle**.

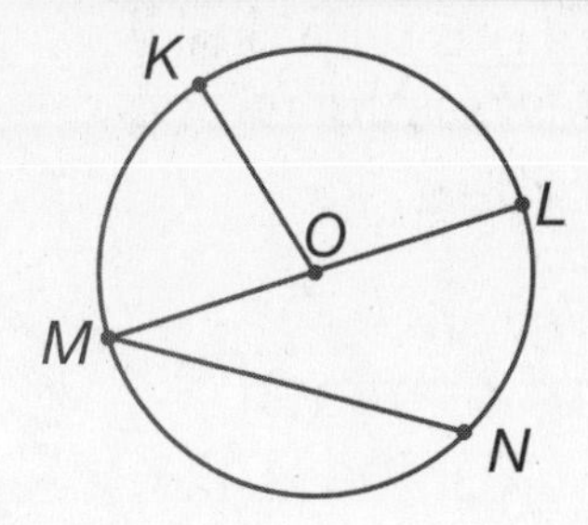

All points of the circle are the same distance from the **center**. Point *O* is the center. A circle is named by its center.

A **radius** is a line segment from the center of the circle to any point on the circle. Line segments $\overline{OK}$, $\overline{OL}$, and $\overline{OM}$ are the radii of circle *O*.

A **chord** is a line segment from one point of a circle to another point. Line segments $\overline{LM}$ and $\overline{MN}$ are chords.

A **diameter** is a chord that passes through the center of the circle. Line segment $\overline{LM}$ is a diameter of circle *O*.

Do I Understand?

1. How can you classify $\overline{MN}$?

____

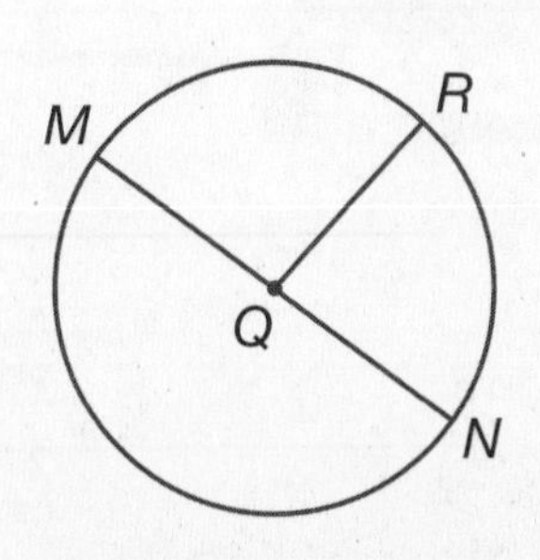

ANSWER: 1. diameter

Compare and Order

To determine whether a number is greater than, less than, or equal to another number.

What the Symbols Means

$>$ **is greater than**
$<$ **is less than**
$=$ **is equal to**

Compare Whole Numbers

Compare the digits from left to right.

6,792 ◯ 6,785

The thousands and hundreds digits are the same.

Compare the hundreds.

6,7**9**2	$9 > 8$,
6,7**8**5	so $6{,}792 > 6{,}785$

Compare Decimals

To compare decimals, align the numbers on the decimal point.

7.32 ◯ 7.3

The ones and tenths digits are the same.

Compare the hundredths.
Insert a 0 to 7.3.

7.32	$2 > 0$,
7.3**0**	so $7.32 > 7.3$

Do I Understand?

Compare.
Use $>$, $<$, or $=$.

1. 9.315 ◯ 9.35

ANSWERS: 1. $<$

Compare and Order
(Continued)

Order Numbers

Numbers can be ordered from least to greatest or from greatest to least. Order the following decimals from least to greatest:

37.26, 37.42, 30.79

Tens	Ones	.	Tenths	Hundredths
3	7	.	2	6
3	7	.	4	2
3	0	.	7	9

Order the digits from left to right.
Since $0 < 7$, 30.79 is the least number.
Compare 37.26 and 37.42
Since $2 < 4$, $37.26 < 37.42$
The order from least to greatest is:
30.79, 37.26, 37.42.

Compare Fractions with Like Denominators

Fractions with like denominators can be compared by their numerators. The greater the numerator, the greater the fraction.

For example, $\frac{1}{8} < \frac{3}{8}$.

Compare Fractions with Like Numerators

Fractions with like numerators can be compared by their denominators. The greater the denominator, the less value the fraction has.

For example, $\frac{2}{3} > \frac{2}{5}$.

Compare Fractions with Unlike Denominators

To compare fractions with unlike denominators, it is helpful to find equivalent fractions.

$\frac{5}{8} \bigcirc \frac{7}{12}$

First, find the **least common denominator (LCD)**. The LCD is the least common multiple (LCM) of the denominators.
The LCD of $\frac{5}{8}$ and $\frac{7}{12}$ is 24.

Write equivalent fractions with 24 as a denominator.

$\frac{5}{8} \times \frac{3}{3} = \frac{15}{24}$ $\frac{7}{12} \times \frac{2}{2} = \frac{14}{24}$

Compare $\frac{15}{24}$ and $\frac{14}{24}$.

$\frac{15}{24} > \frac{14}{24}$, so $\frac{5}{8} > \frac{7}{12}$.

Compare Integers

Integers can be compared using a number line. The number that is farther right on a number line has a greater value. Any positive number is greater than any negative number.

$-4 \bigcirc -2$.

−4 −3 −2 −1 0 1 2 3 4

-4 is to the left of -2 on the number line, so $-4 < -2$.

Do I Understand?

Compare. Use $>$, $<$, or $=$.

2. $\frac{3}{5} \bigcirc \frac{3}{4}$ **3.** $\frac{2}{5} \bigcirc \frac{1}{3}$ **4.** $3 \bigcirc -2$

ANSWERS: 2. $<$ **3.** $>$ **4.** $>$

Congruent and Similar Figures

CONGRUENT FIGURES - Two figures that have the same shape and size.
SIMILAR FIGURES - Two figures that have the same shape but may have different sizes.

Congruent Figures

Congruent figures have the same shape and size. The symbol $\cong$ means that two figures are congruent. Below are examples of congruent figures. It does not matter if the figures are reflections or rotations of each other.

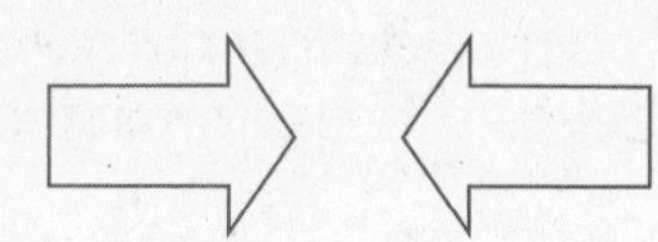

These arrows are congruent.

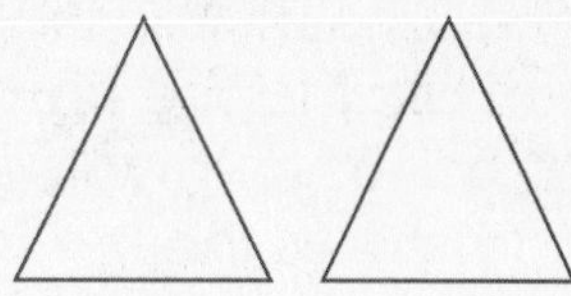

These triangles are congruent.

Similar Figures

Similar figures have the same shape but may have different sizes. Congruent figures are also similar. Below are examples of similar figures that are not congruent.

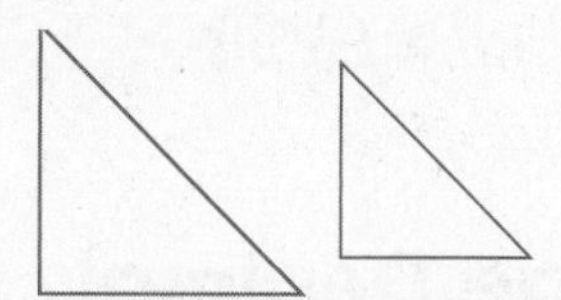

The triangles are similar but not congruent.

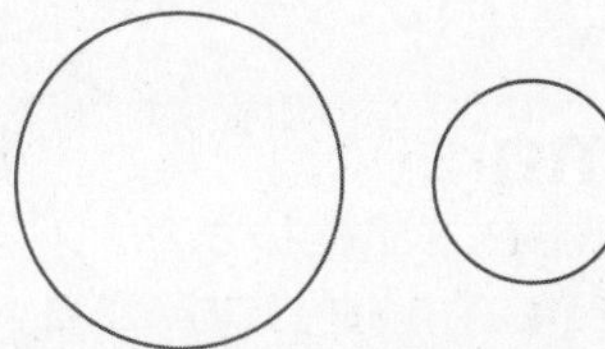

The circles are similar but not congruent.

Sides of Similar Figures

Rectangle *ABCD* is similar to rectangle *EFGH*. You can write a proportion to find the unknown side of a similar figure. Find the length of $\overline{EH}$.

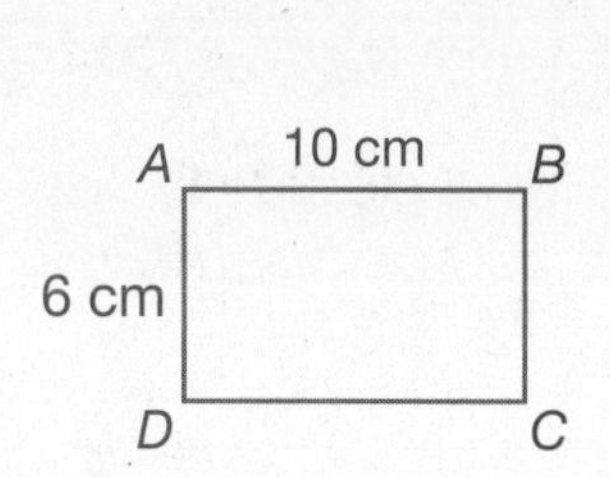

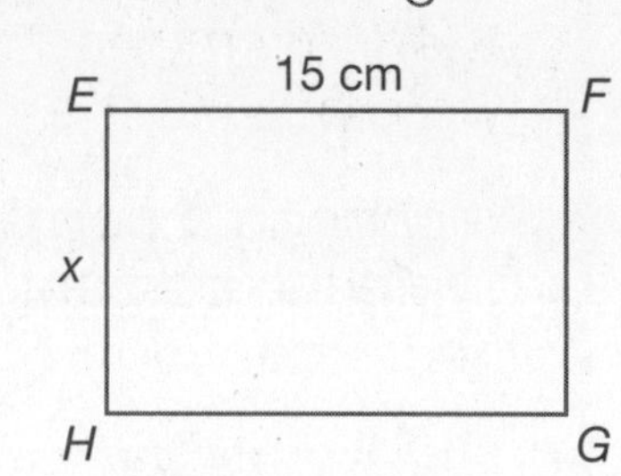

Write a proportion. $\frac{6}{10} = \frac{x}{15}$

Multiply the cross-products. $10x = 90$

Solve for *x*. $10x \div 10 = 90 \div 10$

$x = 9$

The length of $\overline{EH}$ is 9 cm.

Do I Understand?

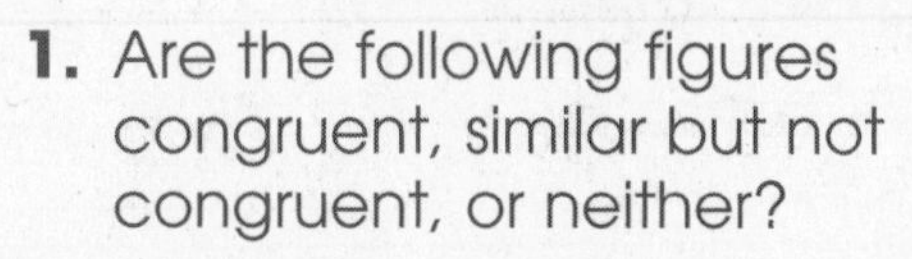

1. Are the following figures congruent, similar but not congruent, or neither?

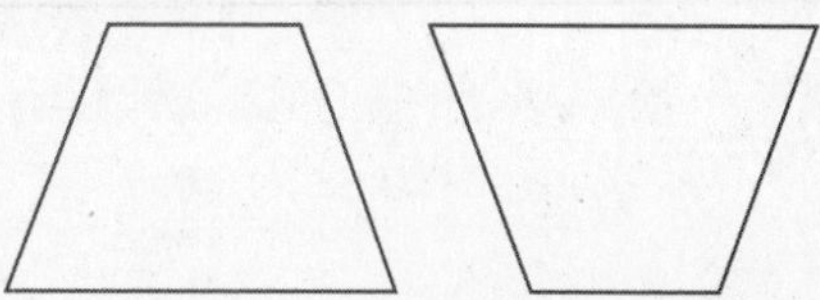

____

ANSWER: 1. congruent

Decimals

A number with at least one digit to the right of a decimal point.

Place Value

A **decimal** is a number with a **decimal point (.)**. A decimal point separates the whole numbers from the part that represents part of one whole. As with whole numbers, each digit to the right of the decimal point has its own value. The place-value chart shows the names of the places.

ones	.	tenths	hundredths	thousandths
4	.	8	5	3

The decimal 4.853 is made up of 4 ones, 8 **tenths**, 5 **hundredths**, and 3 **thousandths**.

Read Decimals

To read a decimal, separate the whole-number part from the part of a whole. Read the part of the whole as a fraction of the number over the least place of the decimal.

Read the decimal 8.272.

Read the whole number part first. The word *and* separates the whole-number part from the part of a whole.

eight and

Read the part of the whole.

two hundred seventy-two thousandths

Change Decimals to Fractions

Change 0.65 into a fraction in simplest form.

Write the decimal as the numerator with its place as the denominator: $\frac{65}{100}$

Simplify the fraction. $\frac{65}{100} \div \frac{5}{5} = \frac{13}{20}$

Change Fractions to Decimals

Change $\frac{5}{8}$ to a decimal.

Divide the numerator by the denominator. The quotient is a decimal.

$5 \div 8 = 0.625$

Change Decimals to Percents and Percents to Decimals

Change 0.72 to a percent.

Multiply the decimal by 100 and insert a percent sign (%). The process is essentially moving the decimal point two places to the right. So, 0.72 = 72%

To change a percent to a decimal, divide the percent by 100 and remove the percent sign. So, 39% = 0.39.

Do I Understand?

1. What is $\frac{3}{8}$ written as a decimal? ____________

2. What is 0.36 written as a fraction in simplest form? ____________

ANSWERS: 1. 0.375 **2.** $\frac{9}{25}$

Division

An operation on two numbers that tells how many groups or how many in each group.

How to Write a Division Problem

There are two ways to write a **division** problem.

$63 \div 9 = 7$

divisor → $9\overline{)63}$ with 7 ← **quotient**

← **dividend**

$$\begin{array}{r} 7 \\ 9\overline{)63} \\ -\,63 \\ \hline 0 \end{array}$$

Division with Remainders

Divide $502 \div 6$.

Divide $50 \div 6$.
Since $6 \times 8 = 48$, there are 8 tens.

Subtract $50 - 48$.
Bring down the 2 ones.

Divide $22 \div 6$.
Since $6 \times 3 = 18$, there are 3 ones.
Subtract $22 - 18$.

$$\begin{array}{r} 83 \text{ R4} \\ 6\overline{)502} \\ -\,48\downarrow \\ \hline 22 \\ -\,18 \\ \hline 4 \end{array}$$

The **remainder** is 4. A remainder is a number less than the divisor that remains after division is completed.

Division by Multidigit Divisors

Divide $926 \div 34$.

Divide the tens.
Multiply 34×2.
Subtract $92 - 68$.
Bring down the 6 ones.

Multiply 34×7.
Subtract $246 - 238$.
The remainder is 8.

$$\begin{array}{r} 27 \text{ R8} \\ 34\overline{)926} \\ -\,68 \\ \hline 246 \\ -\,238 \\ \hline 8 \end{array}$$

Do I Understand?

Divide.

1. $8\overline{)425}$ **2.** $26\overline{)636}$

ANSWERS: 1. 53 R1 **2.** 24 R12

Division

(continued)

Division with Decimals

Dividing a decimal dividend is similar to dividing a whole number. There are two major differences. The first is that it is necessary to place the decimal point in the quotient. The second involves remainders. Instead of writing a remainder, continue dividing until the decimals terminate, or if you are rounding to a specific place.

Divide 25.8 ÷ 4.

$$\begin{array}{r} 6.45 \\ 4\overline{)25.8\mathbf{0}} \\ -\underline{24} \\ 18 \\ -\underline{16} \\ 2\mathbf{0} \\ -\underline{20} \\ 0 \end{array}$$

Divide with Fractions

To divide fractions, it is necessary to write the **reciprocal** of the divisor. The reciprocal is one of two numbers whose product is 1. Then multiply the fractions. Simplify if possible.

Divide $\frac{3}{5} \div \frac{2}{3}$.

Write the reciprocal of the divisor. — The reciprocal of $\frac{2}{3}$ is $\frac{3}{2}$.

Multiply the dividend by the reciprocal of the divisor. — $\frac{3}{5} \times \frac{3}{2} = \frac{9}{10}$

So, $\frac{3}{5} \div \frac{2}{3} = \frac{9}{10}$.

Divide with Mixed Numbers

Use the same steps to divide with mixed numbers as you would with fractions. There is one extra step: convert the mixed numbers into improper fractions.

Divide $3\frac{1}{3} \div 1\frac{7}{8}$.

Convert the mixed numbers into improper fractions. — $3\frac{1}{3} = \frac{10}{3}$ $\quad 1\frac{7}{8} = \frac{15}{8}$

Write the reciprocal of the divisor. — The reciprocal of $\frac{15}{8}$ is $\frac{8}{15}$.

Simplify the fractions, if possible. Multiply the dividend by the reciprocal of the divisor. Convert the quotient back into a mixed number. — $\frac{\overset{2}{\cancel{10}}}{3} \times \frac{8}{\underset{3}{\cancel{15}}} = \frac{16}{9} = 1\frac{7}{9}$

Do I Understand?

Divide.

3. $5\overline{)325.9}$

4. $\frac{4}{5} \div \frac{2}{3}$ ______

5. $2\frac{3}{8} \div 3\frac{1}{2}$ ______

ANSWERS: 3. 65.18 **4.** $1\frac{1}{5}$ **5.** $\frac{19}{28}$

Estimation

Finding an answer that is close to the exact answer.

Estimate by Rounding

Sometimes it is not necessary to find an exact answer. An **estimate** may be all that is required. The most basic way to estimate is to **round** numbers. Rounding is to find the value of a number based on a given place value.

What is 347,528 rounded to the nearest ten thousand? nearest hundred thousand?

To round a number to a given place, follow these rules:

Look at the digit to the right of the place to which you are rounding. If the digit is less than 5, the digit in the place you are rounding remains the same. If the digit is 5 or greater, add 1 to the digit in the place you are rounding. In either case, replace the other digits with zeros.

34**7**,528	Since $7 > 5$, add 1 to the ten thousands place.

So, 347,528 rounds to 350,000 to the nearest ten thousand.

3**4**7,528	Since $4 < 5$, the hundred-thousands digit remains the same.

So, 347,528 rounds to 300,000 to the nearest hundred thousand.

Estimate Sums and Differences

To estimate a sum or difference, round each addend to a given place. Below, the actual answers are given to the left of the estimated answers. See that the estimated answers are close to the actual answers.

$$\begin{array}{r} 35{,}283 \\ +\ 44{,}392 \\ \hline 79{,}675 \end{array} \begin{array}{c} \rightarrow \\ \rightarrow \\ \\ \end{array} \begin{array}{r} 40{,}000 \\ +\ 40{,}000 \\ \hline 80{,}000 \end{array}$$

$$\begin{array}{r} 47{,}128 \\ -\ 22{,}392 \\ \hline 24{,}736 \end{array} \begin{array}{c} \rightarrow \\ \rightarrow \\ \\ \end{array} \begin{array}{r} 47{,}000 \\ -\ 22{,}000 \\ \hline 25{,}000 \end{array}$$

Estimate Products and Quotients

To estimate a product, round the factor to a given place and multiply. For example, to estimate 483×32 round to $500 \times 30 = 15{,}000$. So, 483×32 is about 15,000. To estimate a quotient, it is necessary to use **compatible numbers**. Compatible numbers are numbers that are easy to divide mentally. For example, to estimate $5{,}522 \div 81$, you would not round the dividend to 5,500 or 6,000, you would use compatible numbers, which are 5,600 and 80. Since $5{,}600 \div 80 = 70$, $5{,}522 \div 81$ is about 70.

Do I Understand?

Estimate. Show your work.

1. $\begin{array}{r} 57{,}328 \\ +\ 36{,}920 \\ \hline \end{array}$

2. $\begin{array}{r} 67{,}085 \\ -\ 29{,}183 \\ \hline \end{array}$

3. $\begin{array}{r} 218 \\ \times\ 79 \\ \hline \end{array}$

4. $4{,}720 \div 58$

ANSWERS: 1. 100,000 **2.** 40,000 **3.** 16,000 **4.** 80

Expressions and Equations

EXPRESSION - A group of numbers and symbols that shows a mathematical quantity.
EQUATION - A mathematical statement that has an equal sign in it.

Variables

A **variable** is a symbol that represents a number. Usually a variable will be a letter, but it can also be some other type of symbol.

Evaluate Expressions

An **expression** can be evaluated if you know the value of the variable.
Evaluate $3x + 7$ if $x = 5$.
Substitute 5 for x.
So $3 \times 5 + 7 = 22$.

Solve Addition and Subtraction Equations

An **equation** is a mathematical statement that has an equal sign in it, such as $4x = 20$ or $5 + 7 = 12$. The solution to addition and subtraction equations can be found using **inverse operations**. Inverse operations undo each other. Any operation performed on one side of the equation must be performed on both sides of the equation.

Find the value of x in $12 + x = 21$.

$12 - 12 + x = 21 - 12$ $\quad$ $x = 9$

Find the value of y in $y - 26 = 18$.

$y - 26 + 26 = 18 + 26$ $\quad$ $y = 44$

Solve Multiplication and Division Equations

Like addition and subtraction equations, the solution to multiplication and division equations can be found using inverse operations.

Find the value of n in $4n = 28$.

$4n \div 4 = 28 \div 4$ $\quad$ $n = 7$

Find the value of p in $p \div 5 = 20$.

$p \div 5 \times 5 = 20 \times 5$ $\quad$ $p = 100$

Solve Two-Step Equations

A two-step equation is one where two operations need to be performed. To solve a two-step equation, add or subtract to isolate the variable on one side of the equation. Then multiply or divide to find the value of the variable.

Find the value of q in $3q + 5 = 17$.

Subtract to isolate the variable.

$3q + 5 - 5 = 17 - 5$ $\quad$ $3q = 12$

Divide to find the value of the variable.

$3q \div 3 = 12 \div 3$ $\quad$ $q = 4$

Do I Understand?

1. What is the value of n in $4n - 6 = 18$?

$n =$ __________

ANSWER: 1. 6

Factors and Multiples

FACTOR - a number that is multiplied to get a product.
MULTIPLE - a number that is the product of a number and any whole number.

Factors and Products

Numbers that are multiplied to get a product are called **factors**. A product must have at least two factors, although they may be the same number. Products that have the same two factors are called **square numbers**.

8	×	7	=	56
factor		factor		product

Factors of a Number

The factors of a number are those numbers in which it is possible to find a product.

For example, the factors of 54 are 1, 2, 3, 6, 9, 12, 18, 27, and 54.

Prime Factorization

The **prime factorization** of a number is that number expressed as the product of its prime factors.

For example, the prime factorization of 36 is $2 \times 2 \times 3 \times 3$ or written with exponents as $2^2 \times 3^2$.

Multiples of a Number

A **multiple** is a number that is the product of a number and any whole number.
For example, the first five multiples of 8 are 8, 16, 24, 32, 40, and 48.

Greatest Common Factor (GCF)

The **greatest common factor (GCF)** of 2 or more numbers is the greatest whole number that is a common factor of the numbers. For example, find the GCF of 24 and 32.

1. List the factors of both numbers.
   24: 1, 2, 3, 4, 6, 8, 12, 24
   32: 1, 2, 4, 8, 16, 32
2. Find the common factors:
   1, 2, 4, and 8.

The GCF of 24 and 32 is 8.

Least Common Multiple (LCM)

The **least common multiple** of 2 or more numbers is the least whole number greater than 0 that is a multiple of each of the numbers. For example, find the LCM of 5 and 7.

1. List the first multiples of 5 and 7:
   5: 5, 10, 15, 20, 25, 30, 35, …
   7: 7, 14, 21, 28, 35, …
2. Find the common multiple: 35

The LCM of 5 and 7 is 35.

Do I Understand?

1. What is the prime factorization of 20?

   ____

2. What is the GCF of 27 and 45?

   ____

ANSWERS: 1. $2^2 \times 5$ **2.** 9

Fractions

A number that names part of a whole or a group.

Parts of a Fraction

The **denominator**, or bottom number, tells how many equal parts there are in a **fraction**. The **numerator**, or top number, tells how many of those equal parts are being considered.

$\frac{3}{8}$ ← **numerator** (3) ← **denominator** (8)

Use Fractions

A fraction can name parts of a whole or part of a group

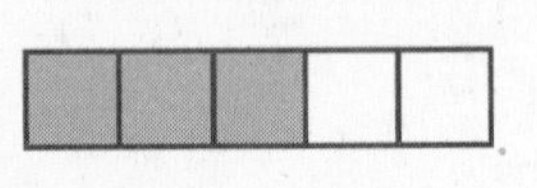

The fraction $\frac{3}{5}$ represents the part of the rectangle that is shaded. The fraction $\frac{4}{9}$ represents the black marbles.

Equivalent Fractions

Equivalent fractions are two or more different fractions that name the same amount. To find an equivalent fraction, multiply or divide the numerator and denominator of the fraction by the same number.

For example, $\frac{2}{3}$ and $\frac{6}{9}$ are equivalent fractions since $\frac{2}{3} \times \frac{3}{3} = \frac{6}{9}$.

Simplest Form

A fraction written in **simplest form** has 1 for the only number that evenly divides into both the numerator and denominator. For example, write $\frac{9}{12}$ in simplest form.

$$\frac{9}{12} \longrightarrow \frac{9 \div 3}{12 \div 3} = \frac{3}{4}$$

Mixed Numbers and Improper Fractions

A **mixed number** is a number that has a whole-number part and a fraction part. An **improper fraction** is a fraction that has a numerator that is greater than or equal to the numerator.

To convert a mixed number into an improper fraction, multiply the whole-number part by the denominator and then add the numerator to the product. The denominator remains the same. For example,

$$3\frac{2}{5} = \frac{(3 \times 5) + 2}{5} = \frac{17}{5}.$$

To convert an improper fraction to a mixed number, divide the numerator by the denominator. The remainder will be the numerator of the fraction part. For example,

$$\frac{21}{4} = 21 \div 4 = 5\frac{1}{4}.$$

Do I Understand?

1. What is $\frac{12}{15}$ written in simplest form?

____

2. What is $3\frac{7}{12}$ written as an improper fraction?

____

ANSWERS: 1. $\frac{4}{5}$ **2.** $\frac{43}{12}$

Functions

A relationship in which one quantity depends on another quantity.

Function Rules

A **function** is a relationship in which one quantity depends on another quantity. A function has a rule that must be followed for every set of values. If the rule does not work for each set of values, then it is not a function.

Function Tables

A function table is used to display functions.

x	0	1	2	3	4	5
y	3	4	5	6	7	8

The rule of this function is $y = x + 3$.

A function table can be extended if you know the rule of the function. For example, in the function $y = x + 3$, find the value of y if $x = 12$.

$y = 12 + 3$, so $y = 15$.

A function can also be a negative number. For example, find the value of y if $x = -5$.

$y = -5 + 3$, so $y = -2$.

Graph Functions in Four Quadrants

A function can be graphed in all four quadrants. Convert the values to ordered pairs. Use the values in the function table on the left:

(0, 3), (1, 4), (2, 5), (3, 6), (4, 7), (5, 8)

The ordered pair (−5, −2) is also part of the function. Plot the points and draw a line.

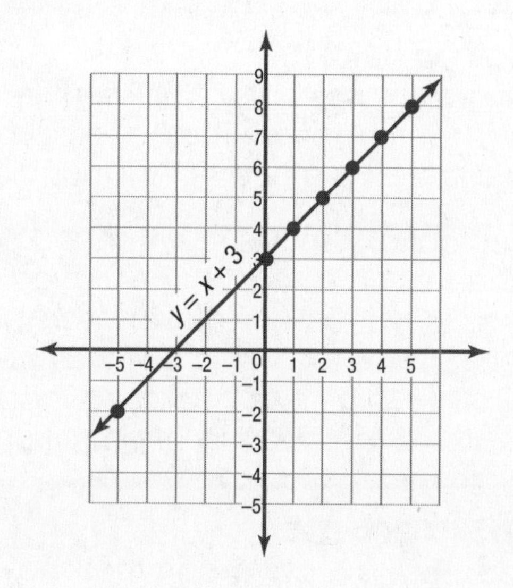

Do I Understand?

1. What is the rule of this function table?

x	1	2	3	4
y	5	10	15	20

____

ANSWER: 1. $y = 5x$

Graphs

A drawing that shows information.

Pictographs

A **pictograph** uses a picture or symbol to compare information. A **key** tells how many items each symbol represents. This pictograph shows how many vehicles were sold.

To read a pictograph, multiply the value of the key by the number of symbols. If there is a half symbol, take half the value of the key. There were 550 SUVs sold.

Auto King Vehicle Sales This Quarter

Vehicle Type	Number Sold
Sedans	🚗🚗🚗🚗
SUVs	🚗🚗🚗🚗🚗½🚗
Trucks	🚗🚗🚗½🚗
Mini Vans	🚗🚗🚗🚗🚗

Each 🚗 = 100 vehicles.

Bar Graphs

A **bar graph** uses bars of different lengths to compare information. This bar graph shows the number of members in various clubs.

The vertical axis shows the number of members each club has. The vertical axis is in intervals of 8. If a bar falls between two numbers, it has the value half way between the two numbers that it falls between. There are 52 members in intramurals.

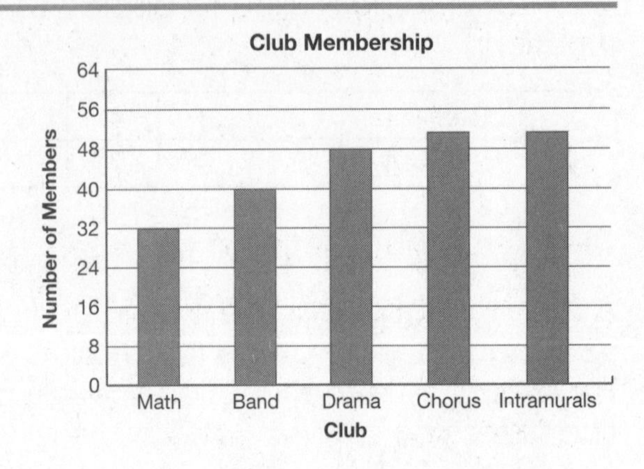

Histograms

A **histogram** is a bar graph that shows a range of data. Unlike a bar graph, there are no gaps between the bars, unless the **frequency** for that interval is 0.

In a histogram, the horizontal axis must have equal intervals without overlaps. This histogram has a range of 10. A number cannot appear in two bars.

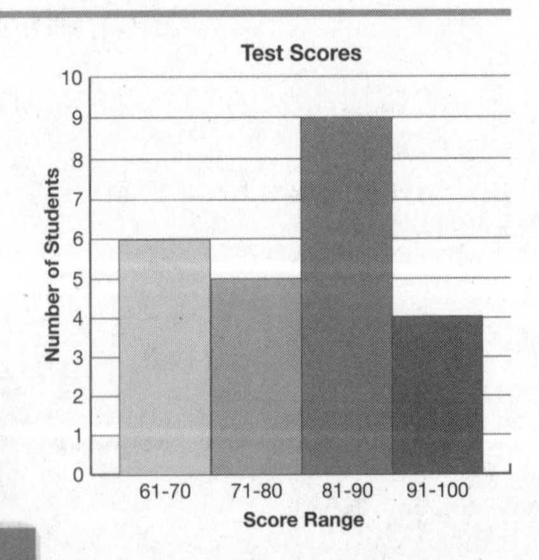

Do I Understand?

1. Use the pictograph. How many more minivans were sold than trucks?

________ minivans

2. Use the bar graph. How many more members are in the chorus than in the math club?

________ members

ANSWER: 1. 150 **2.** 20

Graphs
(continued)

Line Graphs

A **line graph** is read like a coordinate grid. Line graphs are used to show change over time. The points are connected by a line, which shows the change. This line graph shows the temperature in °F for each hour from 12:00 noon to 6:00.

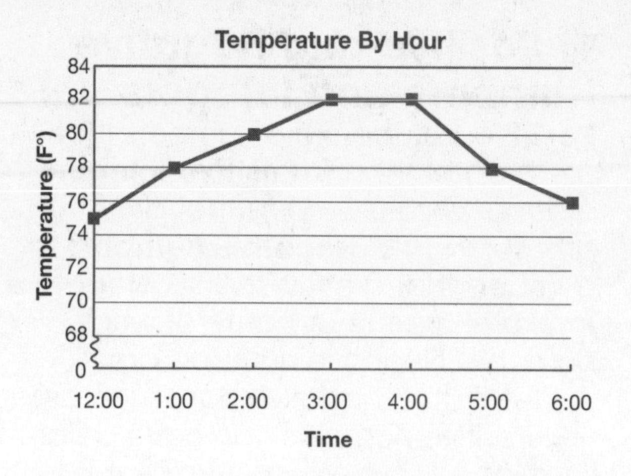

To find the temperature at 3:00, find the point above 3:00. Then look to the left to find the value of the dot.
At 3:00, the temperature was 82°F.

Circle Graphs

A **circle graph** shows the parts of a whole. This circle graph shows grades earned on the last math test.

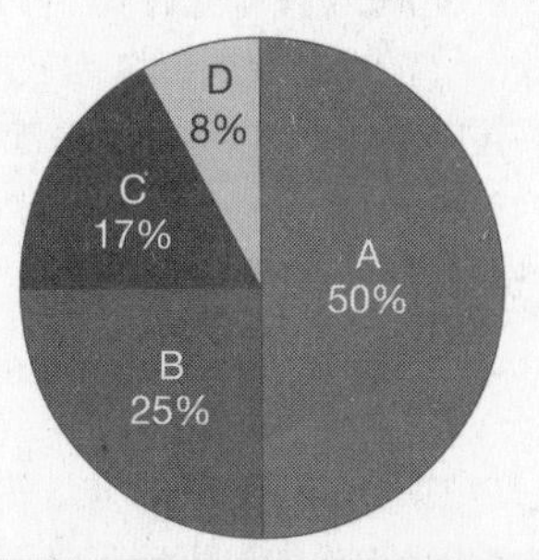

The larger the section of a circle graph, the greater its part of the whole. If you add the percents of a circle graph they will add to 100%, although because of rounding may be a little above or below 100%.

Stem-and-Leaf Plots

A **stem-and-leaf plot** is used to organize data. It separates the ones place from the other places in a number. This stem-and-leaf plot shows the number of pages read yesterday by 12 members of the book club.

The stems represent the tens place and the leaves represent the ones place. So, 1 | 5 = 15. One member read 15 pages.

Number of Pages Read

Stems	Leaves
1	5 8 6
2	4 9
3	5 7 7
4	2 8
5	3 6

1|5 = 15

3. Use the line graph. What was the range of temperatures?

____

4. Use the circle graph. If 24 students took the test, how many earned a B?

__________ students

ANSWERS: 3. 7°F **4.** 6

Integers

A whole number or its opposite.

Positive and Negative Numbers and Integers

Positive numbers are numbers that are greater than 0. **Positive integers** are the whole numbers that are greater than 0. **Negative numbers** are numbers that are less than 0. **Negative integers** are the opposite of whole numbers. Negative numbers are written with a negative sign, such as −3. Positive numbers can have a sign, such as +4, or no sign, such as 4.

Compare Integers

The number line shows how negative integers are related to positive integers.

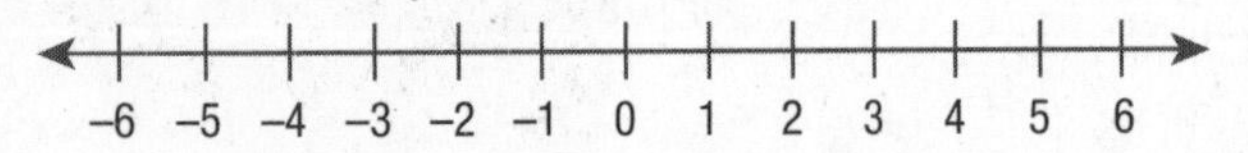

On a number line, the greater number is always to the right of the lesser number. Any positive number is greater than any negative number.

Absolute Value

The **absolute value** is the distance of a number from 0 on a number line. Absolute value is written as $|x|$. The absolute value of $|-5| = |5|$.

Add Integers

If two addends are each negative, add as you would with positive numbers, but include the negative sign. For example, $-4 + -6 = -10$.

If one addend is positive and the other is negative, subtract the number with the lesser absolute value from the number with the greater absolute value. For example, $5 + -7 = -2$. Keep the sign with the greater absolute value.

Subtract Integers

Use parentheses to avoid confusing the negative sign for subtraction.

Positive - Positive
The difference can be positive, 0, or negative. $7 - 5 = 2$ $5 - 7 = -2$

Positive - Negative
The difference is always positive.
$5 - (-3) = 5 + 3 = 8$

Negative - Positive
The difference is always negative.
$-4 - 5 = -9$

Negative - Negative
The difference can be positive, 0, or negative. $-3 - (-4) = -3 + 4 = 1$

Subtracting a negative number is like adding a positive number.

Do I Understand?

Zeke

Solve.

1. $6 + -5$ ____________

2. $-3 - 2$ ____________

ANSWERS: 1. 1 **2.** –5

Lines

A straight path that goes in two directions without end.

Lines

A **line** is a straight path that goes in two directions without end. This line can be read as either $\overleftrightarrow{AB}$ or $\overleftrightarrow{BA}$.

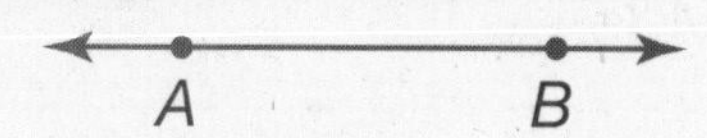

Line Segments

A **line segment** is a part of a line that has two endpoints. This line segment can be named as either $\overline{MN}$ or $\overline{NM}$.

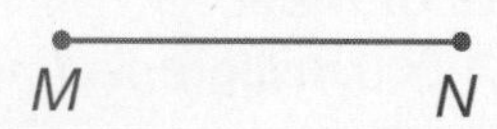

Rays

A **ray** is part of a line that has one endpoint and goes in one direction without end. A ray is read with the endpoint first. This ray is read $\overrightarrow{YZ}$.

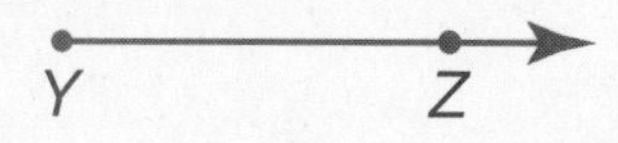

Types of Lines

Parallel lines never meet and remain the same distance apart. The symbol || represents two lines that are parallel. **Intersecting lines** are lines that cross. **Perpendicular lines** are lines that intersect at a right angle. The symbol ⊥ represents two lines that are perpendicular.

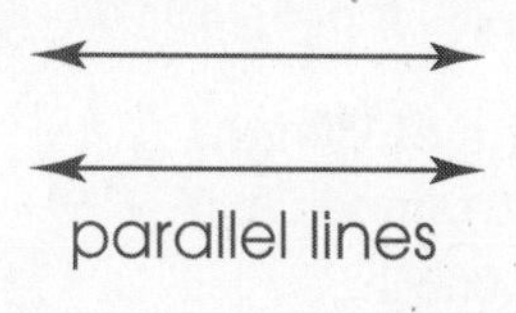

parallel lines

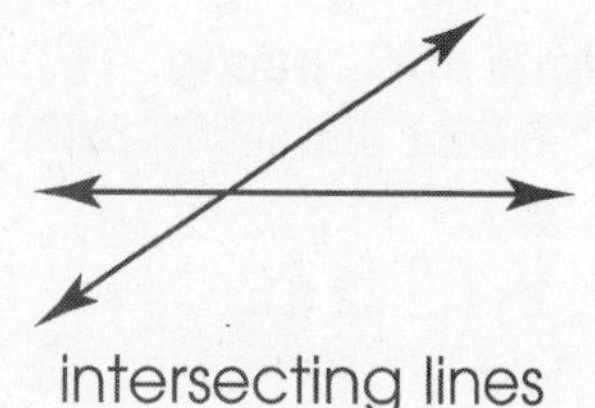

intersecting lines

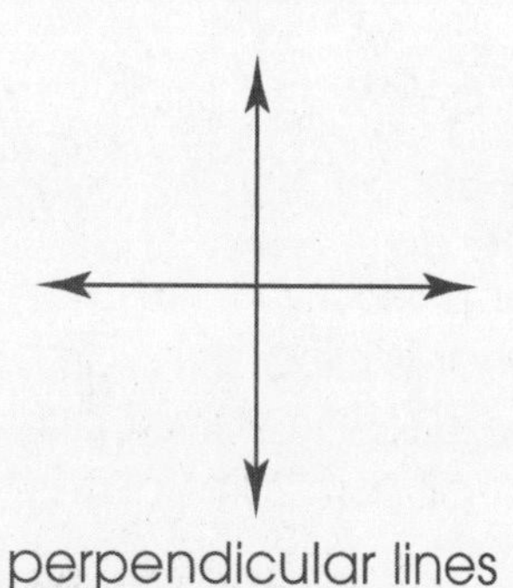

perpendicular lines

Do I Understand?

1. How many right angles are formed when perpendicular lines meet?

____

2. What part of a line has two endpoints?

____

ANSWERS: 1. 4 **2.** line segment

Measurement

The measures of length, capacity, weight/mass in the customary and metric systems.

Customary Measurement

The customary system of measure is used in the United States. Here are the most common customary units of measure.

Customary Units of Length		
1 foot (ft)	=	**12 inches (in.)**
1 yard (yd)	=	36 in. or 3 ft
1 mile (mi)	=	5,280 ft or 1,760 yd

Customary Units of Weight		
1 pound (lb)	=	**16 ounces (oz)**
1 ton (T)	=	2,000 lb

Customary Units of Capacity		
1 cup (c)	=	8 **fluid ounces (fl oz)**
1 pint (pt)	=	2 c or 16 fl oz
1 quart (qt)	=	2 pt or 32 fl oz
1 gallon (gal)	=	4 qt or 128 fl oz

The line segment below is 1 inch long.

____

A piece of paper is about 1 foot long. The width of a door is about 1 yard long. A mile is the distance that an adult can walk in about 20 minutes.

A small eraser weighs about 1 ounce. A basketball weighs about 1 pound. A small car weighs about 1 ton.

Metric Measurement

The metric system is based on the number 10. When you change from one unit to another, you usually multiply or divide by 10.

Metric Units of Length	
1 centimeter (cm)	= 10 **millimeters (mm)**
1 meter (m)	= 100 cm or 1,000 mm
1 kilometer (km)	= 1,000 m

Metric Units of Mass	
1 gram (g)	= 1,000 **milligrams (mg)**
1 kilogram (kg)	= 2,000 lb

Metric Units of Capacity	
1 liter (L)	= 1,000 **milliliters(mL)**

The line segment below is 1 centimeter long.

____

A meter is a little longer than a yard.

A kilometer is the distance that an adult can walk in about 10 minutes.

A hardcover book has a mass of about 1 kilogram.

A liter is a little larger than a quart.

Do I Understand?

1. How many pints are equal to 80 fluid ounces? __________ pints

2. How many grams are equal to 4 kilograms? __________ grams

ANSWERS: 1. 5 **2.** 4,000

Multiplication

A shortcut for repeated addition.

The Parts of a Multiplication Problem

These are the parts of a multiplication problem.

$$\begin{array}{r} 7 \\ \times\ 8 \\ \hline 56 \end{array}$$

- multiplication sign → ×
- 7 ← factor
- 8 ← factor
- 56 ← product

Multiply by 1-Digit Numbers

Multiply 82×7.

Follow these steps:

Multiply the ones. Regroup if necessary.

$$\begin{array}{r} ^{1} \\ 82 \\ \times\ 7 \\ \hline 4 \end{array}$$

Multiply the tens. Add the extra ten.

$$\begin{array}{r} ^{1} \\ 82 \\ \times\ 7 \\ \hline 574 \end{array}$$

Multiply by 2-Digit Numbers

First, find the **partial products**. Then add the partial products.

Multiply 654×43.

$$\begin{array}{r} 654 \\ \times\ 43 \\ \hline 1962 \\ +\ 26160 \\ \hline 28{,}122 \end{array}$$

- 1962 ← Multiply 654×3
- 26160 ← Multiply 654×40

Multiply with Decimals

Multiply as you would with whole numbers, with the difference of placing the decimal point. The sum of the number of decimal places in the factors is equal to the number of decimal places in the product.

$$\begin{array}{r} 2.75 \\ \times\ 0.5 \\ \hline 1.375 \end{array}$$

- 2.75 ← 2 decimal places
- 0.5 ← 1 decimal place
- 1.375 ← 3 decimal places

Multiply with Fractions

First, simplify the factors if possible. Next, multiply the numerators and then the denominators. Write the product in simplest form.

Multiply $\frac{3}{8} \times \frac{5}{12}$.

$$\frac{\cancel{3}^{1}}{8} \times \frac{5}{\cancel{12}_{4}} = \frac{5}{32}$$

Multiply with Mixed Numbers

The first step is to convert the mixed numbers into improper fractions. Then multiply as you would with fractions.

Multiply $2\frac{2}{3} \times 3\frac{1}{4}$.

$$2\frac{2}{3} \times 3\frac{1}{4} = \frac{\cancel{8}^{2}}{3} \times \frac{13}{\cancel{4}_{1}} = \frac{26}{3} = 8\frac{2}{3}$$

Do I Understand?

Anna

Find the product.

1. 58×9
2. 379×28
3. 4.63×2.08
4. $\frac{7}{8} \times 1\frac{2}{3}$

ANSWERS: **1.** 522 **2.** 10,612 **3.** 9.6304 **4.** $1\frac{11}{24}$

Numbers

A number can be used to tell how many, the order, or to identify.

Write Whole Numbers

There are different ways to write **whole numbers**. The number 687,239 can be written in the following ways:

standard form
687,239

word form
six hundred eighty-seven thousand, two hundred thirty-nine

expanded form
600,000 + 80,000 + 7,000 + 200 + 30 + 9

The number 687,239 can also be written in a place-value chart.

Thousands					
Hundreds	Tens	Ones	Hundreds	Tens	Ones
6	8	7	2	3	9

Exponents

An **exponent** is a number, called a **power**, that tells how many times a **base** is used as a factor.

In the exponent 3^4, 3 is the base and 4 is the exponent. It is read "three to the fourth power." It means the same as $3 \times 3 \times 3 \times 3 = 81$.

Square Numbers and Cube Numbers

A number to the second power is said to be squared. The product of a number that is squared is called a **square number**. Examples of square numbers include 1, 4, 9, 16, and 25.

A number to the third power is said to be cubed. The product of a number that is cubed is called a **cube number**. Examples of cube numbers include 1, 8, 27, 64, and 125.

Prime and Composite Numbers

A **prime number** is a whole number greater than 1 that has only 1 and itself as factors. Examples of prime numbers include 2, 3, 5, 7, 11, and 13.

A **composite number** is a whole number greater than 1 that has at least 3 factors. Examples of composite numbers include 4, 6, 9, 12, and 15.

Do I Understand?

1. What is 500,000 + 40,000 + 300 + 70 + 2 written in standard form? ______________

2. Is 53 a prime or composite number ______________

3. What is 7^3? ______________

ANSWERS: 1. 540,372 **2.** prime **3.** 343

Ordered Pairs

A pair of numbers that gives the location of a point on a graph.

A **coordinate grid** is used to name points on a graph. The points are called **ordered pairs**. There are 4 **quadrants** in a coordinate grid. The quadrants are labeled I, II, III, and IV below.

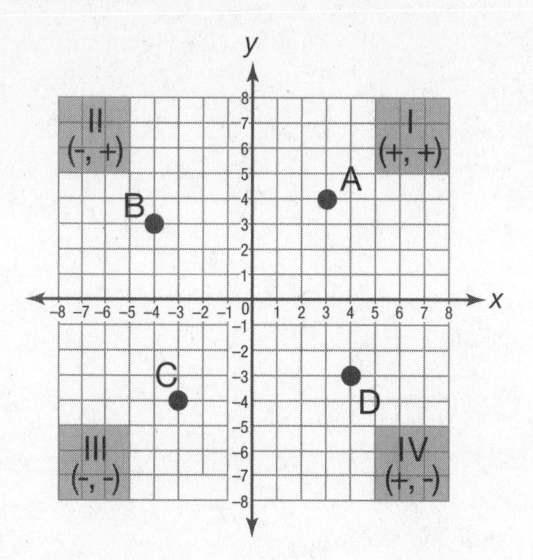

To read an ordered pair, start at the **origin**, which is located at (0, 0). The first coordinate names the distance to the right or left of 0. The second coordinate names the distance above or below 0.

Point *A* is located at (3, 4).
Point *D* is located at (4, −3).

Do I Understand?

Use the coordinate grid above to name the ordered pair.

1. Point *B* __________

2. Point *C* __________

ANSWERS: 1. (−4, 3) **2.** (−3, −4)

Percents

Per hundred.

Meaning of Percent

A **percent** is a ratio of a number per 100. The symbol for percent is %.

Relate Percents to Fractions and Decimals

To write a percent as a fraction, write the percent as a fraction with a denominator of 100. Then simplify the fraction. For example, $35\% = \frac{35}{100} = \frac{7}{20}$.

To write a percent as a decimal, write the percent as a numerator with a denominator of 100. Then write an equivalent decimal.
For example, $47\% = \frac{47}{100} = 0.47$.

To write a decimal as a percent, multiply the decimal by 100 and insert a percent sign.
For example, $0.32 = 0.32 \times 100 = 32\%$.

To write a fraction as a percent, divide the numerator by the denominator to convert to a decimal. Then convert to a percent.
For example, $\frac{3}{10} = 3 \div 10 = 0.3 = 30\%$.

Do I Understand?

1. Write 55% as a fraction in simplest form.

____

2. What is 70% of 40? __________

ANSWERS: 1. $\frac{11}{20}$ **2.** 28

Perimeter and Circumference

PERIMETER - the distance around the outside of a closed figure.
CIRCUMFERENCE - the distance around a circle.

How to Find the Perimeter

To find the **perimeter** of a closed figure, add the lengths of each of the sides. In this figure some of the sides are not given. They can be determined from the other sides.

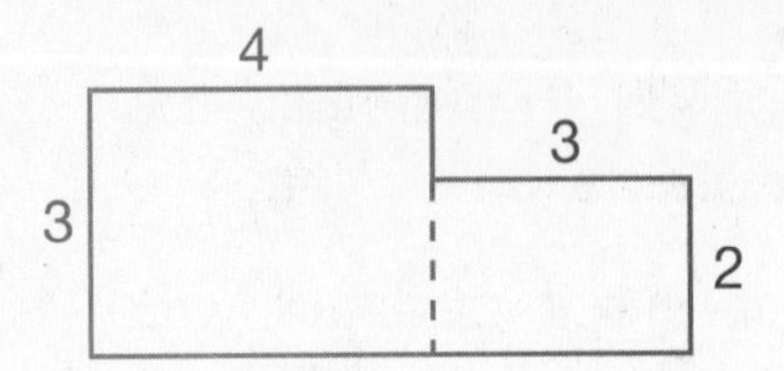

$P = 4 + \underline{1} + 3 + 2 + \underline{7} + 3 = 20$

The perimeter of the figure is 20 units.

Perimeter of a Rectangle

To find the perimeter of a rectangle, use the formula:
$P = 2l + 2w$.
Multiply the length times 2. Multiply the width times 2. Then add the products to find the perimeter.

4

3

$P = (2 \times 4) + (2 \times 3) = 8 + 6 = 14$

The perimeter of the rectangle is 14 units.

Perimeter of Regular Polygons

A **regular polygon** is a polygon with all congruent sides and angles. The perimeter of a regular polygon can be found by multiplying the length of the sides by the number of sides.

6 cm

$P = 6 \text{ cm} \times 5 = 30 \text{ cm}.$

The perimeter of this pentagon is 30 centimeters.

Circumference of a Circle

Circumference measures the distance around the outside of a circle. Use the formula $C = 2\pi r$ to find the circumference. Use 3.14 to represent π (**pi**, pronounced pie) and r is the radius of a circle.

8 in.

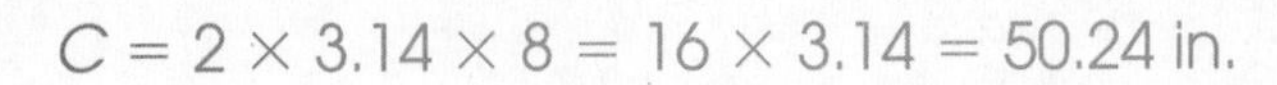

$C = 2 \times 3.14 \times 8 = 16 \times 3.14 = 50.24$ in.

The circumference of this circle is 50.24 inches.

Do I Understand?

1. What is the perimeter of a rectangle with a length of 29 inches and a width of 17 inches? ______________ inches

2. What is the circumference of a circle with a radius of 12 millimeters? ______________ millimeters

ANSWERS: 1. 92 **2.** 75.36

Polygons

A closed figure made of line segments.

Examples of Polygons

A **polygon** is a closed figure made of line segments. If a figure has a curved side then it is not a polygon. Polygons are **two-dimensional figures**.

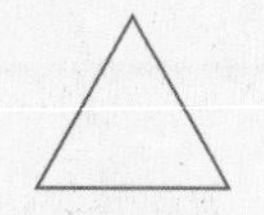

triangle
3 **sides** and 3 angles

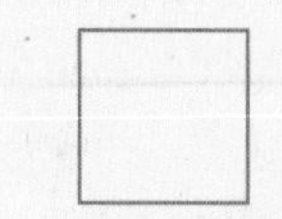

quadrilateral
4 sides and 4 angles

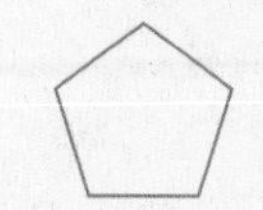

pentagon
5 sides and 5 angles

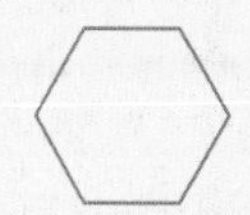

hexagon
6 sides and 6 angles

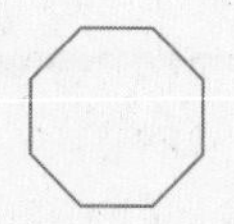

octagon
8 sides and 8 angles

Classifications of Triangles

The sum of the angle measures of a triangle is equal to 180°.

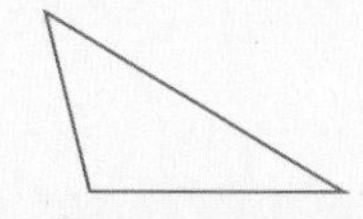

scalene triangle
No sides or angles are equal.

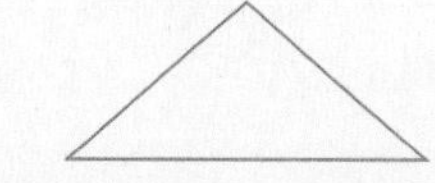

isosceles triangle
At least 2 sides and angles are equal.

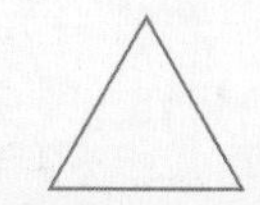

equilateral triangle
3 sides and angles are equal.

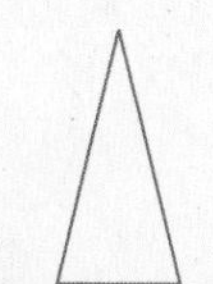

acute triangle
All angles are less than 90°.

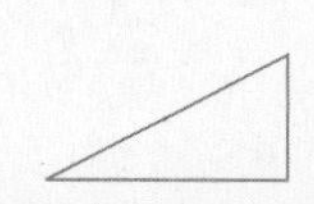

right triangle
One angle is a right angle.

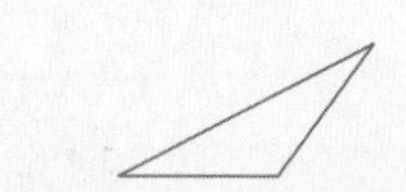

obtuse triangle
One angle is an obtuse angle.

Classification of Quadrilaterals

The sum of the angle measures of any quadrilateral is equal to 360°.

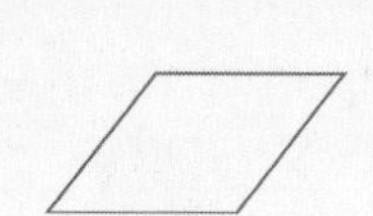

parallelogram
both pairs of opposite sides are parallel

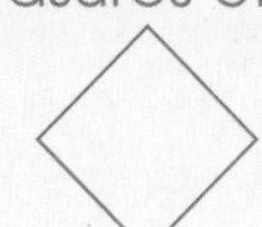

rhombus
parallelogram with all sides the same length

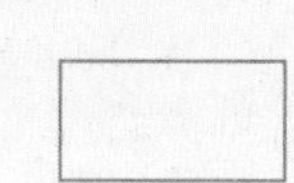

rectangle
parallelogram with 4 right angles

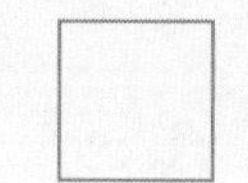

square
rectangle with all sides equal

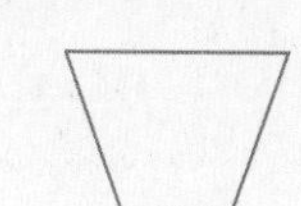

trapezoid
exactly 1 pair of parallel sides

Do I Understand?

Anna

1. A triangle has angle measures of 20°, 75°, 85°. Classify it as specific as possible.

____________________________ triangle

ANSWER: 1. scalene, acute

Probability

The chance that an event will happen.

Certain, Likely, Unlikely, and Impossible

Probability measures the chance of an event happening. An event can be **certain**, **likely**, **unlikely**, or **impossible**.

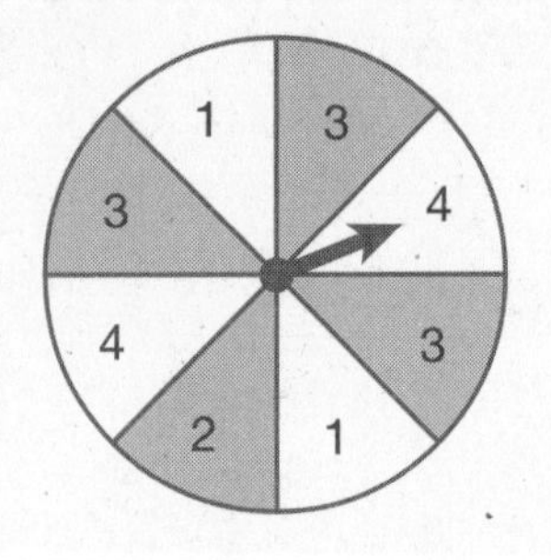

An event that is certain must happen. It is certain that you will spin a number less than 4. A likely event is one that will probably happen, but might not. It is likely that you will spin a 3 or a 4.

An unlikely event is one that probably will not happen, but could. It is unlikely that you will spin a 2. An impossible event is one that cannot happen. It is impossible to spin a 5.

Probability Written as a Fraction

Probability can be written as the following fraction:

$$\frac{\text{the number of favorable outcomes}}{\text{the number of possible outcomes}}$$

The number of **possible outcomes** is each of the possible outcomes. In the bowl of marbles at right, there are 10 marbles, so the **sample space** is 10 possible outcomes. Therefore, 10 is the denominator.

The number of **favorable outcomes** is the desired outcome. To find the probability of picking a white marble, count the number of white marbles. There are 2 white marbles, which is the numerator.

$$\frac{\text{the number of white marbles}}{\text{the total number of marbles}} = \frac{2}{10} = \frac{1}{5}$$

The probability of pulling a white marble is $\frac{1}{5}$. This can be written as $P(\text{white}) = \frac{1}{5}$.

Probabilities of Compound Events

A **compound event** includes two or more simple events. For example, find the probability of tossing heads on a coin and a 3 on a cube numbered 1 to 6.

The probability for tossing heads on a coin is $\frac{1}{2}$. The probability of tossing a 3 on the cube is $\frac{1}{6}$. $\frac{1}{2} \times \frac{1}{6} = \frac{1}{12}$. The probability of tossing heads and a 3 on the cube is $\frac{1}{12}$.

Do I Understand?

Use the spinner.

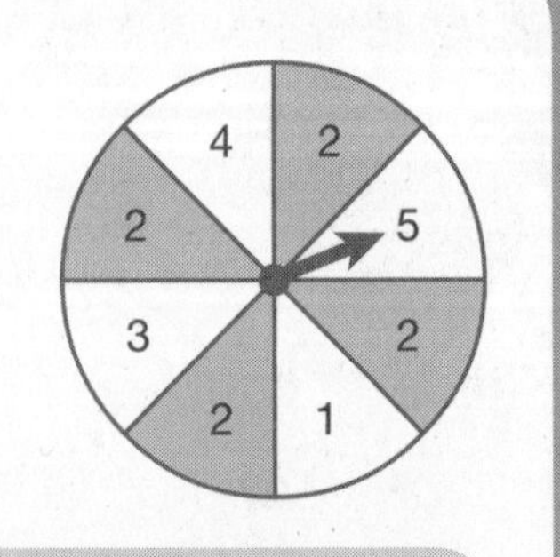

1. It is ______________________________ that the spinner will land on an even number.

2. What is the probability of the spinner landing on 2? ________________

ANSWERS: 1. likely **2.** $\frac{1}{2}$

Properties of Addition and Multiplication

Commutative Property

The **commutative property of addition** states that the order of the addends does not change the sum. For example: $25 + 18 = 18 + 25$.

The **commutative property of multiplication** states that the order of the factors does not change the product.
For example: $15 \times 12 = 12 \times 15$.

Associative Property

The **associative property of addition** states the grouping of the addends does not change the sum.
For example:
$75 + (25 + 56) = (75 + 25) + 56$.

The **associative property of multiplication** states the grouping of the factors does not change the product. For example:
$12 \times (5 \times 7) = (12 \times 5) \times 7$.

Identity Property

The **identity property of addition** states that when one addend is 0, the sum is equal to the other addend.
For example: $32 + 0 = 32$.

The **identity property of multiplication** states that when one factor is 1, the product is equal to the other factor. For example: $27 \times 1 = 27$.

Zero Property of Multiplication

The **zero property of multiplication** states that when 0 is multiplied by a number, the product is 0.
For example: $22 \times 0 = 0$

Distributive Properties of Multiplication

The **distributive property of multiplication over addition** states that to multiply a sum by a number, you can multiply each addend by the number and add the products.

For example:
$42 \times 7 = (40 \times 7) + (2 \times 7)$

$280 + 14 = 294$

The **distributive property of multiplication over subtraction** states that to multiply a difference of two numbers by a third number, multiply the first two numbers by the third and then find the difference of the products.

For example:
$78 \times 9 = (80 \times 9) - (2 \times 9)$

$720 - 18 = 702$

Do I Understand?

1. Use the associative property of addition to find the sum of $67 + 33 + 85$. ____________
2. Use the distributive property to find the product of 87×8. ____________

ANSWERS: 1. 185 **2.** 696

Ratios and Proportions

RATIO - a comparison of two quantities.
PROPORTION - an equation stating that two quantities are equal.

Ratios

A **ratio** is a comparison of two quantities. A ratio can compare a part to a whole, a part to a part, or a whole to a part. Look at the spinner at right.

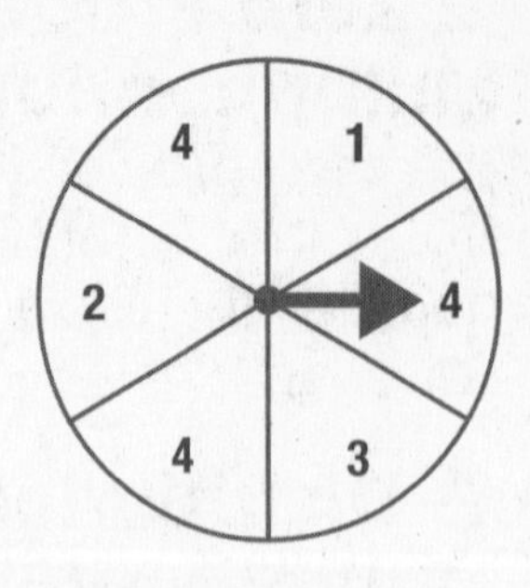

The ratio of even numbers to all numbers is 4 to 6. That ratio can also be written as 4:6 or $\frac{4}{6}$. Like fractions, ratios can be written in simplest form, so the ratio of even numbers to all numbers can also be written as 2 to 3, 2:3, or $\frac{2}{3}$.

The ratio of even number to odd numbers is 4 to 2 or 4:2 or $\frac{4}{2}$.

The ratio of all numbers to even numbers is 6 to 4 or 6:4 or $\frac{6}{4}$.

Equivalent Ratios

Equivalent ratios can be written as fractions. Use the least common denominator (LCD) to compare ratios.

The LCD of $\frac{6}{8}$ and $\frac{9}{12}$ is 24.

Since $\frac{6}{8} \times \frac{3}{3} = \frac{18}{24}$ and $\frac{9}{12} \times \frac{2}{2} = \frac{18}{24}$, the ratios are equivalent.

Write and Solve Proportions

A **proportion** shows that two quantities are equal. A proportion is a way to find equivalent ratios.

Suppose a runner has run 6 miles in 33 minutes. At that rate, how long will it take the runner to run 10 miles? To write and solve a proportion, follow these steps:

Write a proportion.	$\frac{6}{33} = \frac{10}{m}$
Find the **cross products**.	$6 \times m = 33 \times 10$ $6m = 330$
Solve for *m*.	$6m \div 6 = 330 \div 6$ $m = 55$

It will take 55 minutes for the runner to run 10 miles.

Rates

A **rate** is a ratio that compares amounts. For example, a car can travel 240 miles on 15 gallon of gas. How many miles per gallon does the car get? To find the rate, write a ratio of the miles to the gallons and then divide the miles by the gallons: $240 \div 15 = 16$. The car gets 16 miles per gallon. Finding the rate per 1 of a unit is called its **unit rate**.

Do I Understand?

1. What is the ratio of vowels to consonants in the word ALGEBRA? __________

2. An 8-fluid ounce can of soda costs $0.76. At that rate, how much would a 12-ounce can of soda cost? __________

ANSWERS: 1. $\frac{3}{4}$ **2.** $1.14

Solid Figures

A figure that has depth.

Examples of Solid Figures

Solid figures are figures that are not flat. They have depth. Solid figures are called **space figures** or **three-dimensional figures**. Solid figures can be classified by the number of curved surfaces, flat sides, **faces**, **edges**, and **vertices**.

A face is a flat surface. An edge is where faces meet. A vertex is where the edges meet. The following solid figures have only flat faces.

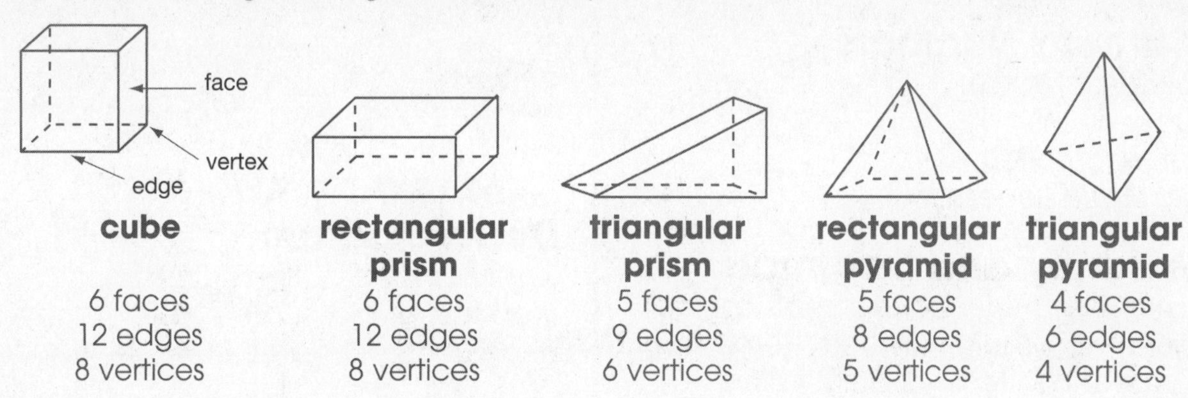

The solid figures that have curved surfaces are shown below.

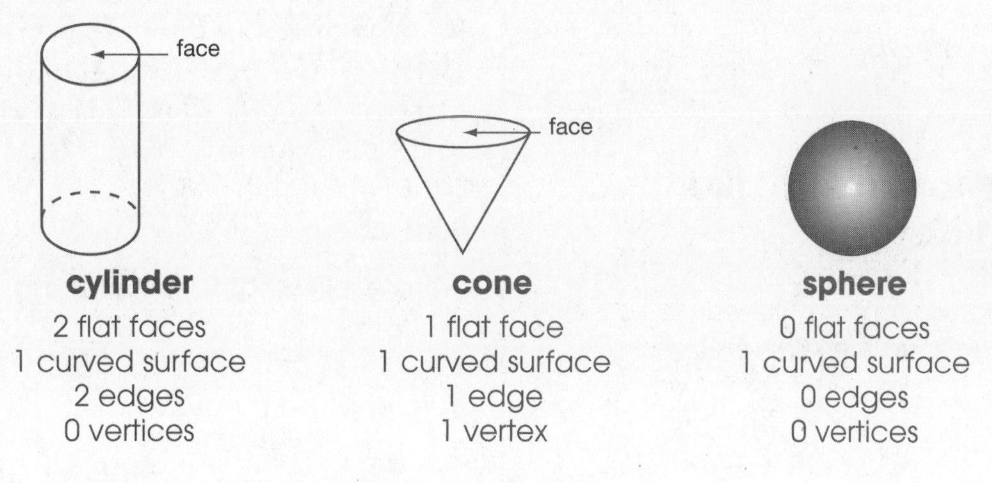

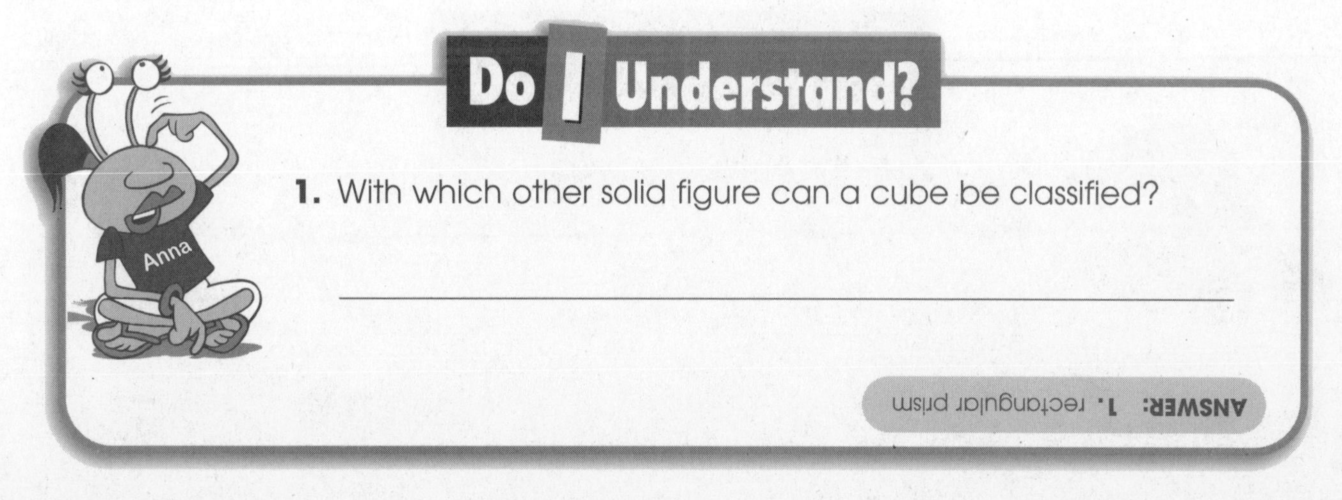

Subtraction

An operation on two numbers that tells how many are left when some are taken away.

Parts of a Problem

These are the parts of a subtraction problem.

```
  294 ←—— minuend
− 177 ←—— subtrahend
  117 ←—— difference
```

Whole Numbers

To subtract whole numbers, subtract from right to left. Regroup if necessary.

```
   16
  7 6̶ 16
  8̶7̶6̶
− 489
  387
```

Money and Decimals

Subtract money and decimals as you would with whole numbers. Remember to place the decimal point in the difference.

```
   6 10
   3̶7̶.0̶5
 − 14.73
   22.32
```

```
    11
   8 1̶ 15
  $9̶.2̶5̶
 − 4.38
  $4.87
```

Fractions with Like Denominators

Subtract the numerators. The denominator remains the same unless the fraction can be simplified.

$$\frac{9}{10} - \frac{3}{10} = \frac{9-3}{10} = \frac{6}{10} = \frac{3}{5}$$

Fractions with Unlike Denominators

Subtract $\frac{5}{6} - \frac{3}{4}$.

Write equivalent fractions using the LCD.

$$\frac{5}{6} = \frac{10}{12} \qquad \frac{3}{4} = \frac{9}{12}$$

Subtract the numerators.

$$\frac{10}{12} - \frac{9}{12} = \frac{1}{12}$$

Mixed Numbers with Like Denominators

Subtract the fraction part first, and then the whole-number part. It may be necessary to rename a whole number as an improper fraction.

$$3\frac{7}{10} - 1\frac{9}{10} = 2\frac{17}{10} - 1\frac{9}{10} = 1\frac{8}{10} = 1\frac{4}{5}$$

Mixed Numbers with Unlike Denominators

First find the LCD. It may be necessary to rename the whole-number part as an improper fraction.

Subtract $2\frac{1}{2} - 1\frac{5}{6}$.

Write equivalent fractions using the LCD.

$$2\frac{1}{2} = 2\frac{3}{6} = 1\frac{9}{6}$$

Rename the minuend and subtract.

$$1\frac{9}{6} - 1\frac{5}{6} = \frac{4}{6} = \frac{2}{3}$$

Do I Understand?

Subtract. Write the answer for problem 2 in simplest form.

1. \$92.36 − \$24.42 ______

2. $2\frac{3}{5} - 1\frac{1}{2}$ ______

ANSWERS: 1. \$67.94 **2.** $1\frac{1}{10}$

Surface Area and Volume

SURFACE AREA - the total area of the surface of a solid figure.
VOLUME - the amount of space that a solid figure encloses, expressed in cubic units.

Surface Area of Rectangular Prisms

A rectangular prism has 6 faces. The **surface area** of a rectangular prism is the sum of the area of all 6 faces. The rectangular prism above can be drawn as a **net**.

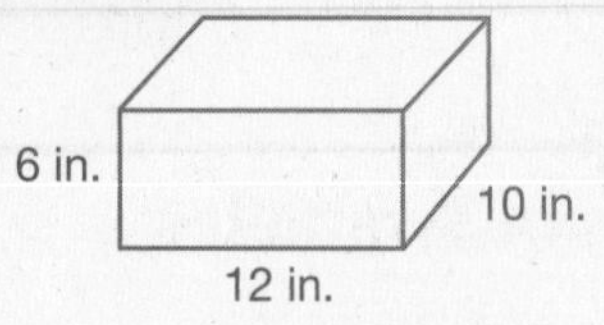

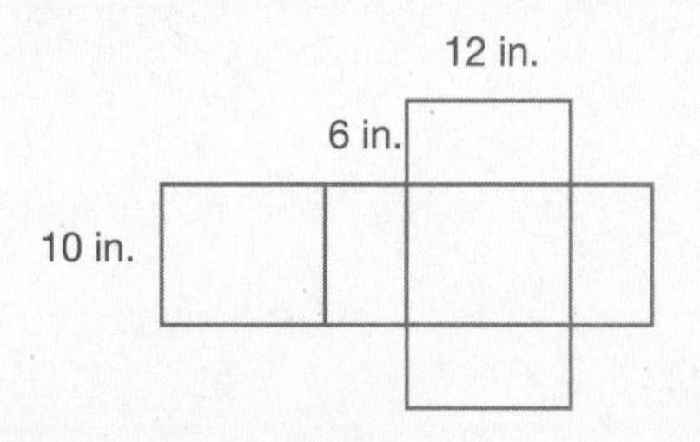

To find the surface area, find the area of each of the faces.

$10 \text{ in.} \times 6 \text{ in.} = 60 \text{ in.}^2$
$10 \text{ in.} \times 6 \text{ in.} = 60 \text{ in.}^2$
$12 \text{ in.} \times 6 \text{ in.} = 72 \text{ in.}^2$
$12 \text{ in.} \times 6 \text{ in.} = 72 \text{ in.}^2$
$12 \text{ in.} \times 10 \text{ in.} = 120 \text{ in.}^2$
$12 \text{ in.} \times 10 \text{ in.} = 120 \text{ in.}^2$

Add the areas:
$60 + 60 + 72 + 72 + 120 + 120 = 504$.

The surface area of the rectangular prism is 504 in.^2.

Volume of a Rectangular Prism

Volume is measured in **cubic units**. Find the volume of the rectangular prism on the left.

To find the volume of a rectangular prism, use the formula
Volume = length × width × height.

$V = lwh$
$V = 12 \text{ in.} \times 10 \text{ in.} \times 6 \text{ in.}$
$V = 720 \text{ in.}^3$

The volume of the rectangular prism is 720 in.^3.

Surface Area and Volume of a Cube

To find the surface area of a cube, find the area of one of the faces and multiply by 6.

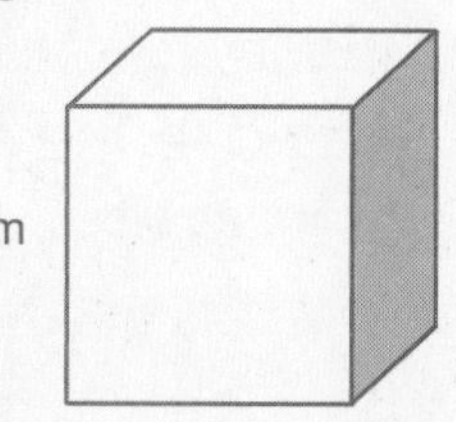

$SA = 6 \times (5 \text{ cm} \times 5 \text{ cm})$
$SA = 6 \times 25 \text{ cm}^2 = 150 \text{ cm}^2$

To find the volume of a cube, use the formula $V = s^3$.

$V = 5 \text{ cm} \times 5 \text{ cm} \times 5 \text{ cm}$
$V = 125 \text{ cm}^3$

Do I Understand?

A rectangular prism has a length of 8 cm, a width of 6 cm, and a height of 5 cm.

1. Find the surface area. ____________________

2. Find the volume. ____________________

ANSWERS: **1.** 236 cm^2 **2.** 240 cm^3

Symmetry

A figure in which both sides of the line match exactly.

Line of Symmetry

A figure has a **line of symmetry** if it can be folded so that both sides match. Some figures do not have any lines of symmetry. Other figures have more than 1 line of symmetry.

Examples of Lines of Symmetry

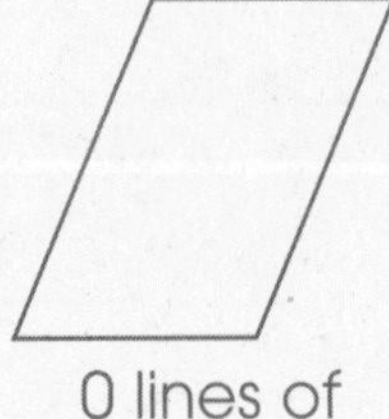

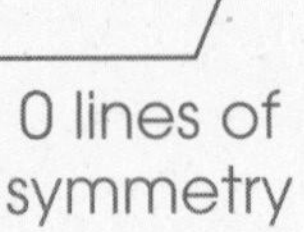

0 lines of symmetry

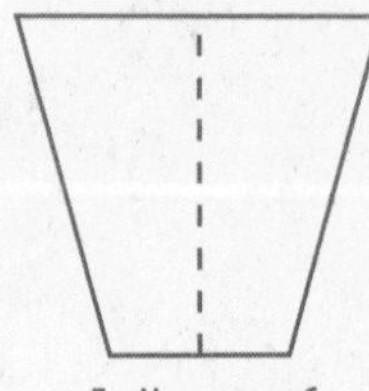

1 line of symmetry

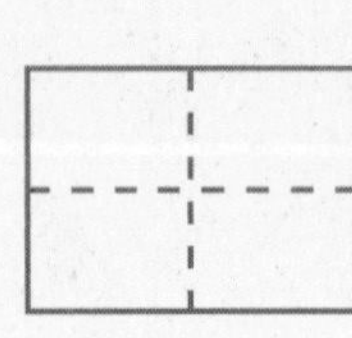

2 lines of symmetry

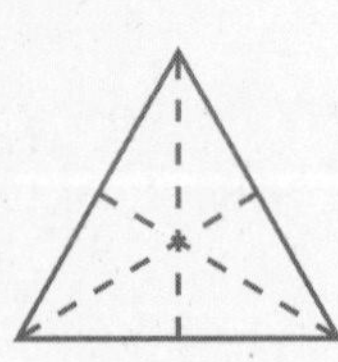

3 lines of symmetry

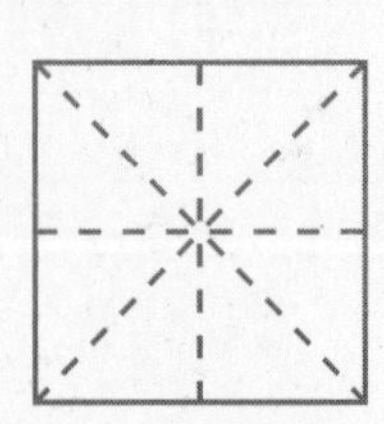

4 lines of symmetry

Each of the lines creates congruent parts. The figures can be folded along any of those lines and the halves will match exactly.

Rotational Symmetry

A figure has rotational symmetry if it can be turned with a $\frac{1}{2}$ turn or less and have the figure match the original position. For example, a rectangle has rotational symmetry.

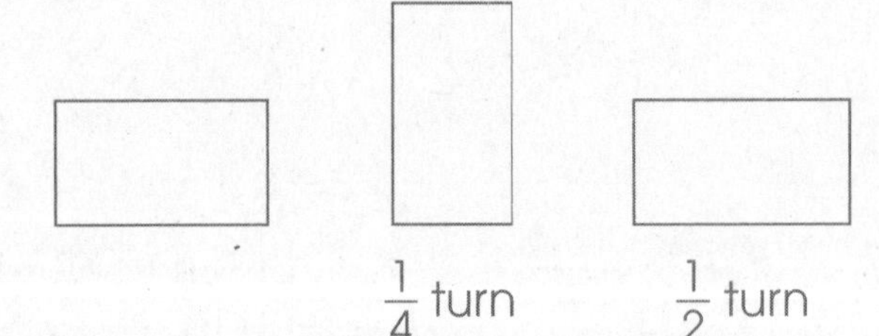

As you can see, the rectangle after $\frac{1}{2}$ turn looks exactly like it did at the beginning.

Do I Understand?

Use this figure.

1. How many lines of symmetry does the figure have? ______________
2. Does the figure have rotational symmetry? ______________

ANSWERS: 1. 6 2. Yes

Transformations

The movement of a figure.

Translations

A **translation**, or slide, moves a figure along a line.

Triangle *ABC* was translated 5 units right to form triangle *DEF*. Each ordered pair has a difference of 5 in its **x-coordinate**. Its **y-coordinate** does not change at all.

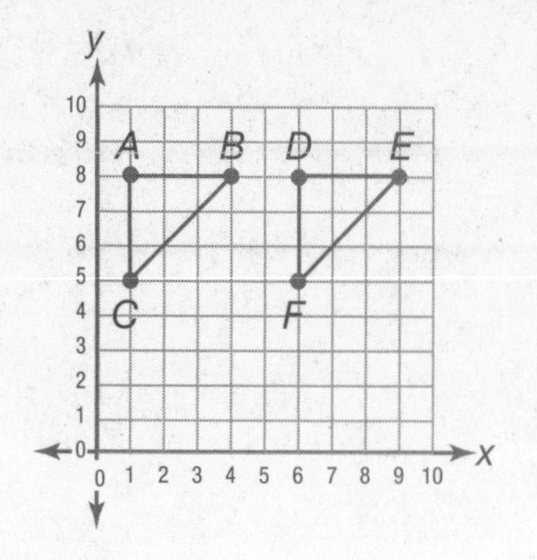

Reflections

A **reflection**, or flip, produces a mirror image of a figure.

Triangle *GHI* was reflected across $x = 5$ to form triangle *JKL*. The *x*-coordinates changed, but the *y*-coordinates remained the same.

If the triangle were reflected across a line on $y = 9$, the *x*-coordinates would remain the same and the *y*-coordinates would change.

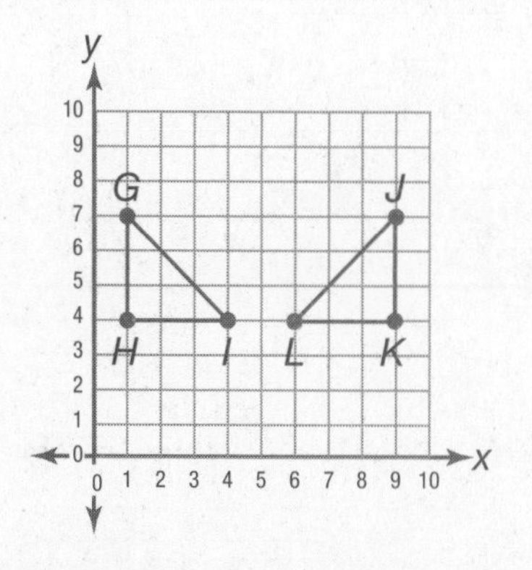

Rotations

A **rotation**, or turn, turns a figure around a point.

Triangle *MNO* has been rotated 90° at point (5, 5) to form triangle *PQR*. The ordered pairs went from (1, 8), (1, 5), and (3, 5) to (8, 9), (5, 9), and (5, 7).

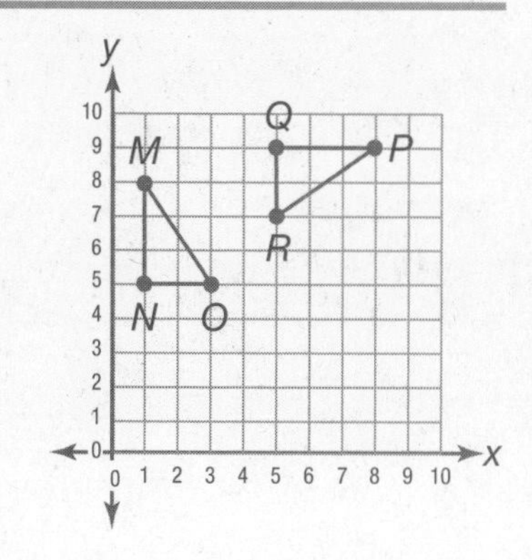

Congruent Figures

The shape and size of a figure does not change when the figure is translated, reflected, or rotated. The figures are congruent.

Do I Understand?

1. If triangle *ABC* were reflected across $y = 4$, what would be the ordered pairs of the triangle that is formed?

____

ANSWERS: 1. (1, 3), (1, 0), and (4, 0)

Glossary

absolute value the distance from 0 on a number line. *(p. 20)*

acute angle An angle less than 90°. *(p. 4)*

acute triangle A triangle with 3 acute angles. *(p. 27)*

addend A number to be added. *(p. 3)*

angle A figure formed when two rays meet at the same endpoint. *(p. 4)*

area The number of square units needed to cover a region. *(p. 5)*

associative property of addition The grouping of the addends does not change the sum. *(p. 29)*

associative property of multiplication The grouping of the factors does not change the product. *(p. 29)*

average The sum of the addends divided by the number of addends. Also known as the mean. *(p. 6)*

B

bar graph A graph that shows data by using bars of different lengths. *(p. 18)*

base A polygon's side or a solid figure's face by which the figure is measured or named for. *(p. 5)*.

base A number that is raised to a given power. *(p. 24)*

capacity The amount a container can hold. *(p. 22)*

center The point that is the same distance from all points on a circle. *(p. 7)*

centimeter (cm) A metric unit of length; 1 centimeter = 10 millimeters. *(p. 22)*

certain An event that must happen. *(p. 25)*

chance The likeliness of an event happening. *(p. 25)*

chord Any line segment that connects two points on a circle. *(p. 7)*

My Math Words

circle A plane figure having all points the same distance from a fixed point called the center. *(p. 7)*

circle graph A graph that shows data by using parts of a circle. *(p. 19)*

circumference The distance around a circle. *(p. 26)*

commutative property of addition The order of the addends does not change the sum. *(p. 29)*

commutative property of multiplication The order of the factors does not change the product. *(p. 29)*

compatible numbers Numbers that are easy to mentally compute with. *(p. 13)*

composite number A number that has more than 1 and itself as factors. *(p. 24)*

compound event A series of two or more simple events. *(p. 28)*

cone A pointed solid figure with a circular base. *(p. 31)*

congruent figures Two figures that have the same shape and size. *(p. 9)*

coordinate grid A graph used to show location of points by using ordered pairs. *(p. 25)*

cross product A product of the numerator of one fraction and the denominator of another fraction. *(p. 30)*

cube A solid figure with 6 square faces. *(p. 31)*

cube number A number that is raised to the third power. *(p. 24)*

cubic units The volume of a cube, one of whose sides is the given unit of length. *(p. 33)*

cup (c) A customary unit of capacity; 1 cup = 8 fluid ounces. *(p. 22)*

cylinder A solid figure with 2 congruent faces that are circular. *(p. 31)*

data Information. *(p. 7)*

decimal A number with a decimal point in it. *(p. 10)*

decimal point (.) A period separating the ones from the tenths in a decimal. *(p. 10)*

My Math Words

Glossary

degree (°) Unit used for measuring angles. *(p. 4)*

denominator The number below the bar in a fraction. It tells how many equal parts in all. *(p. 16)*

diameter A chord that passes through the center of a circle. *(p. 7)*

difference The answer to a subtraction problem. *(p. 32)*

distributive property of multiplication over addition To multiply a sum by a number, you can multiply each addend by the number and add the products. *(p. 29)*

distributive property of multiplication over subtraction To multiply a difference of two numbers by a third number, you can multiply each of the first two numbers by the third and then find the difference of the products. *(p. 29)*

dividend A number to be divided. *(p. 11)*

divisor The number by which the dividend is divided. *(p. 11)*

edge A line segment where two faces of a solid figure meet. *(p. 31)*

equation A number sentence that shows that two quantities are equal. *(p. 14)*

equilateral triangle A triangle with three congruent sides. *(p. 27)*

equivalent fractions Two or more different fractions that name the same amount. *(p. 16)*

estimate An answer close to the exact answer. *(p. 13)*

expanded form A way of writing a number as the sum of the values of its digits. *(p. 24)*

exponent The number that tells how many times a base is used as a factor. *(p. 15)*

expression A group of numbers and symbols that shows a mathematical quantity. *(p. 14)*

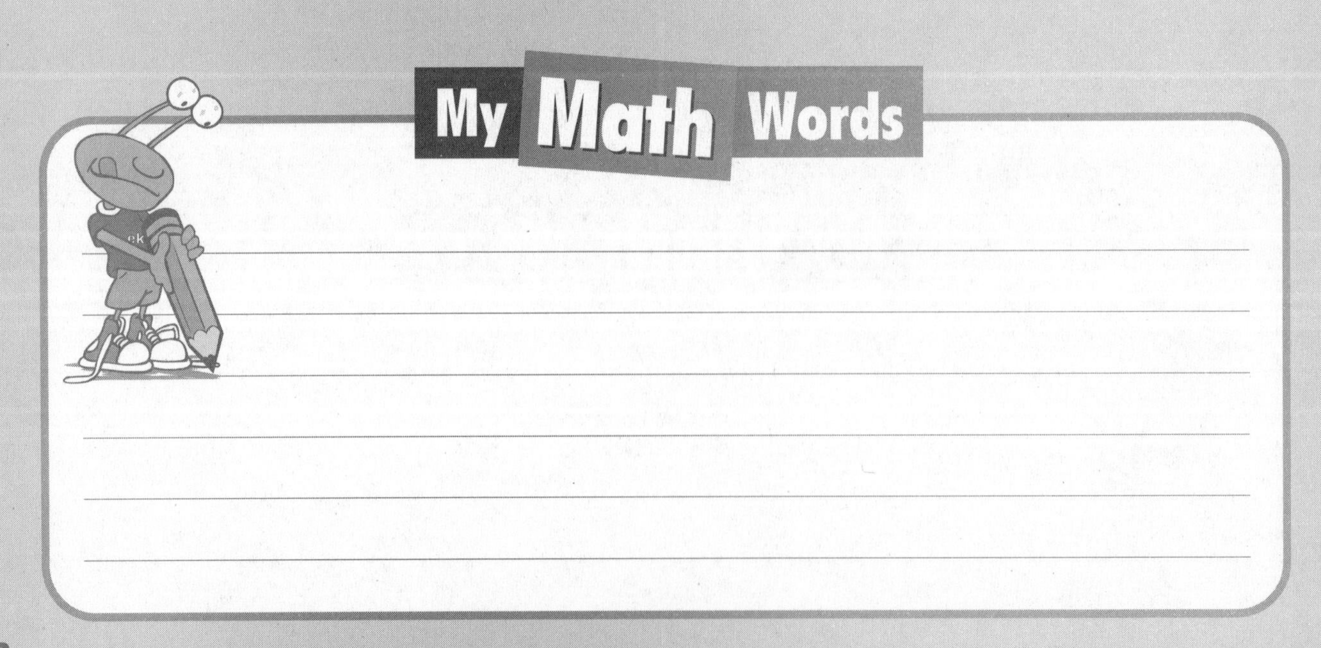

face A flat side of a solid figure. *(p. 31)*

factor Numbers that are multiplied to give a product. *(p. 15)*

favorable outcomes The desired outcomes of a probability experiment. *(p. 28)*

fluid ounce (fl oz) A customary unit of capacity. 8 fluid ounces = 1 cup. *(p. 22)*

foot (ft) A customary unit of length; 1 foot = 12 inches. *(p. 22)*

fraction A number that names part of a whole or a group. *(p. 16)*

frequency The number of times a response occurs or something happens. *(p. 18)*

function A relationship in which one quantity depends upon another quantity. *(p. 17)*

gallon (gal) A customary unit of capacity; 1 gallon = 4 quarts. *(p. 22)*

gram (g) A metric unit of mass; 1 gram = 1,000 milligrams. *(p. 22)*

greatest common factor (GCF) The greatest factor that is common to two or more numbers. *(p. 15)*

hexagon A polygon with 6 sides and 6 angles. *(p. 27)*

histogram A bar graph that shows the frequency of data for intervals. *(p. 18)*

hundredth A decimal place equal to 0.01. *(p. 10)*

identity property of addition When one addend is 0, the sum is the same as the other addend. *(p. 29)*

identity property of multiplication When one factor is 1, the product is the same as the other factor. *(p. 29)*

impossible An event that cannot happen. *(p. 28)*

improper fraction A fraction that has a numerator that is greater than or equal to the denominator. *(p. 16)*

My Math Words

Glossary

inch (in.) A customary unit of length; 12 inches = 1 foot. *(p. 22)*

integer All the positive and negative whole numbers and 0. *(p. 20)*

intersecting lines Lines that meet or cross each other. *(p. 21)*

interval The difference between numbers on an axis of a graph. *(p. 18)*

inverse operations Operations that are opposites such as addition and subtraction, and multiplication and division. *(p. 14)*

is equal to (=) A symbol used to show that two quantities have the same value. *(p. 7)*

is greater than (>) Symbol to show that the first number is greater than the second number. *(p. 7)*

is less than (<) A symbol used to show that the first number is less than the second number. *(p. 7)*

isosceles triangle A triangle with at least 2 equal sides. *(p. 27)*

key In a pictograph, the key tells how many items each symbol represents. *(p. 18)*

kilogram (kg) A metric unit of mass; 1 kilogram = 1,000 grams. *(p. 22)*

kilometer (km) A metric unit of length; 1 kilometer = 1,000 meters. See chart *(p. 22)*

least common denominator (LCD) The least common multiple of two or more denominators. *(p. 8)*

least common multiple (LCM) The least whole number greater than 0, that is a multiple of each of two or more numbers. *(p. 15)*

length The measurement between two endpoints. *(p. 22)*

like denominators Denominators that are the same number. *(p. 3)*

likely An event that will probably happen, but might not. *(p. 28)*

My Math Words

line A straight path that goes in two directions forever without end. *(p. 21)*

line graph A graph that uses a line to show how something changes over time. *(p. 19)*

line of symmetry A line on which a figure can be folded so that both sides match. *(p. 34)*

line segment A part of a line with two endpoints. *(p. 21)*

liter (L) A metric unit of capacity; 1 liter = 1,000 milliliters. *(p. 22)*

mass The amount of matter in an object. *(p. 22)*

mean The sum of the addends divided by the number of addends. Also known as the average. *(p. 6)*

median The middle number in an ordered group of numbers. *(p. 6)*

meter (m) A metric unit of length; 1 meter = 100 centimeters. *(p. 22)*

mile (mi) A customary unit of length; 1 mile = 5,280 feet. *(p. 22)*

milligram (mg) A metric unit of mass; 1,000 milligrams = 1 gram. *(p. 22)*

milliliter (mL) A metric unit of capacity; 1,000 milliliters = 1 liter. *(p. 22)*

millimeter (mm) A metric unit of length; 10 millimeters = 1 centimeter. *(p. 22)*

minuend The number which the subtrahend is subtracted from. *(p. 32)*

mixed number A number that has a whole-number part and a fraction part. *(p. 16)*

mode The number that occurs the most in a set of data. *(p. 6)*

multiple The product of a number and any whole number. *(p. 15)*

negative integer An integer less than 0. *(p. 20)*

negative number A number less than 0. *(p. 20)*

net A two-dimensional pattern that can be folded to make a three-dimensional figure. *(p. 33)*

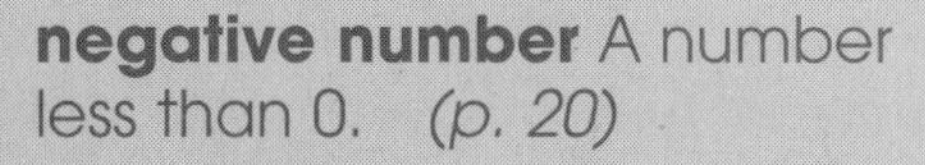

Glossary

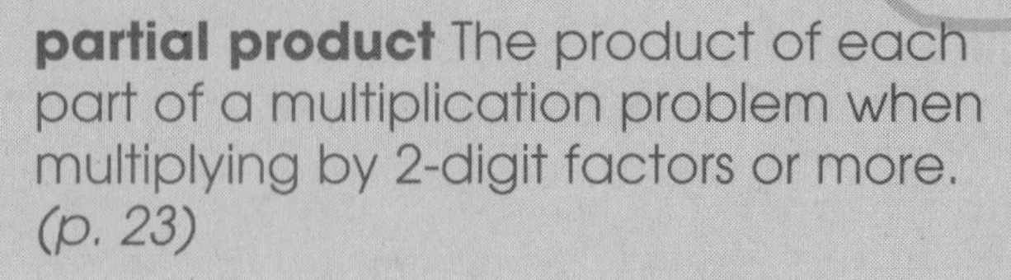

numerator The number above the bar in a fraction. It tells how many parts are being considered. *(p. 16)*

obtuse angle An angle greater than 90° and less than 180°. *(p. 4)*

obtuse triangle A triangle with one obtuse angle. *(p. 27)*

octagon A polygon with 8 sides and 8 angles. *(p. 27)*

ordered pair A pair of numbers that gives the location of a point on a graph. *(p. 25)*

origin The point of a coordinate grid where the horizontal and vertical axes meet, known as (0, 0). *(p. 25)*

ounce (oz) A customary unit of weight; 16 ounces = 1 pound. *(p. 22)*

parallel lines Lines that stay the same distance apart and never meet. *(p. 21)*

parallelogram A quadrilateral with both pairs of opposite sides parallel. *(p. 27)*

partial product The product of each part of a multiplication problem when multiplying by 2-digit factors or more. *(p. 23)*

pentagon A polygon with 5 sides and 5 angles. *(p. 27)*

per For each. *(p. 6)*

percent Per hundred. *(p. 25)*

perimeter The distance around the outside of a closed figure. *(p. 26)*

perpendicular lines Lines that meet or cross at a right angle. *(p. 21)*

pi (π) The ratio of the circumference of a circle to the diameter of a circle. It is approximated as 3.14. *(p. 26)*

pictograph A graph that shows data by using symbols. *(p. 18)*

pint (pt) A customary unit of capacity; 1 pint = 2 cups. *(p. 22)*

polygon A closed figure made of line segments. *(p. 27)*

positive integer An integer greater than 0. *(p. 20)*

positive number A number greater than 0. *(p. 20)*

My Math Words

possible outcomes Any of the results that could happen in an experiment. Also known as the sample space. *(p. 28)*

pound (lb) A customary unit of weight; 1 pound = 16 ounces *(p. 22)*

power A number obtained by raising a base to an exponent. *(p. 24)*

prime factorization A way of expressing a whole number as a product of its prime factors. *(p. 15)*

prime number A number with only 1 and itself as factors. *(p. 15)*

probability The chance that an event will occur. *(p. 28)*

product The answer to a multiplication problem. *(p. 23)*

proportion An equation stating that two ratios are equivalent. *(p. 30)*

protractor A tool used to measure angles. *(p. 4)*

quadrant One of the four sections of the coordinate grid formed by the two axes. *(p. 25)*

quadrilateral A polygon with 4 sides and 4 angles. *(p. 27)*

quart (qt) A customary unit of capacity; 1 quart = 2 pints. *(p. 22)*

quotient The answer to a division problem. *(p. 11)*

radius A line segment from the center of a circle to any point on the circle. *(p. 7)*

range The least number subtracted from the greatest number in a data set. *(p. 6)*

rate A ratio that compares measurements or amounts. *(p. 30)*

ratio A comparison of two quantities. *(p. 30)*

My Math Words

Glossary

ray A part of a line with one endpoint and which goes on forever in one direction. *(p. 21)*

reciprocal One of two numbers whose factors is 1. *(p. 12)*

rectangle A parallelogram with 4 right angles. *(p. 27)*

rectangular prism A solid figure with 6 faces, 12 edges, and 8 vertices. *(p. 31)*

rectangular pyramid A solid figure with 5 faces, 8 edges, and 5 vertices. *(p. 31)*

reflection A transformation of a figure across a line producing a mirror image. *(p. 35)*

regroup To rename a number. *(p. 3)*

regular polygon A polygon with all sides and angles equal. *(p. 26)*

remainder A number less than the divisor that remains after division has ended. *(p. 11)*

rhombus A parallelogram with 4 equal sides. *(p. 27)*

right angle An angle that measures 90°. *(p. 5)*

right triangle A triangle that has one right angle. *(p. 23)*

rotation A transformation that turns a figure around a point. *(p. 35)*

rotational symmetry A figure that matches itself after $\frac{1}{2}$ turn or less. *(p. 34)*

round To find the value of a number based on a given place value. *(p. 13)*

sample space The set of all possible outcomes of a probability experiment. *(p. 28)*

scalene triangle A triangle that does not have equal sides or angles. *(p. 27)*

side One of the line segments of a polygon. *(p. 27)*

similar figures Figures that have the same shape but may have different sizes. *(p. 9)*

simplest form A fraction whose numerator and denominator have only 1 as a common factor. *(p. 16)*

My Math Words

solid figure Any figure that has depth. *(p. 31)*

space figure Another name for a solid figure. *(p. 31)*

sphere A solid figure that is the set of all points that are the same distance from a given point called the center. *(p. 31)*

square A rectangle with 4 congruent sides. *(p. 27)*

square numbers The product of two factors that are the same. *(pp. 18, 24)*

square units The area of a square, one of whose sides is the given unit of length. *(p. 5)*

stem-and-leaf plot An arrangement of numerical data that separates the ones digits from the other digits. The ones digits are called leaves and the other digits are called stems. *(p. 19)*

straight angle An angle that measures 180°. *(p. 4)*

standard form A way of writing a number using only digits. *(p. 24)*

subtrahend The number that is subtracted from the minuend. *(p. 32)*

sum The answer to an addition problem. *(p. 3)*

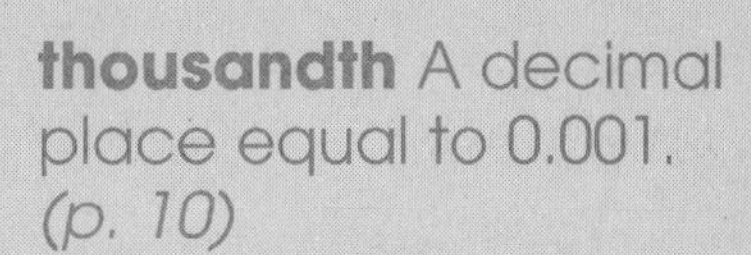

tenth A decimal place equal to 0.1. *(p. 10)*

thousandth A decimal place equal to 0.001. *(p. 10)*

three-dimensional figure Another name for a solid figure. *(p. 31)*

ton (T) A customary unit of weight; 1 ton = 2,000 pounds. *(p. 22)*

transformation The movement of a figure. *(p. 35)*

translation A transformation that moves a figure along a line. *(p. 35)*

trapezoid A quadrilateral with exactly 1 pair of parallel sides. *(p. 27)*

triangle A polygon with 3 sides and 3 angles. *(p. 27)*

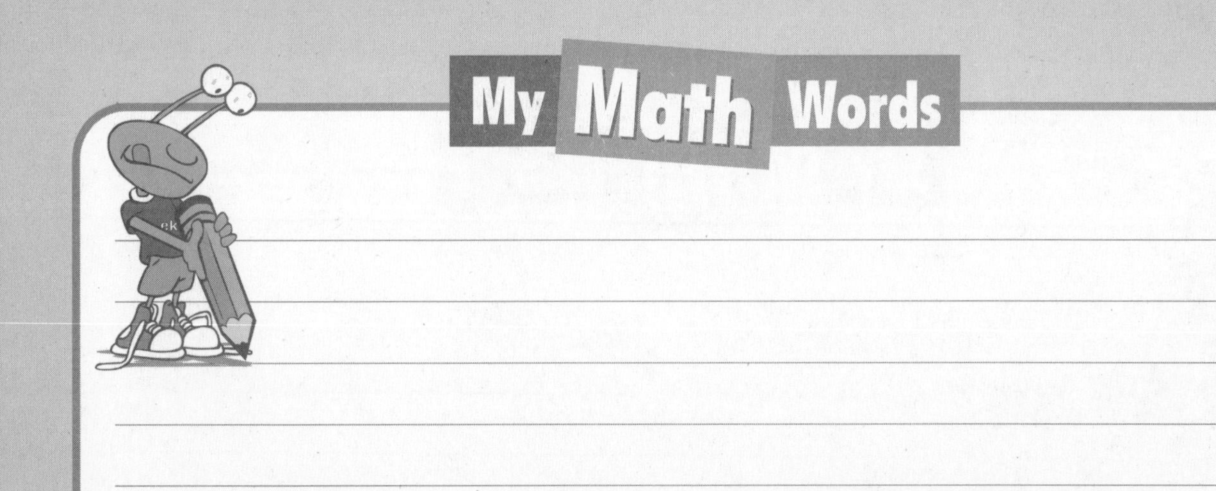

Glossary

triangular prism A solid figure with 5 faces, 9 edges, and 6 vertices. *(p. 31)*

triangular pyramid A solid figure with 4 faces, 6 edges, and 4 vertices. *(p. 31)*

two-dimensional figure A figure that has only length and width. *(p. 27)*

unit rate A rate in which the second measurement or amount is 1 unit. *(p. 30)*

unlikely An event that probably will not happen, but could. *(p. 28)*

variable A letter or symbol used to represent a number. *(p. 14)*

vertex (plural: vertices) The point where the rays meet in an angle. *(p. 4)* A point where 3 or more edges meet in a solid figure. *(p. 31)*

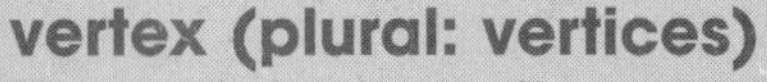

volume The amount of space that a solid figure encloses. *(p. 33)*

weight A measurement that tells how heavy an object is. *(p. 22)*

whole number Any of the numbers, 0, 1, 2, 3, and so on. *(p. 24)*

word form A way of writing a number using words. *(p. 24)*

x-coordinate The first number in an ordered pair. *(p. 35)*

yard (yd) A customary unit of length; 1 yard = 3 feet. *(p. 22)*

y-coordinate The second number in an ordered pair. *(p. 35)*

zero property of multiplication When zero is one of the factors, the product is 0. *(p. 29)*

My Math Words

Math Abbreviations

centimeter	cm
cup	c
day	d
fluid ounce	fl oz
foot	ft
gallon	gal
gram	g
greatest common factor	GCF
hour	h
inch	in.
kilogram	kg
kilometer	km
least common denominator	LCD
least common multiple	LCM
liter	L
meter	m
mile	mi
milligram	mg
milliliter	mL
millimeter	mm
minute	min
month	mo
ounce	oz
pint	pt
pound	lb
quart	qt
second	s
ton	T
week	wk
yard	yd
year	y

Larger Units of Time

1 minute (min)	=	60 seconds (s)
1 hour (h)	=	60 minutes
1 day (d)	=	24 hours
1 week (wk)	=	7 days
1 month (mo)	=	between 28–31 days
1 year (y)	=	12 months or 365 days
1 leap year	=	366 days

Temperature Equivalencies

°Fahrenheit		°Celsius
32	Water freezes	0
68	Room temperature	20
98.6	Normal human body temperature	37
212	Water boils	100

Math Symbols

$+$	addition
$+3$	positive 3
$-$	subtraction
-3	negative 3
$\times$	multiplication
$\div$	division
$\overline{)}$	division
$=$	is equal to
$>$	is greater than
$<$	is less than
.	decimal point
$	dollars
¢	cents
%	percent
π	pi
2:3	ratio of 2 to 3
$P(A)$	probability of event *A*
3^2	3 to the second power
(2, 3)	ordered pair (2, 3)
"	inches
'	feet
°	degree
°C	degrees Celsius
°F	degrees Fahrenheit
$\overleftrightarrow{AB}$	line ***AB***
$\overrightarrow{AB}$	ray ***AB***
$\overline{AB}$	line segment ***AB***
$\angle A$	angle ***A***
∟	right angle
$\triangle ABC$	triangle ***ABC***
$\perp$	is perpendicular to
$\parallel$	is parallel to
$\approx$	approximately
$\cong$	is congruent to

Math Formulas

Formula	
Perimeter of a rectangle	$P = 2l + 2w$
Perimeter of a square	$P = 4s$
Circumference of a circle	$C = 2\pi r$
Area of a rectangle	$A = lw$
Area of a square	$A = s^2$
Area of a parallelogram	$A = bh$
Area of a triangle	$A = \frac{1}{2}bh$
Area of a circle	$A = \pi r^2$
Volume of a rectangular prism	$V = lwh$
Surface Area of a rectangular prism	$SA = 2lw + 2lh + 2wh$
Surface Area of a cube	$SA = 6s^2$
Probability	$P = \frac{\text{number of favorable outcomes}}{\text{number of possible outcomes}}$